Sailors in the Sky

Sailors in the Sky

Memoir of a Navy Aircrewman in the Korean War

by JACK SAUTER

with a foreword by
EDWARD PEARY STAFFORD
Commander, U.S. Navy (Ret.)

McFarland & Company, Inc., Publishers
Jefferson, North Carolina, and London

Front cover photograph: Douglas Skyraider landing on the
  USS *Lake Champlain*, 1953.

Frontispiece: The author, September 1953, USS *Lake Champlain.*

British Library Cataloguing-in-Publication data are available

Library of Congress Cataloguing-in-Publication Data

Sauter, Jack, 1929–
    Sailors in the sky : memoir of a navy aircrewman in the
  Korean War / by Jack Sauter.
      p.   cm.
    Includes bibliographical references and index.
    ISBN 0-7864-0113-3 (sewn softcover : 50# alk. paper)
    1. Korean War, 1950–1953—Personal narratives, American.
  2. Korean War, 1950–1953—Aerial operations, American.
  3. Korean War, 1950–1953—Naval operations, American.
  4. Flight crews—United States—Biography.   5. Sauter,
  Jack, 1929–   . I. Title.
  DS921.6.S28   1995
  951.904'2—dc20
  [B]   95-19567
                                                    CIP

Manufactured in the United States of America

McFarland & Company, Inc., Publishers
  Box 611, Jefferson, North Carolina 28640

This book is dedicated to Marianne,
the love of my life

This work is also for the thousands
of Navy and Marine Corps aircrewmen,
alive and dead, who helped preserve
the freedom we enjoy today,
and especially John Finn,
Chief Aviation Ordnanceman (Aircrewman),
Medal of Honor, 7 December 1941

Foreword

SAILORS IN THE SKY is about young enlisted men who fly from air-craft carriers. But since they do that for only a minuscule proportion of their total time embarked, the book is essentially a sea story. And it is a sea story of the genre of *Two Years Before the Mast* and *The Sand Pebbles*, a story told by a fully involved participant with the good fortune to be educated, intelligent, and articulate.

All the timeless aspects of the classic sea story are here: the camaraderie, the crowding and discomfort, the loneliness and bore-dom, the dangers, the excitement of foreign ports seen for the first time, the importance of mail and liberty and food and pay, and the poignant ambivalence of a sailor's feelings for his ship.

The setting is the early fifties. Times and ships and aircraft and electronics have changed in the ensuing forty years, but other equally significant aspects of life at sea in a man-of-war have not and will not change: the risks inherent in the handling of volatile fuels and high explosives, the challenges of flying from and returning to a moving deck in foul weather, the long hours or just plain hard work for which ten times the pay scale could not compensate, and the awesome responsibility shouldered by young men that has no par-allel in civilian life and constitutes a maturing process without equal in any other field.

All these factors are treated here, and with the involving inti-macy of a first-person narrative.

Perhaps the most significant single point made in the telling of this story of the sea is the vital role played by enlisted aircrewmen in naval aviation, a role generally unrecognized despite a long tradi-tion of gallantry and heroism. (As a former pilot and commander of early warning aircraft with twenty-two-man crews, this writer is especially conscious and appreciative of that role and is aware of the general ignorance of its importance.) Flying from carriers, a few dozen petty officers with less than a year's training who man search radars in the backs of single-engine aircraft completely assume responsibility for the safety of an entire task force from enemy attack in time of war and carry out similar duties in a time of fragile peace, from the Korean littoral to the Norwegian Sea.

There is a lesson in this sea story, and perhaps a welcome reaffirmation of faith in what young Americans can do, at sea and wherever and whenever the need is there.

EDWARD PEARY STAFFORD
Commander, U.S. Navy (Ret.)

Contents

Preface

I STARTED TO WRITE THIS BOOK one cold rainy night in Bonita Beach, Florida. It was January 1990. I had just finished reading a moving military memoir, and I remember being particularly impressed by the author's experiences as an OCS trainee. I immediately recalled my own boot camp trials in August 1950, and I was astonished at how much detail I could conjure up. I picked up a legal pad and started to write. By the time the eleven o'clock news came on, I'd filled twenty pages.

In those early weeks, I never thought about writing a book: I just kept filling those yellow pages with memories. I had never written anything other than letters to friends or an occasional article for a club, but I didn't think about what I was attempting: I just kept filling those legal pads.

A year later my kids gave me a word processor for Christmas and that was another hurdle. I had never learned to type, so I transferred the whole first draft, all 470 pages of it, with one finger. *Sailors in the Sky* was the hardest thing I ever attempted, but at the same time, the most gratifying.

There were times the book dominated my life. I would get ideas while driving to work, and I went nuts trying to scribble notes and cope with New York City traffic at the same time. On other occasions, I would awaken in the middle of the night (with that perfect sentence to end the chapter) and go into the bathroom,where I had a pad and pen stashed away. This happened so often that my wife thought I was experiencing prostate problems.

The creation of *Sailors* had almost as exciting an odyssey as the story itself. A second heart attack in March 1992 almost ended it forever, and the resulting depression from open-heart surgery nearly caused me to toss the whole thing into the fireplace, much like Rudolfo in the first act of Puccini's *La Bohème*.

Four months earlier, as my son Keith was editing the manuscript, a power drop wiped out everything on the word processor. Fortunately I had made a copy and thus partially avoided what could have been a major setback. But *Sailors* seemed to have a life of its own and has survived every possible disaster.

Why write a book about one's service memories? Is anyone out there really interested in what happened to a bunch of aircrewmen over forty years ago?

I guess the answer to those questions relates to one's perspective. When I started to scribble those first few lines five years ago, I had just turned sixty. To most people this is a time to ease up and start planning for retirement, a time to take a closer look at Social Security instead of sailing into uncharted waters. But in spite of the drawbacks, sixty had a lot going for it.

Life didn't have nearly the distractions it had twenty years before, when I was putting three kids through college and was deeply involved in the day-to-day operations of my insurance business. Things are quieter now. Two heart attacks taught me I wasn't immortal, and I started to reorder my priorities.

Sixty was also a time for reflection: a rest stop where one could "balance one's books." I looked back to the people and events that had shaped my life, searching for the key that would somehow reveal the first fundamental change.

For most of the men in my generation or older, the great dividing line was their "rendezvous with destiny": World War II or Korea. Establishing service ties is often the initial link in a male friendship, making us brothers under the skin. Educational backgrounds and sectional differences pale before the bonds of khaki or blue. In the nineteen forties and fifties, it was, for practically all of us, a rite of passage.

The service offered many rewards: a sense of closely knit community and imperishable bonding that was, in many ways, far stronger than marriage itself. Along with the loneliness and the fear, we shared a thousand and one joys and deprivations, and through it all we enjoyed a sweet freedom never again to be tasted. This was the great allure of that never-never land called the military. And this is what makes it so hard to explain to those who weren't there.

Who can forget the endless chow lines, the "dirty details," the excitement of strange new lands, and those never-to-be-forgotten times when death looked us straight in the eye?

My last reasons for writing are more personal. Most military memoirs are written by officers. Capable though they were in their own milieu, they knew little of the gritty day-to-day experiences of a sailor. The barriers, both social and professional, were just too great.

Only one who was there can truly speak for the whitehat. Although officers, mostly pilots, drift in and out of this narrative, it is foremost an enlisted man's story, with an enlisted man's viewpoint.

In writing this account, I have tried for the most part to view these happenings with the eyes of a twenty year old. I know that's not entirely possible, but by primarily using original source material I think I have come pretty close. I have avoided hindsight in all situations except the chapter called "A Summing Up," where it's appropriate. While everything in this book is true, I have changed most of the names in order to protect the privacy of my former shipmates.

Finally, in the vast catalog of naval exploits from World War II to Vietnam, the significant role of navy aircrewmen has been virtually ignored. While *Sailors in the Sky* is in no sense a formal history, I have tried to give my branch at least a modicum of recognition. Shortly before I wrote these words, a great U.S. naval armada supported our forces in Desert Storm. Flying in Grumman Hawkeye E2Cs from carriers like the *Eisenhower, Kennedy* and *Midway*, enlisted ACs provided early warning protection for the fleet. Their duties may have been infinitely more sophisticated than those of their predecessors who manned the flimsy biplanes catapulted from battleships and cruisers, or those who flew Skyraiders in Korea, but they are merely the present-day embodiment of "sailors in the sky." Let us not forget those who wear wings, but who fly in aircraft that do not: those aboard the "choppers" or "whirlybirds." Pilots know that it is the helicopter aircrewman who often rescues them after an ejection or ditching. Recognition is long overdue for the thousands now on active duty and the untold number who showed the way. In a small way, I hope this account will help balance the ledger.

While there are many days and nights I would not want to repeat, I look back on the navy with only pride and a strong sense of fulfillment. Those four years changed most of us like no other period in our lives. Within this great fraternity, my shipmates and I shared a variety of adventures only fully appreciated by those who answered the call. In spite of the chickenshit, the boredom, and the grinding loneliness, most of us only recall the good times. These experiences are readily familiar to anyone who had to leave home and family and adjust to military life. For all of us, it was a "coming of age" in the truest sense.

No book is solely the work of one person, and I'm deeply grateful for the help I received from many quarters. Commander Edward Stafford, the author of *The Big "E,"* was kind enough to read my first draft and later graciously contributed a foreword. His two memoirs, *Subchaser* and *Little Ship; Big War*, set the high standard I always aimed for.

To ensure historical accuracy, I followed the well-worn path to Dean Allard and the Operational Archives Branch of the Naval Historical Center in Washington, D.C. Here, Bernard F. Cavalcante helped me immeasurably and provided me with the official history of Composite Squadron 12 (VC-12) and the action reports of the USS *Lake Champlain* (CVA-39) and Carrier Air Group 4 during their Korean deployment. This information was invaluable for helping me remember such things as the names of our sister ships in Task Force 77 and which oiler or ammo ship kept us in the fight.

To recall the more personal day-to-day happenings, I relied on two main sources: the 68 letters I sent to my parents and the more than 124 letters to Marianne, the girl who later became my wife. For an overview of life on the *Lake Champlain*, I am indebted to the late John Williford, shipmate, confidant, and true friend, who edited *The Champ*, the ship's weekly. John, who died in March 1993, left me with a special slice of history in the pages of his newspaper, and in a sense he lives on in *Sailors in the Sky*. Both *The Keel*, the boot camp record of Company 248, Great Lakes, August 1950, and *The Champ*, the cruisebook of the USS *Lake Champlain*, April–December 1953, afforded me a rich tapestry of detail, and their vivid photographs triggered many forgotten memories.

Many whitehats were invaluable in transmitting that special "I was there" conviction to the story, and each one deserves my gratitude. John Robben read my manuscript from cover to cover and was unstinting both in his encouragement and his time. My closest friend on board *CVA-39*, John is also a published writer and thus doubly valuable to me. He was also of primary importance in helping me make my initial literary contact. After more than four decades, he remains a true shipmate in the best meaning of the word.

Don Roller, an old friend from high school days and later in VC-12, was kind enough to read my rough copy; he gave me some rare insights into the early days of the squadron. George Walls, another aircrewman from VC-12 who flew with me in Korea, recalled many of the humorous incidents that occurred at Quonset Point and onboard ship. The late Les McCarty, a former chief quartermaster, was helpful in explaining the workings of a carrier bridge as it related to flight operations.

After *Sailors* was written, Paul Fargis of Stonesong Press played a critical role in putting me on the right road to a publishing contract.

He never let me get discouraged and always seemed to come up with a new tack to keep me persevering. He remains a key player in an inner circle of writers who were never lacking in faith or support.

Taking first place in my family circle was my son Keith. A true "Man Friday," he did everything from correcting the worst misspellings on God's good earth to copyediting the manuscript. He persevered through a power drop that nearly wiped out a year's work and was always ready with fresh ideas. In short, he was the indispensable man. While she was not as directly involved as Keith, my wife Marianne's help was almost too great to measure. Many of her insights were incorporated into the final draft, but more important, she allowed me to take over her favorite room for close to three years. In far more concrete ways, she kept up my morale. I should also add that without all those letters to her, there would probably be no book. My lifelong companion, she has been a loving wife and true friend for over forty years.

In spite of all the help, at some point an author has to admit that fate played a large role in leading me to consider writing a book, when I had never written anything before. I was lucky to be on the *Champ* during her only combat deployment and to sail most of the way around the world. And fortunate, too, to have met shipmates like Roller and Robben, Murphy and Walls, Ott, Williford, Williams and Stein. I never planned any of this, it just happened. If I had had a different counselor at Great Lakes or Millington, I might have spent the war on a supply ship or some stateside billet doing paperwork. Not that there is anything wrong with those jobs or ships, but it's far easier to make an interesting story out of flying from a carrier deck or walking the teeming streets of Hong Kong than it is to describe a day filling out requisitions. I was lucky, incredibly lucky.

Lastly, I owe a great deal to being born into a family where nothing was ever thrown away. Maybe it was the Depression syndrome, I don't know. In any case, those "genes" inspired me to collect the countless Plans of the Day, flight schedules, menus, matchbook covers, nightclub programs, and the thousand-and-one bits and pieces that are the meat and potatoes of any remembrance.

They weren't pilots, they weren't bombardiers, they weren't even in the air force. They were unlikely airmen, for they were sailors, sailors in the sky.

In the thirties and forties, they froze in open cockpits, manning the guns and radios. And in World War II, they died by the hundreds flying in slow torpedo bombers in places like Midway and the Philippine Sea. Others gave their lives facing rearward in SB2Cs or Dauntlesses, as their planes flew through murderous flak and swarms of Japanese fighters to hit the target.

They continued to die in Korea and the Cold War. Some were shot down in F3Ds or Skyraiders in combat, others were lost operationally with "cold-cat shots," and still others disappeared alone in their P2V patrol planes when the Russians claimed they strayed over their air space in the Bering Sea. They still serve and die today in such essential aircraft as the E2C Hawkeye. Accepting the same risks as their pilots, they nonetheless share the same uniform and quarters as regular blue jackets.

Uncomplaining and immensely proud, they were recognized only by a set of silver wings (later gold), a few extra dollars in their paycheck and the envy of their shipmates. These then are navy aircrewmen, unsung but not forgotten.

Prologue

THEY ARE ALL GONE NOW: the ships of my youth, the great carriers I served on more than forty years ago. Sailing in peace and war, these great ships seemed indestructible. Now, the last one has been retired, and there is a void in my life.

The USS *F.D. Roosevelt* and *Lake Champlain* were scrapped in the early seventies, and after a fabulous career spanning nearly fifty years, the *Midway*, my first ship, went into the reserve fleet in April 1992. As long as the *Midway* remained active, so did a part of me that said, "If she can do it, so can I. I'm still very much the man I was in 1952." Sure, she underwent some extensive rebuilding, but then so had I, with open-heart surgery. Now she's gone, and suddenly I feel much older.

As an aircrewman flying from those decks, I shared that special love of the sailor for his ship. These magnificent vessels would provide us with many things: a place to work, a place to sleep, and for me, a welcome deck to return to. But most of all, they would be a home away from home.

They carried me from the Arctic Ocean to the China Seas, from the boulevards of Paris to the steaming streets of Hong Kong. But my most important journey, the one that would change me forever, was within myself. This cruise was simply called "growing up," and for me and a large part of my generation, it was done in the navy.

Yes, they are gone. And yet there are constant reminders. In New York City, a mighty carrier rests at a pier not far from 42nd Street. An impressive symbol of naval aviation, the USS *Intrepid* was one of the great Essex class ships that ranged the Pacific and brought the war to the doorstep of Japan. Now a memorial, her silent flight deck holds a melange of aircraft that fought from World War II to Vietnam. The planes and carriers may have changed, but the spirit of those who sailed in them remains the same.

I never served on the *Intrepid*, but except for the number painted on her "island," she could be the *Lake Champlain*'s double. Seeing that familiar silhouette reawakens within me images and memories going back four decades. The roar of city traffic fades, replaced now by the high-pitched scream of jets hurtling into the night sky off Korea. In my mind's eye, I see the long chow lines snaking through the hangar deck. I am greeted again by that familiar odor: an evocative blend of frying bacon, lubricating oil, and the strong unmistakable smell of the sea.

BOOK ONE

Chapter 1

Taking the First Step

In THE SPRING OF 1950, I was twenty and had just completed my third year of night college at Fordham University. During the day, I shuffled papers for an insurance company in lower Manhattan. The money I earned paid my tuition and barely supported what little social life I could arrange between reports and papers. Travel was not something I gave a great deal of thought to, and in my entire life, I'd never ventured more than forty miles from New York City. Events unfolding in a tiny far-off country would soon change all that, however, not only for me, but for thousands of others in my generation.

Like its predecessor, this war started on a Sunday. Within a few days, it was clear that America would commit a large force to stop the aggression in Korea. In less time than one usually takes to pick out a suit, my buddies and I decided to become part of that force. We trooped down to 346 Broadway in lower Manhattan to enlist in the navy. We hoped that by joining as a group, we'd have a better chance of staying together. It was not to be.

Our plans started to unravel almost immediately. Dick Landy and I had reserve commitments and had to obtain releases to go on active duty. Corky Kern had a problem requiring a second medical, and chronic asthma kept Larry from enlisting. Dick, Corky, and I were all in boot camp together, but like paratroopers who jump from the same plane, we scattered to the wind. I entered the navy on 6 August 1950.

The letter I received a few days before that date spelled out little of what to expect; it only asked me to bring my high school diploma, toilet articles, and six dollars. I've often wondered how the navy arrived at that figure, but as it turned out, it was more than enough.

Forty-six of us crowded into a large room just inside the recruiting office. For all our high-spirited bravado, it was a sober group that waited to be sworn into the navy, and the sound of a typist could be clearly heard in the next room. A chief torpedoman, resplendent in his immaculate light tan uniform, mounted a small stand. He looked every inch the man we all yearned to be. On his chest, below the twin dolphins of a submariner, he wore two rows of ribbons, many encrusted with battle stars. Although he'd been obviously engaged in this routine every day since the war started, he made it seem as if we were the first to answer the call. His manner was serious, but he injected just enough humor to ease the tension in every one of us.

"I hope you've all thought this out." he bellowed. "This is no Sunday School picnic you're going on. This is four years! And remember one thing. You may be your mother's pride and joy, but when you lower your right arm, your ass belongs to Uncle Sam." There was scattered laughter, but it was shallow, much like what you'd hear in a doctor's examining room.

After the formal ceremony, he added a few words of his own, and I've never forgotten them. "The navy has always been made up of volunteers. You're here because you want to be, and that's the kind of men we want. Those of us in the service know what you're giving up. For the rest of your lives, you'll probably never do anything as important or as unselfish as what you're doing today. The gratitude of every American goes with you. Learn your jobs well, for heaven knows, the navy needs you. Good luck and God bless you."

And so we gave up four years. It was as easy as that.

Because I was the oldest, and the only one with prior military experience (a couple of years in the National Guard), I was put in charge of this group heading for Great Lakes Naval Training Center, just north of Chicago. The navy sent us by Pullman, and besides the large manila envelopes containing all our records, I was entrusted with countless railroad tickets, meal chits, and taxi vouchers. Our train didn't leave Hoboken until 6 P.M. (soon to be 1800), so we had that first day in the service pretty much to ourselves. I made sure everyone knew how to take the Hudson River ferry to the terminal and told them all to be an hour early. I must have looked a little worried as they melted away, for the chief walked over and said, "I wouldn't be too concerned, son, you need more than six bucks to get in trouble in this town."

I spent the balance of the day saying a last good-bye to my close friend Bruce at his office near City Hall and wandering around Broadway. Excited at the thought of breaking all ties, I still had some grave misgivings. It's not easy to walk away from twenty years of home and security without some doubts, but I knew the time for choice was over. I boarded the ferry for the ride to Hoboken and what turned out to be my last view of New York City for over a year.

Fortunately, the chief's prophecy came true, for my detail was patiently waiting for me on the New Jersey side of the river.

We had two cars to ourselves, and when the other passengers discovered our destination, everything was "on the house." Some kindly mother types even bought us magazines and candy along the way. I wasn't exactly called "Pop," but being a few months shy of twenty-one, I probably seemed ancient to my men, most of whom were seventeen year olds. They'd have their share of restless nights soon enough, but now there was just too much going on for them to feel lonely. I told them to have a good time, short of wrecking the New York Central, and to remember one thing: I had their records, and they'd all better be with me when we delivered ourselves to the navy. I worried about losing some when we changed trains in Chicago, but the muster came out right in the end.

During that night on the train, we were all living in a make-believe world. We were a cocky bunch, trying hard (but not too successfully) to live up to our newly acquired roles. We might be in the navy, but we obviously weren't sailors.

I guess none of us realized what a momentous step we'd taken. For the next four years, we would be completely subject to every whim of the service. The recruiting chief's remark about our ass belonging to Uncle Sam would turn out to be all too true, but mercifully, none of us were yet aware of it. In a burst of patriotic fervor, buttressed by the ever-present spectre of the draft, we'd surrendered a fair chunk of our youth. Some of us would later call this period the "best years of our lives." Unknowingly, we'd also traded the Bill of Rights for something called the Articles for the Government of the Navy. These articles would shortly be referred to as "Rocks and Shoals," and we'd all get to know them well.

After making certain none of my brood had fallen off the train, I retired to my lower bunk and turned out the reading lamp. I'd traveled on trains before, but never in a Pullman or overnight. In the films of my youth, sleeping car scenes were de rigeur, and it wasn't hard to get caught up in the romance of it all. As I lay tucked away in that dark cocoon, it almost seemed like a movie.

As the small towns of rural America flashed by, rows of cars stood impatiently behind winking lights and ringing bells at railroad crossings. Through countless kitchen windows, I saw families clustered round their tables, eating and talking. After a while, as I dozed off, the distance between towns stretched longer and longer, and only the whoosh of a passing train awakened me. Soon I was in a deep sleep. It had been a long and tiring day, crowded with emotion and filled with the promise of a whole new world to come.

Chapter 2

Civies to Blues

GREAT LAKES NAVAL TRAINING STATION was a beehive of activity when we arrived in the fading light. Just inside the Main Gate, a yeoman took a quick muster and relieved me of all those official records I'd so zealously guarded. I happily became just one more faceless recruit in what was to become Company 248. It was too late to issue us uniforms, so in our various civilian outfits we were hustled off to a cavernous mess hall for our first real taste of navy chow. Those in power evidently wanted us to think we'd made the right choice, because this dinner was memorable. The food went downhill fast after that, but I doubt if anyone noticed.

At 0530, we awakened to what would become a familiar summons over the next four years: the sound of a bugle call. Immediately, we moved onto the fast track. We traded our hair for uniforms, and long needles punctured our arms. Blues, whites, blankets, and dungarees filled our seabag, and when we couldn't hold anymore, they placed dog-tags around our neck. All this in the first morning.

In a large drill hall, we were instructed in the fine art of stenciling every item of clothing with our name. Invariably, some "boots" painted their names on the outside of their white hats. Fortunately, hats were only a buck and a half. Except for dress blues and peacoats, everything was dirt cheap. Later, when we were doing all our laundry by hand, one recruit never seemed to have any wash. When I asked him how he managed this feat, he said he just discarded all his soiled underwear and socks and bought new ones at the Ship's Store. As an added benefit to all this scrubbing, our dungarees and blue work shirts were slowly fading. While this didn't exactly transform us into "old salts," it did remove this stigma of the new arrival, the dark blue, or "dirty shirt."

There were 120 men in Company 248. A few weeks before, the companies were half that size, and Great Lakes didn't appear to be ready for the transition. With the officers and chiefs trying to cope with five times the number they'd been accustomed to, we sometimes wondered if they were making it up as they went along. We were the last of the peacetime units, and the people after us received less training and a smaller uniform allowance. There were waiting ships out there, and we were here to man them.

Our company was made up mostly of New Yorkers, with a sprinkling from Philadelphia and Chicago. We were housed in two-story barracks built in 1942. These buildings had been vacant since the end of the last war, and the new arrivals were filling them all. Our camp was named after a heroic naval aviator, Admiral Moffat. Other sections were called Dewey, Downes, and Porter. Before we could bunk down, we were issued soap, swabs, and rags, and we proceeded to hold what is commonly known in the navy as a "field day."

It took us about six hours, and I don't know if we got more water on ourselves than on the deck, but the old planks soon sparkled. Someone had an RCA 45 record changer playing in the corner, and I heard the refrain of two songs over and over: "Goodnight Irene" and "Tennessee Waltz." I can never again hear these sad melodies without thinking of a hot August night when a bunch of soaking recruits became a company, in spirit as well as in name.

Mr. Kurzack was our company commander. If he had a first name, we never knew it. All recruit commanders, although enlisted men, were addressed as "Mister." He was a gunner's mate first class and had the widest grin this side of Joe E. Brown. He lived just off the base in comfortable navy housing with his wife and worked an 8 to 4 routine. This probably accounted for his good humor, since there weren't too many billets ashore for navy gunners.

From his perfectly rounded white hat to his gleaming black shoes, he was the sailor personified. He looked as though he'd just stepped out of cellophane, and next to our baggy issue, the contrast was even greater. Although he stood only 5'7", his lack of height was more than offset by a perfectly proportioned body, hardened by years of manhandling fifty-pound shells. "Popeye" is who he looked like, and "Popeye" is what we called him (behind his back).

Nothing in his appearance prepared us for his most distinctive quality, his speech. When asked, "Do you think we'll get liberty soon?" he'd answer, "Sure, and you shit too." This, we soon learned, meant no. If you didn't have a good sense of direction, he complained, "You couldn't find your ass with both hands on a clear day." To the hapless recruit who couldn't tell left from right and messed up our morning parade, he'd shout, "Shitbird, don't you want me to make chief?" Ironically, he so thoroughly fitted the image of a sailor, one could never imagine him in the jacket and tie of a chief.

More than anything, Popeye loved to talk. If we expected to feel his wrath at our sloppy drill or messy quarters, he could easily be defused by asking him what it was like in the "Old Navy." Soon he'd be happily back on the Yangtze River, bewitching us with tales of opium dens and fantastic White Russian women who did things we couldn't even imagine. Carried away by memories, he'd often stay after hours. By spinning yarns about ships and men long gone, Popeye made us believe the navy could truly be an adventure.

Inside the barracks, the time-honored sorting out process began. Much like the first day of school, there were leaders and followers, but more important, instant friendships were made. They had to be. These next twelve weeks were going to be full of surprises, and some of them would be downright unpleasant. We needed all the support we could get.

A few men had buddies. They'd been more successful than my group in sticking together. For the rest, it was a "do it yourself" indoctrination. Fortunately, I'd been away to two National Guard summer camps, so I knew a little of what to expect. But there I had many friends, and no matter how bad it got, I could always count on being back in the "real world" two weeks later. Here, there was no such luxury. The transition was frighteningly thorough at every level: new faces, new home, new routine. Our only consolation was that we were all in the same boat, and no one wanted to be the first to complain or drop out. The pressure to stay with the group was tremendous.

The lack of privacy was the first jolt to our tender sensibilities. We were always exposed. In all the barracks, not one place existed where one could be totally alone. But we discovered that privacy was not shaped by walls and doors, it was rooted in the mutual understanding that everyone is entitled to his own personal space, even if it was only your bunk. As a result, no one sat on your mattress without your permission, and this alcove became the one inviolate spot to read your mail or just stare into space.

For the most part, though, the lack of privacy was keenly felt by those who'd never experienced communal toilets or showers at home. The men who'd frequented gyms or engaged in team sports strolled to their first navy shower "au naturel" and never batted an eye. The more insecure recruits were probably dying inside. What to do? Was it worse to show yourself to everyone and try and fit in, or wrap yourself in a towel until you reached the shower stall? For those who chose the latter course, they got a double-whammy when they discovered there were no stalls.

If anyone was worried about his size and how he'd stack up, it didn't take more than an hour in the barracks to discover there were no great surprises here. All the tension disappeared with the observation that, at least in this sector, most men were created equal. After a few days, only two boots continued to wait until after lights out to take their douche, as it was quickly dubbed. I'd had my baptism two years earlier in the National Guard, but I could sympathize with all these poor souls. Sometimes, lying in my bunk after taps and thinking back on the day's activities, an old song would recur to my memory. Those Irving Berlin lyrics about there being no private rooms or telephones for army recruits could have just as easily been applied to us.

Other nights, in the welcome darkness, one could hear the sounds of quiet sobbing. For some, the transition was almost too painful. Although it occasionally awakened us, we remained silent and let the suffering recruit come to terms with his own loneliness. There are times when men are better left alone.

I always had trouble matching names with faces, and none of those sure-fire memory courses seemed to work for me. The navy came to my aid in an unexpected way. The imprinting of our monikers on every piece of clothing was, I'm sure, for purposes of theft prevention and easy laundry separation. For me, it had the added advantage of locking in each face with the matching name. There was no escaping. One could be identified in the shower by his dogtags, and if you were really inquisitive, you could even determine your buddy's religion and blood type. No secrets here.

Removing our last shreds of privacy was part of the navy's method of indoctrination. Loyalty to one's unit in particular, and to the service in general, was the goal. Individuals just didn't exist.

Our days were filled with classes covering subjects like the types of guns on a cruiser or destroyer and the organization of the navy. Other sessions included semaphore, watchstanding, and General Orders. Some of it was familiar from the National Guard and appeared more suited to the infantry, but ours not to reason why.

Everyone looked forward to the training films. When the lights went out, half the class would drop off to sleep. Once the recruit next to me was awakened in the middle of a particularly gory scene from *The Fleet That Came to Stay*, a vivid documentary about the kamikaze attacks on our ships off Okinawa. These weren't the heavily censored clips from *Victory at Sea*; this was the real thing. There were burned bodies stacked like cordwood, and blood flowed from shattered gun tubs. All in living color. The suddenly awakened recruit bolted upright and said, "Holy Shit! Where do I transfer to the infantry?"

Other classes covered seamanship, line-handling, and the difference between a bollard and a bitt. Also, how to avoid all those scheming civilians ashore who only wanted to separate you from your hard-earned dollars. These people included everyone from credit jewelers to ladies of the night. No one dozed off during a full-length film devoted to the hazards of dealing with the opposite sex. It was entitled *Don't Take a Chance*. Gonorrhea was about as familiar to most of us as Einstein's Theory. Later, another VD film (usually shown just before chow) depicted the ravaged anatomy of a sailor who was foolish enough to succumb. It was so vivid that it prompted one of our class to shout, "What did his girl have, leprosy?"

Not all classes were held indoors, and perhaps our most memorable afternoon was spent fire-fighting. Since fire is a constant threat at sea, this was a "no holds barred" session. We learned about the different types of fires and how to control them. Later, we were split into groups using CO_2 and foam, and finally we were broken down into hose teams to fight larger fires.

Inside massive steel structures built to resemble ship's compartments, oil and gasoline blazes were started. We rotated our positions on the hose team, and one soon discovered the advantage of being "nozzle man." At the conclusion we could have all been signed to play in a minstrel show, and the singed eyebrow became a badge of honor.

In the barracks, a sort of makeshift government evolved, completely separated from the official navy. Included was our own police force, appropriately called "the armed guard." Although armed with little more than their fists and some webbed belts, they were a formidable lot who dispensed quick justice. Composed of five burly recruits from South Philadelphia, they could have easily formed their own defensive football line. They made it possible for one to leave valuables on one's bunk while taking a shower and find them there upon returning.

When our one and only thief was caught, he was worked over by the armed guard in the dryroom (a laundry space) and emerged minus a few teeth. His uniforms and seabag were cut up and labeled "thief." Before he could replace them, there was a full-scale Captain's Inspection.

The "Four Striper" gave a quick glance at the telltale clothing and asked the recruit how he got those bruises on his face. "Fell off a ladder, Sir," was his reply, and the captain continued walking down the line. No action was taken by the officers or Mr. Kurzack. I think the navy preferred our handling these "family" situations in our own way. A few weeks later, this misfit was transferred out, along with a chronic bed-wetter. No one told us they were going. One afternoon when we returned from the drill grinder, they were gone with all their gear.

Other than this one incident, discipline was rarely a problem. We rose at 0530, and went flat out till 1600 with an hour for dinner. Our activities included calisthenics, swimming, running, and marching, especially the latter. We marched everywhere: to class, to chow, to church. If they could have figured out a way, we would probably have marched to the head.

Close order drill took up an hour of every day. For me this required no effort. My rifle balanced easily on my shoulder, and my body answered the commands like a well-oiled robot. After all, I'd been marching one way or another for the previous ten years.

When I was a kid, I'd learned all the rudiments of military drilling in a rifle company with a group of sea scouts known as the American Bluejackets. Later, in the same organization, I joined the band. Here we engaged in far more complicated steps than anything the navy did. Counting bars of music, we sometimes spread so far over the hall that most onlookers doubted we'd ever get back in formation. When I was seventeen, I enlisted in the venerable Seventh Regiment (National Guard) in New York City. In their honor guard, the movements were even more intricate. I enjoyed marching, especially to music, and my rifle, with its sweet smell of oil and leather, took on a nearly mystic quality.

I'm often asked how with such an ingrained love of the navy, I ever got into an infantry regiment. Aside from the fact that my best friend Larry was already in the regiment (his boss was a company commander), I guess it all boiled down to time and scheduling. There was a Naval Reserve chapter in my part of the Bronx, but they only met on weekends. With my college regimen of four nights a week, I desperately needed my Saturdays and Sundays, not only for papers and book reports, but to preserve my sanity.

During the summer, we spent two weeks on maneuvers. For those who were really gung ho (me and my buddies), there were also "firing weekends" every few months at Camp Smith, just outside New York. Here we became proficient with an assorted array of weapons including the M1 rifle, carbine, BAR (automatic rifle), .45 pistol, and machine gun. Later, as part of a mortar platoon, I lugged the base plate to an .81 mm mortar more miles than I care to remember.

This regimen, while a far cry from the real thing, gave me some appreciation of what the infantry was like. We fired live ammunition, ate C-rations out of a can, and lived in pup tents in the rain. Such experience, apart from demonstrating a little of what my relatives had lived through in World War II, also taught me in no uncertain terms that the infantry was a good place not to be.

So, aside from separation from home and family, boot camp held no secret terrors. I never told anyone in Company 248 about my past military adventures, and when our recruit drill leader gave the command, "to the rear, march" on the wrong foot, I kept my mouth shut.

After the evening meal, we commenced washing our personal laundry by hand. The white canvas leggings, or "boots," were the worst, since they were scuffed by the black work shoes we wore. This took the better part of an hour, since no soiled clothing was permitted to be stored. Those with any energy left wrote a few letters, but most of us were long asleep when taps sounded at 2100.

One did not have to be in boot camp long to discover that all recruits were not created equal. Two groups were afforded special treatment: athletes and musicians. If you could catch or throw a football better than most, you were plucked from the ranks and joined an elite echelon representing Great Lakes Naval Training Station on the gridirons of the Midwest. With a pool of talent tremendously swelled by the war, we fielded some pretty good teams in that autumn of 1950. As no football game is complete without a band, that's where I came in.

There was no lack of applicants, since membership definitely had its privileges. It enabled one to pass up such character-building programs as a week in the scullery. Here one toiled from 0400 to 2000, cleaning GI cans with scalding hot water and scraping grease from encrusted pans. Scores of men aspiring to be Harry James or Gene Krupas preceded me at the audition, and almost all were quickly returned to their companies. The two bands had room for about 130, and over a thousand tried out.

It took me only a moment to see I had no problem. The band had four sets of bells (or glockenspiels), but no players. The chief in charge said, "There's some music. Let's see what you can do." I said I didn't need any music and started to play "The Stars and Stripes Forever," one of the many pieces I'd memorized during my ten years in a marching band. After a few bars, he said, "You're in. Report to me at the drill hall in Camp Porter tomorrow at 1400." So music came to my rescue again. Seven years earlier, it had been my passport to a parochial school I'd never have made with my flimsy academic credentials.

Among the perks of being a band member was a jump on the rest of the company when it came to liberty in Chicago. After the football games, we were free until 11 P.M. Regular recruits time off wouldn't commence until after the seventh week of boot camp. When it finally came, the navy wasn't exactly generous. Each Saturday, following a meticulous barracks inspection and a full dress parade, we were granted a modicum of freedom. Subtracting an hour each way for the Skokie Line, we netted about eight hours in the Windy City. It doesn't sound like much, but after fifty days of confinement, those minutes were golden. Since just about every member of our company was below the legal drinking age, we spent most of our time wandering around State Street or one of the parks that adjoined the lake. We must have looked really tender because I don't recall anyone ever mentioning being approached by any of those forbidden girls, the ones so aptly described in our training films.

One of my shipmates, Bill Buckingham, had been a steward on Capital Airlines. Chicago being one of their regular stops, Bill knew his way around. He was easily the most sophisticated man in the barracks (which wasn't saying much), and he belonged to that unfortunate group of young men who lose their hair early on. While he would have gladly passed up the distinction, it made him look six or seven years older, and it opened a lot of doors. One evening the Palmer House welcomed us. He knew the manager and the maitre d', and we were neither asked for ID, nor presented with a bill. I felt ill at ease in such regal surroundings, but Bill just winked and said, "Relax, Jack. Even if we've forgotten, these people know there's a war on. This uniform will give us a lot of entrée for quite a while, so sit back and enjoy it. Just think about what it's costing you." The couple at the next table sent over a bottle of wine. After a couple of glasses, I decided Bill was right, and I sat back to revel in what was no doubt the premier dining experience of my life.

By now the company was settling in, and a few individuals started to stand out. Jack Tanzer had the bunk below mine. He was from some mysterious place called Bensonhurst, pronounced "Bensonhoist," which I later discovered was part of Brooklyn. When he learned I came from the Bronx, it amused him no end. Although we'd both been born and raised in New York City, neither of us had set foot in the other's borough. Jack soon became the court jester of Company 248.

One of Jack's favorite tricks was to call out as he passed a group of lonely recruits (there were always groups of lonely recruits), "Anybody here from Chicago (or Michigan, or Ohio)? When some happy face replied yes, he'd say, "That's too bad. I'm from Brooklyn." It never failed to get a laugh, even when you knew it was coming.

On a long chow line, Jack would take out his wallet and reveal several snapshots of two spectacularly built nudes. When asked if he knew them, he'd say, "Sure, they're my sisters" (of course they weren't). He always claimed to have enlisted to escape from two beautiful girls, both of whom he had promised to marry. He said he didn't have the heart to disappoint either of them.

One day we had a welcome break in the monotony of our regular drill and classes. We were bussed to the rifle range. After the National Guard, I expected a two-hundred yard affair, complete with pits and large targets. Instead, we were issued .22s and used a short indoor range. The navy didn't expect us to become Sergeant Yorks, they just wanted us to become familiar with firearms. I scored twelve out of twelve. Having qualified with the M1 and carbine in the course of many "firing weekends," it was no big achievement. "Popeye" was elated, however, and true to the crossed barrels on his sleeve, said I should strike for gunners mate.

Deep down, what I really wanted to be was a boatswain's mate, handling lines and running small boats. To me, that was the real navy. During my classification interview, I was steered away from this romantic, and (according to my counselors) highly impractical course, and was guided into aviation. According to the personnelman, boatswains wore size 45 jumpers and size three hats. Later I learned that the navy couldn't survive without BMs, and many were sharp as a tack. After I related this story to one, he said, "And how many personnelmen did Columbus have?" Visions of tying fancy knots faded when I discovered the navy was really run by fire-control types and people with "wings": officers wore them on their chests, sailors on their sleeves.

After the interviews and test results, I knew I would be headed back to school for a long, long time before setting foot on a ship. That ship, if and when it came, would clearly be an aircraft carrier.

About two weeks later, I received a letter from Don Roller, a high school buddy who'd gone into the navy two years earlier. Don's advice confirmed that I'd made the right decision. He was an AT, aviation electronics technician, a rating he chose before enlisting. He knew exactly what he wanted to do, but I was just bumping along, hoping I'd fall into the right niche. I wondered if we'd ever run into each other, and we promised to keep in touch.

The last few weeks of recruit training turned out to be real fun. Summer's humidity slowly but surely faded into a cool, breezy autumn. With skies that could have come from calendars, the air was dry and clean (perfect drying weather for our laundry). After our last drill on the grinder at 1600, we knocked off our wash and went to chow. Afterward we were free until taps at 2130.

By now we were comfortably attuned to the regimen, so we

began to enjoy the diversions of the base. Movies were available nightly, and on occasion there was a live show. In spite of this, everyone griped about being confined to the base. Having just spent three years in night college, four days a week (with a military drill on the fifth), I didn't know what to do with my newfound freedom.

One evening just before sunset, I found myself walking towards the recreation hall where the movies were held. While adjacent to the main parade ground, I noticed a detail readying a saluting cannon, while another stood by to lower the flag. As a bugler sounded attention, everything in sight came to a halt, and only the fading sound of a bus could be heard away in the distance. The sharp report of the cannon echoed off the administration buildings as the first notes of "Retreat" came clearly across the field. As all hands saluted, the National Colors came slowly but steadily down toward the Honor Guard. This team was precision trained. The last note was just dying as the broad red and white stripes reached the outstretched hands of the detail. The whole ceremony had taken a little less than a minute.

When it was over, I had no desire to move. I wanted to savor the moment and make it last. In Carnegie Hall, there had been times when the music was so moving one didn't wish to break the spell. For me, this was such a moment.

At summer camp with the Guard, "Retreat" was included in Evening Parade, and it was part of an involved formation that brought out the whole regiment. Here, it was one on one: just you and the flag. This military angelus always brought me up short, with the chills-up-the-spine and hair-on-end routine. No matter how many times I experienced it, I was always left with a deep feeling of satisfaction. Some might call it a high. These emotions are not easy to explain; you just have to live them. At the same time, I reflected on what I was doing here.

Boot camp had been a whirlwind of new adventures. We had little time for contemplation or anything else. We all slept the sleep of the dead. Watching the colors made me feel that I had finally severed the last links to my former life. At summer camp, I was just playing at something for two weeks. Now I was part of a unique brotherhood, wedded to that flag for the next four years.

The navy had begun by teaching us to take care of ourselves, and to many, this was a revelation. Then they taught us our responsibility to our fellow shipmates (staying alert during fire watches was the first lesson). When our training was complete, it probably didn't dawn on many that, in a sense, the whole purpose of this indoctrination was to teach us how to take care of the country.

It had been traditional to grant each recruit ten days leave before he reported to his first duty station. In the fall of 1950, with ships coming out of mothballs almost daily and our forces battling in Korea, the navy didn't have that option. There were guns to be manned and ships to be filled. Most of Company 248 was at sea within a month of leaving Chicago, assigned primarily to destroyers and minesweepers.

I had a much longer wait before I saw blue water, and I wasn't to see home on a regular leave for over a year. My parents came out to spend the graduation weekend with me in the end of October. My mother couldn't believe that after all this training, I looked exactly as she had last seen me in uniform when I was playing the bells in a marching band. Like the other parents, mine were proud, and it was my father's first time on a military base. He was on a train to Yaphank in November 1918 when the armistice was signed. Behind their smiles, too, was the unspoken relief that they were witnessing this graduation at Great Lakes, rather than Camp LeJeune or Fort Benning.

My orders were to Aviation Primary School, Naval Air Technical Training Command, Memphis, Tennessee. It sounded impressive. Before I could leave, however, my naval career almost underwent a dramatic change. Personnel informed me that my grades on GCT (General Classification Test) were such that I'd been chosen to take the entrance exam to the Naval Academy. I started to wonder how I'd like a career as an officer, but I never had the chance to find out.

After raking leaves for a week, my orders were finally cut for Memphis. Someone had noticed that I would be an ineligible candidate for Annapolis because I'd turn twenty-one before the class began. I accepted this return to my original course without much disappointment. I'd been in the service long enough to adjust to whatever came my way. It was my first and most important lesson.

Chapter 3

Tennessee Waltz

MEMPHIS WAS STILL WARM in early November when I completed my second Pullman experience in three months. At the air base, I had my first encounter with a holding barracks. This is where you end up when you are caught between starting classes. In the army it's called a "repo-depot," and it's best described as being in limbo, or "no-man's-land." In my case, I had eleven days to wait before the navy turned me into an "airedale."

The military had a theory that if you've nothing to do, you'll end up in trouble. (The nuns used to say, "An idle mind is the devil's workshop.") And don't forget, you're getting paid the 5th and 20th of each month. Enter the make work projects.

Some of us were employed painting road markers, while others picked up cigarette butts from the parade ground. They called this a Naval Air Technical Training Command? Highly skilled technicians we might eventually become, but we were still in the navy.

I was detailed (with six other "holdees") to clean and paint a recreation hall that had lain dormant since just after World War II. At first glance, the hall was a wreck. It had become a storage area for every piece of equipment that had to be put under cover five years before. Obviously, the people who stored this stuff were only thinking of going home, and no one imagined it would be used again.

The windows hadn't been opened since V-J Day and were rusted shut. We decided to split up and see if we could find anything that would help us put this hall back in commission. One by one, we made discoveries. Bob found a large floor fan and the power to run it. By opening both doors, we managed to cool the hall down from the low 90s to a more livable level. Lou located some benches and tables, so we had a place to sit. Since we were going to milk this detail for more than a week, we figured we might as well be comfortable.

By the third day, we had scoured the walls and floors with an eye-stinging solution, and now we were ready to paint. The supply department hadn't issued us any drop cloths, so we started to look for rags or old tablecloths; anything that would cover the refrigerator and bar area. While moving some sheets of plywood, we discovered a small door leading to what was probably a boiler room. It took us a while to pry this rusted door loose, but finally it opened.

The odor that greeted us was like that of some ancient crypt, and we half expected to find a body or two. Someone fashioned a work light, and two of our party entered the anteroom. In what seemed like seconds, we heard an unearthly scream, and I thought our fears about finding bodies had come true. Quickly we learned we were sitting on a treasure: over twenty cases of beer. The cartons had almost disintegrated in the dampness, but the bottles were intact.

After the excitement died down, we realized that this would have to be our secret. We removed two dozen bottles and placed them in the rear of the giant refrigerator. We stored some soda in the front, so on a chance opening of the cooler, our secret would remain secure.

It took forever for that Griesedieck beer from St. Louis to cool down. Some of the boys opened a few bottles to see if it was fit to drink. At least, that's what they told the rest of us. I'd never been a beer drinker, but I must admit that in that steaming room it tasted like the nectar of the gods. One of our more enterprising sailors strolled over to the mess hall and casually revealed that he had beer to trade for some steak sandwiches, coffee, and pie. The cooks thought this was a fine idea. It was hot as hell in the galley, and beer was like manna from heaven. After all, weren't the different ratings supposed to work together? That's what it said in the Bluejackets Manual.

We were the only group of new students who were sorry to see the classes start.

An P school stood for "Aviation Primary," but when it was pronounced, it sounded more like we were going to handle canned goods instead of airplanes. This eight-week course, designed as an introduction to the "airedale" navy, was also an intense review of the basic skills required in all the aviation ratings. We learned, among other things, the theory of flight, basic electricity, physics, algebra, survival, and a brief introduction into our future job codes. From An P, we'd go on to more specialized courses that prepared us to be technicians in our assigned trades. These final schools, which qualified us to work on aircraft, ranged in length from eight to twenty-eight weeks.

One of the courses was "hand tools," and it nearly ended my

career before it started. The stereotype of the typical male American teenager tinkering with the engine of his old jalopy obviously didn't fit me. Not only had I never owned a car, but as a child of the Depression, neither had my father. Growing up in an apartment, I rarely saw anything more exotic than a hammer or a pair of pliers. It was with some trepidation, then, that I entered the shop class.

We were doubled up at huge wooden work benches, a vise at either end. My partner was "Big Hal," one of those who'd found the beer. When he placed a file in the palm of his calloused hand, it looked like it belonged there. Our instructor walked down the aisle, pushing a cart loaded with roughly cut steel blocks, each about the size of a brownie. Our task was to file these lumps into smooth cubes. We were also provided with a T-square to help us fashion the perfect cube.

Hal fastened his lump into the vise and, with a few deft strokes, finished it. It was perfect. I filed and filed and filed, but every time I'd get one end right, the other one was out of line. It was as if I was sawing the legs off a chair, trying to get them level, but only making them shorter in the process. I started to sweat as the lump grew smaller and smaller. Hal glanced over at my vise and quipped, "Jack, if you're not careful, you're going to be arrested for making counterfeit dimes." Later, when the instructor moved away, he picked up another block and quickly duplicated his perfect cube for me.

A few days later in a physics class, I saw him struggling with some formulas and offered to help after chow. With this, a team was born, and neither of us experienced any problems for the remainder of the school.

Halfway through Aviation Primary, we were given our evaluation interviews and were asked to list our preferences for advanced service schools. These choices and our final grades would determine our careers for the next three-and-a-half years. My counselor noticed in my records that I'd been a journalism and history major in college. He wondered why I hadn't tried for "journalist," a navy rating. I'd never given it much thought, but since I couldn't type, it eliminated me from consideration. Strange how the navy mind works. I'd met scores of people who could type up a storm, but couldn't put two sentences together.

When my counselor and I discovered we had similar college backgrounds, the initial tension eased and we established a quick rapport. He made me aware of how many billets there were for each school and what my odds were. He knew my class standing, which was prized information. My first choice was aerographer, or weatherman. I had no chance, he revealed, because there were only two openings, and both were claimed by classmates with far better grades. Since I'd never given much thought to any other job, I leaned on his expertise. He looked at my test scores and said with a smile, "John, with your mechanical ability, I'd never want to fly in a plane you'd done engine work on." Aviation Machinists School was going to claim 40 percent of the class, and those who didn't make their first choice, would surely end up there. I thought about my afternoon with the lump and shuddered.

Looking at my GCT (General Classification Test) and my math scores, which were in the top 5 percent of the navy, my counselor said electronics was the course for me. I said I didn't know a damn thing about electronics or electricity. Laughing, the counselor confided he hadn't known anything about sex, but had had two kids in two years. Besides, he could guarantee a berth in Aviation Electronics, or AT school. Thus, the path of my navy career was laid out by a chance encounter.

About this time, the war in Korea appeared to be in its final phase, and the Eighth Army was deep inside the North. It looked as if the whole thing would be wrapped up by Christmas. Everyone in barracks N72 listened to the news with mixed emotions. We were all glad the end seemed near, but on the other hand, we hadn't even seen the ocean, and our adventure might well be over before it even started.

The Chinese had a trick or two up their sleeves, however, and by Christmas it looked like the Battle of the Bulge all over again. The squadron I was to join two years later was in the thick of things during the Hungnam evacuation, but at the time I wouldn't have given any odds I'd ever see a ship, much less Korea.

Once I realized I was going to stay here a while (AT school, twenty-eight weeks, was just across the road), I decided to explore Memphis. In the fall of 1950, it was still a small city, with a much more relaxed atmosphere than Chicago. The parks adjoining the Mississippi were ideal for quiet walks, and many other sections, like Beale Street (of jazz fame), had real charm. The town was mobbed by sailors from Millington (as the base was known to the locals), and the parade of blue grew larger with each passing week.

I soon discovered I was a Yankee. I bristled at this title, not because of any North-South feeling, but because it suggested a baseball team I loathed. When I heard people saying "damn Yankees," I wanted to agree with them, until I found it was me they were talking about.

All of us from outside the South soon realized we were like tourists in some foreign land. The natives were friendly enough, but

we really didn't speak the same language. Men had names like Earl
or Clyde (there weren't too many of those in the Bronx), and the girls
were called Emma Lou Mary or Barbara Anne Rose. One could run
out of breath just making introductions.

All these differences quickly faded against the excitement of our
newfound freedom, however. One night in four we stood fire watches;
otherwise we were free to do all the things sailors are supposed to
do, but rarely accomplish. After four months of eating in mess halls
that somehow all smelled the same, it was heaven ordering a hamburger and soda and having the hamburger served on a plate. I soon
discovered the locals put mustard on their burgers (an unpardon-
able culinary sin back home, since mustard was strictly for hot
dogs), and for every hamburger stand, it seemed there were a dozen
others featuring something called "barbecue." This concoction, if
nothing else, made me grateful to have parents that came from New
York.

Other bits of alien produce found their way onto my plate: black-
eyed peas, hominy grits, and corn bread. These, I might add, also
appeared with some regularity on my mess tray at Millington. In
time I acquired a taste for them, and on the credit side, the cooks,
both in Memphis and on the base, did marvelous things with pork,
one of my favorite meats. In a class by itself were their biscuits, and
there were times I could have made a complete meal out of them.
The only New York bakery products I missed were hard rolls and
crusty bread.

Just like the navy, the local restaurants had a language all their
own. My waitress must have thought I was totally deaf one day when
I ordered fried chicken, and she asked something that sounded like,
"Y'all wan slaa on daa?" Three times she repeated it, her voice growing louder with each request, as if that would help break through to
this dumb Yankee. I'd probably still be sitting there, if a kindly
woman on the next stool hadn't pointed to the cold slaw on her
plate.

But this was only part of the discovery process. In the service,
one soon learned to treasure life's smallest pleasures. The weekends
were special in that we enjoyed our first overnight liberty since joining the navy. Mine soon settled into a familiar pattern.

After our final muster on Friday afternoon, I'd pack a small bag
with toilet articles and a change of underwear. Then I'd catch an
early bus into Memphis and check into the Peabody Hotel, where six
bucks bought me a room with private bath for the weekend. It was
heaven stretching out in the steaming water before dinner, but the
best part of the hotel room was the solitude. Privacy in the navy is

something reserved for Captains and Admirals, and not being able to
get away from it all was the biggest complaint. Just before Thanksgiving, I made the mistake of telling some of my classmates about my
hotel room. I arranged to leave the key on the transom, and I'd often
find sleeping bodies on the floor when I awakened in the morning. No
one worried about thieves: we had little to steal in any event.

Early on in Memphis, I met Corky Kern, one of my N.Y. buddies
with whom I'd enlisted. I'd seen him briefly at Great Lakes, where he
told me he was going to try to get into aviation. He was attending AM
school (Aviation Metalsmith), a twelve-week course. He laughed
when I told him about the now infamous lump.

We both enjoyed having someone from home to talk to. It was a
welcome change, not having to always play the part of a bell-bot-
tomed Errol Flynn, as we did with other "swabbies." Sex took up 99
percent of the conversation in the barracks, and even those who
spent all their free time at the library invented wild stories so they'd
appear to be one of the boys. Most of the students at NATTC were middle class (aviation skimmed the cream off the top), and they tended
to look for girls from their own background. For those who went this
route, their "scoring" mark was probably close to zero, as these were
very closely watched daughters. Of course, hundreds of others were
more democratic and held to no class distinction. They chased everything that breathed.

Corky and I were definitely in that first category. He was a little
different in that he had an ongoing serious relationship with a girl
in New York. I'd written to a few girls, but after six months, their
lives were moving in other directions, and I was just starting to find
myself after a hectic year. Although I was always lonely, settling
down with one steady 1,200 miles away was just not in the cards.
Corky and I shared hotel rooms most weekends and assisted as
altar boys in the local parish at Sunday mass. So much for wild
sailors.

One Sunday the priest saying mass, Father Kelleher, asked us
to join him for breakfast following the service. Over bacon and eggs,
he revealed he'd been a chaplain in World War II. He'd only been out
of the seminary a few months when he volunteered for the navy and
was assigned to a small aircraft carrier (CVL) in the Pacific.

His wartime "parish" was composed primarily of 17 and 18 year
olds, and in spite of all his efforts, he couldn't attract any of the
older men. Attendance at mass was sparse, and he was deeply disappointed. These career men were strong role models for the others,
and he knew that without them leading the way, there was little
chance he could succeed. He'd just about given up when the ship

joined a task force covering the liberation of the Philippines. Here, they encountered the dreaded kamikaze. One plane crashed into the side of the carrier, wiping out two gun crews and injuring scores more. Suddenly, everyone got religion. Father Kelleher lit a cigarette and sat back as he continued.

During a long afternoon of hearing confessions, Father Kelleher encountered a grizzled boatswain's mate, who admitted that he had not seen the inside of a church in 20 years. Reciting his "sins," the bos'n acknowledged cheating at cards, profanity, and chasing women. Then he stopped. "I told him to go on," Kelleher recalled, "but he replied, 'That's all I remember, Padre.' 'Look,' I said, 'you must have more to tell me after twenty years. Why don't I run through the Commandments to help refresh your memory?' The tattooed sailor sat mesmerized while I slowly intoned each one of the ten. When I finished, he looked relieved and said, 'Well, Father, I never killed anyone, or worshiped any false gods, and I was always good to my parents, sending them a few bucks when I had the chance. And that part about my neighbor's wife: well, she was a pig if you ever saw one. But as for all the others, you can mark me down in spades!'"

Kelleher had a faraway look in his eyes when he finished and said he'd never felt closer to God than he did during his two years in the navy. One could truly be a follower of Christ and not have to worry about repairing the boiler, raising money, or keeping on the good side of the bishop. I think he envied us.

Some of my buddies joined scores of other swabbies and rented lockers where they could change into civilian clothes on weekends. I thought this was a waste of money. Besides, it created some extra logistical problems when you shipped out. A full seabag was enough to wrestle with, without having to contend with "civies."

To my mind, it was also pointless to masquerade as something you weren't. Given a choice, I think most local girls would choose a sailor over a civilian. They wanted to meet boys from out of town, and I'm sure that, in this case, distance really did lend enchantment. I liked everything about the uniform, and its individuality guaranteed we were never mistaken for mailmen, or indeed anyone else.

By the time I arrived, the navy was in its winter colors. This meant wearing the woolen flat hat, one of my favorites. It was the perfect companion to a set of dress blues. Soft and yet warm, it could be rolled up and stuffed in a peacoat pocket. A ribbon around the headband proclaimed, "U.S. Navy." I thought this a bit redundant: what else could we possibly be? But best of all, it required no washing. It could be worn for years on end without losing its color or shape.

Other than cleaning, the white hat had the same advantages, and a few more. A true American original, I often wondered about its source. Half the world's navies copied it, and through the years it had found its way into countless fashions for both sexes. During the thirties, an ice cream company marketed the "Dixie Cup," an exact replica of our head gear. Coming full circle, our present-day sailors call their white hats by the same name.

The white hat was pliable enough to be rolled up, and it gave good service in a myriad of roles. Countless stories abounded about castaways on rafts or lifeboats who owed their lives to this hat. It was perfect for bailing out seawater and invaluable as a sun protector. As you stood watch on nights that suddenly turned cold or windy, the open white hat covered your ears, as well as your head.

The jumper and trousers were perfectly designed for minimal pressing. Here, the pants legs were creased, but the crease was inward (unlike for conventional clothing), and on the side of the leg and not in the front. As a result, it didn't lose its shape when you sat down or got caught in the rain. Instead of a hanger (which was often unavailable on board ship), one could fold the pants under a mattress, and they would remain unwrinkled. Likewise, our jumper was folded inside out. It kept the creases intact and prevented the white piping on the collar and cuffs from becoming soiled when the jumper was stored. Its unique shape gave the sailor a tremendous jump on the army and marines, since we possessed the only dress uniform with a permanent open neck. And don't think that wasn't practical in those pre-airconditioned days.

Those thirteen buttons came in for a lot of flak, but even they had their good points. For a start, there were no zippers to get your personal equipment hung up on, and of all the oddities our blues possessed, this one seemed to hold an endless fascination for the opposite sex. If the truth were known, most sailors only opened one side.

Even the long black neckerchief had its function. Aside from decoration (and there was little enough), it came in handy on cold nights to help close up the open collar. In a pinch, it could substitute for a shopping bag, provide a tourniquet, or become the perfect memento to leave a girl at the end of a date.

Of course, there were some drawbacks. The two pockets were so tiny, one had to be incredibly resourceful when it came to stowing personal gear. Our wallets were folded over our waistband, and with the jumper pulled down, they were scarcely visible. Cigarettes, money, and a comb were stashed in our socks. The wide bell-bottoms would hide almost anything. Of course, the marines at the gate knew this too and would often tap our calves with a night stick as we returned from liberty, exerting just enough pressure to break a bottle of booze.

We were very much in the same dilemma as a girl in a skirt and a blouse when it came to carrying our paraphernalia, only we couldn't carry a pocketbook or purse. Among other things, this restriction caused me to switch from a pipe to cigarettes. These minuses aside, I still wouldn't trade my blues for any other uniform.

The Naval Air Technical Training command was spread over a vast area. An P school was on Northside, and the advanced service "preps" took up the remainder (known logically as Southside). There was also a working naval air station, albeit used mostly for training. In my last two weeks here, I'd get to know it well. Seeing and hearing planes all day, there was little doubt we were in the "airedale" navy. On the other hand, Great Lakes was situated hundreds of miles from the ocean, and the only ships we saw were in training films.

The barracks, two-story wooden structures, were all of World War II vintage. Besides the familiar rows of double-decker bunks, there was a spartan lounge comprised of a few battered chairs, couches, and tables. The lounge was used for everything from letter-writing to studying, with an occasional card game thrown in. With fresh memories of boot camp in our minds, these quarters were a quantum leap upward.

I guess the first thing we noticed was the row of washing machines on the first level. No more standing at a basin scrubbing our clothing white. Of course, leggings were a thing of the past, but even so, the presence of the machines told us in no uncertain terms that we were no longer recruits. This alone gave us a tremendous boost psychologically. Instead of a seabag, where it seemed everything one needed was always on the bottom, we had roomy lockers to stow our gear. Photos of family and girlfriends graced these cabinets and added a little color to the drab surroundings. To remind them of what they'd left behind, the more adventurous students pasted up some shapely nudes. Inspections were rare, and when they did occur, it appeared the brass were far more interested in the art work than in the neatness of our uniforms.

About ten days before Thanksgiving, we were notified that all personnel would be granted "basket leave" of four days over the holiday weekend. Basket leave was a navy expression for unofficial time off, an extended liberty so to speak. The downside of this arrangement was a restriction limiting travel to within 500 miles of Memphis. Since every student in the training command had not been

Barracks N72, Aviation Primary School, NATTC, Memphis, Tennessee, October 1950.

home since enlisting, just about all hands ignored this order, thinking the navy would never be the wiser.

As time was short, I booked a round trip on American Airlines, flying to La Guardia Airport on Wednesday evening. It was a great weekend: the thrill of my first plane ride, surprising my family, and looking up my old buddies and girlfriends. This was my first appearance in uniform, and I was given a lot of attention. Everything contributed to this "dream" weekend until Saturday, when an early winter storm cut a swath of destruction through the Midwest and East, toppling trees in New York and dumping a couple of feet of snow around the Great Lakes. La Guardia Field, where I was scheduled to depart Sunday afternoon, was under two feet of water.

Visions of being confined to the brig soon came to mind, and I desperately started calling other airlines. A particularly vivid training film I'd seen in boot camp, about a sailor overstaying his leave, kept recurring in my memory. He ends up a deserter, living a double life. In the film it turns out to be a bad dream, but in my case, 1,200 miles from Memphis, it was all too real. After many anxious phone calls, Eastern Airlines put me on standby for a sold-out flight leaving Newark at 7:15 A.M. Sunday morning.

The bus from the midtown airline terminal took a roundabout journey to Newark, making detours to avoid fallen trees. Finally arriving at the gate, we found the flight was delayed because of high winds and ice patches on the field. Our "full" Constellation eventually took off with exactly six passengers, all military, after skidding halfway down the runway. The weather forced us to fly at 5,000 feet, seat belts fastened all the way. Not even the stewardesses moved about. We stopped at Philadelphia, Washington, Winston-Salem, and Birmingham before landing at Memphis a little before 2 P.M. The weather couldn't have been more different than New York—a beautiful, mild Sunday afternoon. So there I was, after having worried about being AWOL, now deposited back to duty nine hours early.

As it developed, I'd been needlessly concerned. Monday morning found only about eighty men (out of two hundred sixty-eight) present at muster. The missing aviation students were scattered all the way from Maine to Minnesota, trapped in snowbound towns and closed highways. This was my first experience with the Law of Large Numbers. If you're going to break the rules, make sure you have plenty of company. There were so many missing that the navy didn't prosecute anyone who made it back by Friday. They were just charged with official leave. I mourned my "lost weekend" for a while, but it all turned out for the best. I didn't know it at the time, but I would have missed my eventual super assignment (those who were late were put a class behind) had I not been there for that all-important muster.

Chapter 4

Memphis Belle

ONCE BACK IN THE CLASSROOM, An P school drew quickly to a close. True to my counselor's prediction, I was assigned to Aviation Electronics School, one of the longest in the navy: twenty-eight weeks, commencing right after the first of the year. Before it started, the holidays were upon us.

None of us were looking forward to our first Christmas away from home. I'd originally planned to spend it at a hotel, but the thought of being alone on this special night changed my plans. Christmas Eve found me at the "Y," drinking punch, and singing carols around their tree. I intended to catch a late bus back to the base. The navy promised a big turkey dinner the next day, and best of all, there'd be plenty of company.

About eight-thirty, most of the whitehats (sailors) had gone out on the town. I was sitting by a fire in the club meeting room at the "Y" with two other sailors, shooting the breeze. A well-dressed older man (he was probably forty) came in and asked all of us to join him for the holidays. At first we were a little suspicious, but when he mentioned his wife and children, we all agreed to go. The three of us piled into his big Lincoln.

At a brightly lit colonial home, a slender woman in her late thirties greeted us. When we entered, it was apparent our host and hostess could have easily accommodated five times our number. We all perked up when they mentioned their three daughters, but they turned out to be fourteen and under. If nothing else, it simplified matters.

In a few moments, they made us feel like family, in the true sense of the word. Some punch, that bore little resemblance to what we'd been drinking at the "Y," soon had everyone in a festive mood. That Christmas Eve that I spent a thousand miles from home and totally surrounded by strangers was the nearest I'd ever come to the perfect holiday experience.

Later around the tree, each of us received a brightly wrapped package: handkerchiefs and wallets. We felt embarrassed not having anything to exchange, but after a quick conference, we decided to give the daughters our neckerchiefs. It was little enough, but the girls couldn't have been happier. Here was something their friends couldn't duplicate.

Late the next day, after an elaborate turkey dinner with all the trimmings, our host and hostess drove us back to Millington. At the main gate, we were all too choked up to more than mumble thanks before rushing back to our barracks.

A week later, we started a new school and bid farewell to 1950, the most momentous year of our lives. With little fanfare, the first half of the twentieth century also slipped into history.

Aviation Electronics School was like a college level course. We went to classes from 0800 to 1600, with an hour break for noon chow. There was a fair amount of math and electrical theory, but we never got in too deeply. There just wasn't time. The navy was literally taking us from Ohms Law to trouble shooting radar in six months. It was impossible, but somehow it worked. It's called total immersion. In World War II, the services did the same thing with foreign languages, and to a larger extent, flight training. There was plenty of homework and lots of things we did together, like Morse Code. We all fell asleep counting dots and dashes.

Sometimes during the night as I was listening to the rhythmic heavy breathing in the bunks around me, I'd try to imagine what happened to the former occupants of barracks S-54. How many had been shot down or died in kamikaze attacks? At our age, the last war seemed a lot more remote than a mere five years ago. I didn't have much time to explore these possibilities, however, as I settled in for the next seven months.

Dave Bauer and Joe DeFranco were my immediate neighbors, and we became instant friends. Both hailed from Brooklyn, but that's where the similarity ended. Far from being students, they were recalled reservists, veterans of the Pacific. Dave had stayed in Hawaii as a radioman, but Joe had a more adventurous tale to tell. He was a radioman/gunner and flew in the backseat of one of those fabric seaplanes carried on cruisers. Every takeoff, a catapult shot, was powered by the detonation of a five-inch shell. Their best story, though, had nothing to do with the war. It involved how it took them more than two weeks to get from Floyd Bennett Field in New York to Memphis by car.

They were sworn in at Brooklyn just after Christmas and received orders for N.A.S. Minneapolis. Halfway there, they were caught in a howling blizzard outside Cleveland. Joe's 1940 Ford bogged down in a small town amid six-foot drifts, and they spent five days sleeping in a firehouse. Resuming their journey, they finally limped into Minneapolis three days later. Reporting for duty, they were met with blank stares. It seemed some sleepy yeoman had typed N.A.S. "Minneapolis" instead of N.A.S. Memphis. The ice-covered base let them rest a few days until the roads south thawed out.

Tall and dark, with a winning smile, Dave liked to chase the girls. He often invited us along because most young women tended to move in twos and threes. That first Saturday, we went into town. Joe left us, agreeing to meet us for dinner at the Claridge Hotel.

A little shorter than Dave with a smile to match, Joe nevertheless held something in reserve. His eyes gave him away: keen, secret, and impenetrable. He was street smart; growing up in a tough Brooklyn neighborhood, he learned early on never to show his emotions. Beneath that warm Mediterranean facade, Joe was hard as steel. He could be nudged, but never pushed.

When Dave and I arrived about six, Joe was already at the bar, sipping a tall beer. He related his first impressions of Memphis. "It only took five minutes for me to realize this was some strange 'burg.' I walked into grocery stores, but they were like nothin' I'd ever seen. Nothin' smelled right. No garlic, no olive oil, no peppers. I asked a guy behind the counter if he had any hard salami, and he looked at me like I just stepped off the moon. So I said to myself, 'Joe, You're a long way from Brooklyn.' I was about ready to hit myself over the head with a plank, when suddenly there it was. A big sign goin' on and off, drawin' me closer and closer. It flashed 'BILLIARDS! BILLIARDS! BILLIARDS'!

"I stepped inside and walked over to a table where a couple of natives had drawn a small crowd. I just stood there and watched, not sayin' a peep. Finally somebody said, 'Hey sailor, would you like to join us in a friendly game?' I said I'd been watching them for a while, and they looked too good for me. I'd only played billiards at school a few times. When I said the word 'billiards,' they kinda' snickered and figured they had a live one. Well, I played for three hours."

Joe reached under his jumper, and as he pulled out his wallet, his face broke into a big smile. He said, slowly and deliberately, "I cleaned 'em out."

Hal later told me that Joe had probably started playing pool when he was about three. When I said a three year old couldn't reach the table, Hal said that in Joe's part of Brooklyn they had special stools for three year olds.

The three of us usually ended up back in my room at the Peabody, drinking Scotch from a fifth, with tap water and ice. We'd rather have sat with more company at a bar or lounge, but by law, mixed drinks were not served in Tennessee. This rather ridiculous prohibition forced everyone to buy a bottle, when what they really wanted was a drink or two. The rule must have in many cases made the expression "drunken sailor" seem all too appropriate.

The experience of our first billet after boot camp was unsettling, to say the least. Here we were, walking around this strange city, trying for all the world to act like sailors and not fooling anyone. None of us had ever been to sea, and about half the class hadn't even laid eyes on an ocean. But there was this whole folklore about wild sailors who chased women and in general created havoc wherever they went. It was reinforced by Hollywood and countless war stories passed down from fathers and uncles. We were somehow expected to play a part, but we didn't know the script.

Putting a teenager in a set of whites or dress blues doesn't change the boy inside, anymore than a sailor suit changes a four year old. Some of the boys from NATTC tried to use the uniform as a security blanket and had the misguided impression that it would explain away a multitude of sins. The local gendarmes soon quashed that illusion. Anyway, it only took a week or two for most of us to revert back to our familiar selves and accept the fact that we were lonely, homesick, and insecure.

In this guise, the people of Memphis took us to heart. We were treated just like any other bunch of college kids, with one big exception. These mothers and fathers had vivid memories of their war and knew very well this was more than just fun and games. They'd seen hundreds of sailors go through Millington in the early forties and remembered some who hadn't come back. Our boisterous behavior and occasional drunkenness was overlooked, and they even let us date their daughters (after thoroughly checking us out). Rides were easy to come by, and airedales by the score would be picked up at the bus station by drivers heading out on Highway 51. More than once my benefactor was a middle-aged or elderly woman traveling alone.

Back at school, our studies became more intense. For someone who had never had physics, there were plenty of empty spaces to fill. It was like studying a foreign language and starting with French III. There was little time for questions, and a demanding quiz loomed every Friday afternoon. Gradually, concepts that had been quickly memorized without understanding fell into practical use. Seven hours a day, five days a week, plus study in the sack, really made an impression. Now some of our classes were held in shops on bench set-ups and often in the aircraft themselves.

Winter came, and outside activity slowed almost to a standstill. The heating system turned the barracks into a Turkish bath and made it nearly impossible to stay awake during fire-watches. I used many different ploys to keep from dozing off. You had to stretch your mind and concentrate on one thing, or you'd start daydreaming. Only here it was night dreaming, and you could be in real trouble.

After exhausting all the electronic formulas I had to know, I started to recall all the themes from the Beethoven symphonies and concertos, working my way through the "big nine." After that, I'd go on to Brahms. One night I was standing outside the head trying to remember if a particular tune came from Beethoven's 4th or 8th. I was humming away and saying aloud to myself, "It's the 4th. No, it's the 8th," when a sharp cough jolted me out of my half reverie. It was the petty officer of the watch. He didn't say a word, but he gave me the oddest look. He must have thought I was ready for the white coat with no sleeves.

Given a choice, the last watch, 0400 to 0800, was my favorite. If I hit the sack an hour before lights out, I could log an uninterrupted six and a half hours. There's an unwritten law in the navy that says you always relieve a watch fifteen minutes early.

This was also the time night slowly turned to day, and the crystal winter sky never let me down. Always a sucker for sunsets, I could now see the heavens do their act in reverse. At home only milkmen and shift workers could match my front seat, and I didn't have anything to do but watch.

The faintest glow appeared in the sky a little after 5 A.M. Gradually, the thin red streak on the horizon changed into brilliant hues of pink and yellow and gold, while directly overhead, wisps of white cloud became visible for the first time. In the west, the deep black sky created a perfect backdrop to this welcome brightening, and on occasion, it was so beautiful you longed to share the experience. You recalled those early summer evenings when you asked everyone to come out and see this great sunset. Well, I never succumbed to the temptation to share the sunrise. You just didn't wake sailors up before reveille, not if you valued your life.

Speaking of waking up sailors, it was fascinating to watch how well disciplined those who had to answer a call to nature were. A typical sailor would ease himself out of his bunk and shuffle along slowly to the head. He'd return the same path, never fully awakening. One night, I spoke to Big Hal when he was in this state, but the next morning he couldn't remember a word I said. When I queried him, he said, "Hell, Jack, like I always say, never let a midnight piss interrupt a good dream." Sleep was so valuable we all became skillfully adept at perfecting this technique. Some little boys acquire this knack, but they usually lose it by the time they reach eleven or twelve.

Often, on my fire watches, I'd have uninvited company in the guise of a stray dog. The base, being out in the boondocks, was a mecca for wandering animals of all description. Besides "man's best friend," we had cats, raccoons, skunks, opossums, and even the odd fox. Mostly it was a haven for dogs. All sailors are suckers for hungry mutts, and the galley always had a half dozen mongrels waiting patiently for a handout. When it was cold or raining, we'd invite them inside the barracks.

The bedraggled appearance of these dogs spurred on practical jokers, of which we had an oversupply. A watch stander would be told his relief was in, say, bunk 14B. When he went to rouse him, he'd find a smelly canine under the blankets, snoring away. More than once, a dog was slipped in next to a guy with a "snoot full," sleeping off a big night on the town. The next day when he'd start to tell us about it, we'd all act like he was crazy and tell him to lay off whatever he was drinking. If nothing else, these dogs were the best-fed animals in Tennessee.

Leroy, an airman from Florida, had a pet baby alligator about a foot long. He usually left it overnight in a sink in the head, and it gave many a new arrival a shock, especially those with a few drinks under their belt. Another sailor in S-13 wanted to keep a pet snake he'd found on the road, but here we drew the line and made him return it to the woods. It was bad enough having to contend with Palmetto bugs in your shoes in the morning.

Most of my classmates were 18 or 19 and seemed to possess unlimited energy. Many had cars and were cruising around Memphis a couple of nights a week. They'd pull up outside the barracks about one o'clock in the morning, their car antennas draped with bras and panties, like some ace submarine returning from a war patrol. These trophies adorned the inside towel rack of scores of lockers, and no doubt would have raised some eyebrows, were the practice not so widespread. I guess it was regarded as some sort of bluejacket merit badge.

I really envied this bunch. If even one half their tales were true, they were having the time of their lives. As long as the girls of Memphis didn't run out of underwear, it seemed nothing would slow them down.

I didn't own a car, and even if I had, I found the school difficult enough to grasp without coming to class half asleep. This pattern changed a bit in February, when everything started to fall into place, and I realized I wasn't about to flunk out. For me, total immersion took a little extra time.

My classmate, Floyd Barr, took me under his wing. He thought I was a big spender from New York, booking a hotel room every weekend. He slept at the "Y," fifty cents a night for clean sheets and all the coffee and doughnuts you could devour. Most of us in the military never saw the Red Cross, but the "Y's" and the Salvation Army were a Godsend. To this day, I never pass up a fund raiser.

The Memphis YMCA had a dance every Friday and Saturday night—canned music, no alcohol, and well chaperoned. The air was heavy with Tabu perfume, and there was enough pancake makeup to make Pillsbury work overtime. But it was all free, and the girls were pretty much like the ones I knew back home: they were just as nervous as I was. It had been about six months since I had a female in my arms, but it didn't take more than a microsecond for that great feeling to return.

Floyd's partner and mine were girlfriends. Afterward, we invited them for coffee and took them home by bus. I hardly knew this girl (can't remember her name), but she gave me what was then popularly known in New York circles as a French kiss. I'm sure I looked stunned, but she just smiled and said goodnight. On the bus back to the "Y," I excitedly told Floyd, probably sounding like I'd just discovered a new element. He just grinned and said as they can only say in the South, "Sheeet, all the little girls do that down here, from the time they're about ten."

As a reward for getting me out of my rut, I invited him to live in luxury at the Peabody for the balance of the weekend. We talked half the night. He was from some place called Cave City in Kentucky, about as far from the Bronx as you can get. The nearest I'd come to a cave was the IRT subway, and Floyd thought that was amazing, trains running underground. The next morning we both agreed that, although we didn't have any underwear to show for it, it'd been a marvellous night.

This experience was far better than a couple of blind dates I'd been set up with. I should have known better. You could tell a sailor almost anything about a prospective date, including the fact that she has only one leg, and he'd probably still show some interest. But utter the phrase "I don't know about her looks, but my girlfriend says she has a nice personality," and those words were the kiss of death. A month later at another dance I met Kate, a nursing student at Methodist Hospital. She was from Seattle and had just barely chosen nursing over a career as a nun. When I told this to Joe (of billiard fame), he said, "You can really pick 'em, Jack."

Actually Kate and I filled each other's needs almost perfectly. She'd been in Memphis almost six months when we met and was desperately lonely. Our lives were complicated enough without a serious relationship, so we had sort of a built-in safety net. By contrast, a half dozen students were engaged, and one I knew had already set a wedding date.

Neither Kate nor I was ready for sex. Some people would say you don't have to be ready, but I'd never been in a position where I was even close. In my background those situations just didn't exist. There was no peer pressure, and fifteen years of religious education had locked in my values pretty tight. In the back of your mind, too, was always the fear of rejection. After finding a girl who'd go out with you, listen to your troubles, let you kiss and touch her, you didn't want to ruin everything by coming on too strong.

Big Hal, for all his strength, was like jelly next to a woman. After a few drinks, he admitted that once on a date with Kate's girlfriend, he was so nervous that they stood outside the nurses' residence for almost an hour. They hadn't even kissed goodnight. Finally, he got up enough nerve and said, "Elaine, if you don't make the first move, we're going to be here all night."

In spite of all that religious education, I only thought about girls twenty-six hours a day. I may have not been ready to go all the way, but I was very interested in what lay under all that nylon underwear. Sometime later, in the back of a dark movie theatre, my curiosity was satisfied.

Kate and I took long walks along the river bank. I didn't need to spend a dime to have a wonderful time, for often she'd pack lunch and we'd picnic next to the Mississippi. As the barges glided by, I'd notice envious glances from groups of wandering whitehats. They were always searching for a friendly face. Aside from the lack of unbridled passion (whatever that is), we spent five utterly enjoyable months together. My liberties weren't hunting expeditions, and I had a guaranteed date anytime I went to town. After watching knots of dejected sailors shuffling from bar to bar, I knew I'd hit pay dirt.

Back in the barracks, it soon became common knowledge that Jack had a regular girl. When I returned from liberty, Joe and Hal would tease me. "Haven't you gotten into that nurse's skivvies yet?" and "Jack, I think you're overdue for some horizontal refreshment." In the collective folklore of the day, nurses were supposed to be sure things. I guess the fact that they saw a lot of private parts was in some way supposed to turn them on. I was only going with the student variety, but she wasn't ready to jump in the sack. What Kate really wanted was a steady male who'd tell her she was pretty and treat her special. My education went a lot further than it had gone in New York, but somehow we never "crossed the bridge." At the time, what we did seemed more than enough.

The only group of women supposedly easier than nurses were divorcées. I'd never met a divorced woman. Where I came from, they were whispered about, like someone who had a communicable disease, so I really didn't worry too much about missing out. One night in the barracks, we were talking about these two groups, when Floyd said with a real serious look, "You know, I just figured out why we're not scoring. What we really need to look for is a bunch of divorced nurses." He was still laughing when he hit the floor under a rain of pillows.

I made up stories about Kate the same way the others did about their girls. We all had to play the game. If we didn't, we'd somehow be false to our naval heritage. I often wondered what Joe and Dave would have said if I told them Kate and I usually started our Saturday night date by going to confession together.

In March our class members were promoted to airman, the equivalent of corporal in the army. In addition to about twenty bucks more in our pockets, we added a third diagonal green stripe to our left sleeve. Every student on the base wore green (the color of naval aviation) and would not be free to sport red chevrons until being rated third class petty officer. This wouldn't come for at least six months, if and when you passed a service-wide exam. All of us in electronics wore the symbol of the element helium (two atoms entwined and framed by tiny wings) above our three green bars. By popular acclaim, we were all known as "green-eyed monsters."

But there were more than just ATs here. Memphis also housed schools for aviation machinist mate, AD ("mechs"); aviation metalsmith, AM ("tin benders"); aviation bo'sun mate, AB (catapult and arresting gear); aviation storekeeper, AK (supply); and aviation electrician, AE. Talk to anyone who was in naval aviation in the forties and fifties, and chances are he went through Millington.

Whatever else happened, one thing you could be sure of was being paid on the fifth and twentieth of every month. The amount of money in your account was posted on a bulletin board a few days before, and you could draw anything from one dollar up to the full amount. For some reason, we were fingerprinted each payday. If this wasn't bad enough, the instructions on the pay slip directed those without a thumb to use another digit. I'd met a number of sailors who were missing many things (including some of their marbles), but I never ran across anyone who didn't have all his fingers. The navy made a big deal out of this disbursement, and everyone involved in the transaction was heavily armed with a Colt .45 pistol. Most disbursing officers looked about as menacing as a bunch of nearsighted bird-watchers, so this always drew a big laugh. And who the hell was going to hold them up? Anyone trying to pull off a robbery in the middle of a naval base guarded by scores of armed marines would need their head examined.

As lowly students, we didn't draw a lot of money anyway. An airman apprentice earned about $52 a month. From this amount, $6.50 was immediately taken out to pay our government life insurance. It turned out to be more than adequate. Our only expensive pastime was an occasional long distance call to our family. The rates of $5 to $7 per three minutes quickly made letter writers out of nearly everyone. With practically everything provided, about the only item we could add was a Zippo lighter. It was extremely useful for lighting cigarettes in all kinds of weather. Before owning one of these, however, I acquired the knack of cupping my hands and holding a match inside to light a butt. This was a distinctly nautical skill, and it drew admiring looks from every civilian in sight.

Halfway through AT school, I found electronics had opened up a whole new world. My previous exposure to radio was turning the on-off switch and adjusting the volume. Now we explored the insides of these receivers like a group of high-tech surgeons. It was hard to believe that radio waves not only could travel through the air but were transformed into sound by passing through an odd-shaped collection of bits and pieces, most of which could fit easily into a small paper bag. I guess all of us had taken this miracle for granted. We started with a basic radio receiver and progressed all the way up to loran (long range navigation) and radar (radio detection and ranging). Our studies mirrored the history of communications, except that we did in days and weeks what had taken the pioneers years. Every principle we studied was developed shortly before or during our short lifetimes. It was an evolving science, and spectacular breakthroughs were occurring at a dizzying pace. Transistors were just over the horizon. Vacuum tubes would almost disappear, and with them most of the weight that was such a critical factor in aviation technology. Unfortunately, I wasn't in the navy long enough to benefit from this, and a lot of old-fashioned muscle was still needed to haul the gear from the aircraft to the shop.

Safety wire entered our lives, and in some cases left its telltale mark. All the equipment was secured in racks with lock screws. No matter how tightly items were fastened, the engine vibration could work them loose. Tiny holes were punched in the outer edge of the screw locks, and safety wire was threaded through. The ends were tightened with a pair of needle-nosed pliers, and the excess cut away. These razor-sharp points were supposed to be tucked under to avoid injury, but through either haste or carelessness, it wasn't always done. Soon we had the ripped dungarees and long scratches that were the trademarks of every technician.

My favorite part of the class was troubleshooting. I could usually find the defective part on the schematic faster than most, but locating the actual condenser or resistor took me a lot longer.

I became familiar with soldering irons, ratchet and Allen wrenches, and volt-ohm meters. We learned how to work in tiny corners, and some of the alignments demanded the dexterity of a brain surgeon. Now we were way beyond the theoretical. Everything we did had a visible purpose. We were becoming at ease technically, and what's more, we were enjoying it. All those long hours had paid off. The military could be faulted for many things, but I can't think of how they could have improved on our training.

Our instructors were primarily chiefs and first class ATs, and almost all had been in World War II. Sometimes when we completed a lesson early, they'd tell us what it was like to fly off a carrier or spend ten hours in the cramped quarters of a PBY (long-range patrol plane). These bull sessions were more than just time killers. They were constant reminders that what we were studying was deadly serious. Sooner than we imagined, people's lives would be depending on our ability, and some of those lives would be our own.

Electronics wasn't the only thing we were learning. We were also learning a new language (a continuation from Great Lakes). When we took the bus to Memphis, we weren't going to town, we were "hitting the beach," even though the nearest beach was hundreds of miles to the southeast. Ceilings became the "overhead," walls "bulkheads," and floors "decks." Candy was "pogey bait," marines were "jarheads," and toilets became "heads." Nothing was ever mislaid; it was "adrift" and sailors were "whitehats" or "swabbies," never "gobs."

The mess hall had a lingo all its own. Coffee was "Java" or "Joe." Griddle cakes were "collision-mats" (none of us had any idea what a collision mat was). Cold cuts, a regular on the Sunday evening menu, were appropriately called "horse cock."

To be relieved (from a detail or formation) was to be "secured." Since the word to me has always meant "kept in place" or "tied down," I thought "insecured" would have been a better choice.

Most of the expressions eventually made sense and gave all of us, hundreds of miles from the sea, some link to our nautical forebears.

The only one I could never "fathom" (another maritime "bon mot" that made it into general usage), was "ditty bag." This term described a small sack we were issued in boot camp. It was designed to hold our toilet articles and small odds and ends, like cigarettes, pens, and sun glasses. I've often wondered where the word *ditty* originated. It sounded much too feminine to be used in the rough and tumble world of the navy.

Electronics had its own set of mystifying phrases and formulas. To this day, I can recall obscure bits of vacuum tube theory that resulted in something called "mu." I can remember too the significance of things like "screen grid voltage" and "push-pull circuits." Unfortunately, it was all totally useless to me in later life. It was much like the intriguing name of that odd piece from the .30 caliber machine gun (I had to memorize them all when "field stripping" the weapon in the National Guard): "belt feed lever stud cam groove."

Early in May, the afternoons started to get uncomfortably hot. I'd arrived in late autumn, so I wasn't prepared for summer in the deep South. In those pre-airconditioning days, the navy's concession to ninety-plus temperatures was a change from blues to whites. Since issued whites gave you a remarkable resemblance to a Good Humor Man, we all had them fitted. Most of us went straight to Ben's, a local tailor in Memphis, one of about a dozen who was trying to retire early on the military. To them, the term "fortunes of war" had a completely different meaning.

Our trousers were "belled," and the jumpers cut down, with a zipper inserted along the left seam. If the tailor did his job right and you were suitably lean, the result was a sailor any red-blooded American girl would be proud to be seen with (at least that's what ads implied).

On the other hand, these tailor-mades could spell disaster for the heavier "swabbie." After a night of beer drinking, with the resulting perspiration, they often couldn't squeeze the jumper past their shoulders. On occasion, we had to cut some people out of their uniforms.

To suitably launch our new whites, Floyd invited me to an afternoon at the home of his girlfriend's sister, just outside Memphis. Kate came along, and the three girls hit it off right away. Nancy, our hostess, was recently married to a career man just off the carrier *Leyte*, and he filled us with tales of what it was like in the "real" navy.

While we were deeply immersed in talk of ships and planes, the girls were involved in their own milieu. I half wondered if Nancy wasn't setting up her younger listeners to be future navy wives. I had to admit she and Zeke made marriage look inviting. Later, when

Floyd and I were alone, he said, "Just imagine, Jack, he can have it anytime he wants." Boy, did we have a lot to learn!

On another date with Kate, I brought along a copy of *All Hands*, a quasi-official magazine that featured stories aimed exclusively at enlisted men. In this issue, there was a featured article on NATTC, Millington. While I was waiting for Kate to appear, a nurse in the lobby picked up the magazine and doubled up with laughter. I said, "What's so funny?" She replied, barely able to speak, "The name of this magazine, *All Hands*, is a perfect description of every sailor I've ever dated."

One of the most bizarre evenings I spent in Memphis, or in fact anywhere, started as a simple picnic at a lake. Joe and Dave joined Big Hal and me, and Kate generously set up the boys from Brooklyn with two older nurses from Methodist Hospital. Hal commandeered a pickup, and we drove to a state park just across the border in Mississippi. The girls packed some fried chicken and sandwiches, and we supplied the beer, soda, and spirits. We found a picnic area near the lake, and the sun had almost set when we finished eating. While Hal and Elaine changed for a swim, the rest of us separated into twos and followed our natural instincts. Over the next half hour, my night school education continued with Female Psychology II and Anatomy 101. From the sounds coming from the nearby bushes, Hal and Dave had already graduated summa cum laude. Except for the cicadas and the heavy breathing, the night was still.

All at once, screams and loud voices broke the silence. In a second, we were all on our feet, and in the beam of a flashlight, we saw Hal and Elaine running toward us, frantically slapping themselves. At first, I thought they'd stumbled into a hornet's nest, but it turned out to be a lot worse.

As Kate and her friends tried to comfort Elaine, who was nearly hysterical, Hal filled us in. They'd slipped into this warm lake about a hundred yards from the picnic site, and he started to get romantic. Suddenly, Elaine stiffened, whispering, "There's something in this water, and I don't like it." Hal began to tell her it was just her imagination, when he too felt something like a leech clinging to his leg. He brushed it off, but others took its place. Elaine was beginning to shake, and she cried, "Let's get the hell out of here!"

As they struggled to shore, they encountered more and more of these creatures. They didn't bite, but clung tenaciously to their skin. Finally ashore, and in the light, what they saw filled them with rage and disgust. They were covered with what the local fishermen referred to as "Memphis eels."

Unknown to us, our end of the lake adjoined a dead-end road

that doubled as a popular lover's lane. Every spring night, scores of couples discarded their beer cans on the shore, and the by-products of their passion in the lake. The locals knew enough to avoid this end, but we'd arrived late and met no one. This sudden change of events put a damper on the rest of the evening, and we all piled back into the truck. Elaine couldn't get to a shower fast enough, and Hal drove home with clenched teeth, not saying a word.

This was a night we all wanted to forget, but somehow couldn't. Dave said he could only recall one event that came close. It was the time that his best friend fell into a cesspool while looking for an outhouse on his wedding night.

Now the summer bloomed, with a heat and humidity only fully appreciated by those living along the Mississippi. The navy, in its usual logical manner, decided that the best time to instruct us in the ins and outs of the new Uniform Code of Military Justice was while we were standing in the morning sun. A chief droned on in a combination of legalese and navy double-talk as we stood melting away.

The first couple of lectures were so obtuse that half the men thought he was talking about their uniforms. When we tried to hear what punishments were being awarded for various infractions, all we got was, "as the court martial may direct." In actual practice, very few of the students ever got into serious trouble.

The navy had an extremely effective deterrent to crime. Those awaiting special, or summary, courts-martial were held in a brig on the base. Guards were tough marines who looked as though they would have been at home in Auschwitz. Every day during noon chow, these prisoners were marched in in lock-step and ate in full view of all hands. With closely shaven heads and baggy dungarees stenciled with large white P's (for prisoner), they appeared to have lost their last shred of human dignity. We found it hard to imagine a breach of regulations that could warrant such treatment. I'm sure this daily routine made a lasting impression, and I never met a sailor who wouldn't have gladly walked the twenty miles back to the base from Memphis rather than risk being AWOL.

This was just another reminder that we weren't simply a bunch of carefree students filling in idle days and weeks. Isolated from the war, and even the sea, it was easy to forget the oath we had all taken nine months before. I'm sure no one actually thought of it in quite those terms, but once the veneer of training classes was scraped away, we were literally "defending our country against all enemies whomsoever."

Just when we were beginning to feel at home, our studies moved into their final phase. Our sojourn in Tennessee was fast drawing to a close. After nearly a year of classroom lectures, we were finally going to fly. Our last two weeks of AT school were spent navigating the Mississippi from twin-engined Beechcraft, fitted with World War II radar.

Each aircraft had a pilot and copilot up front, and six students with their instructor filled the main cabin. Directly in front of each seat was a radar repeater scope and a plotting board. Using these, we had to trace the snakelike turns of the river.

We had heard for months that this would be the highlight of the school, and our class approached the flight line with great anticipation. Headsets were worn for the first time, along with a harness for a parachute chest-pack. Images from every flying film I'd ever seen flashed across my mind. I tried to look nonchalant, yet all I could think of was how stupid I'd been not to use the head when I had the chance. I'd also taken so much dramamine for airsickness that I felt I was virtually floating across the hot tarmac.

Watching John Wayne or Clark Gable, one didn't smell the oil or exhaust fumes, but it was the aircraft interior that really gave my stomach the flips. Hundreds of students had preceded us, and it seemed each one had left his contribution in this well-worn cabin. Luckily, before the inevitable happened, the engines coughed into life. Now, I was much too excited to think of anything but getting airborne, and soon we were taxiing toward the runway.

Abruptly, we came to a squealing stop as the brakes were locked. The sound of the engines rose to a bone-shaking roar. Just when I thought the props would rip off their housing, the brakes were released and we started our roll down the runway. With each turn of the wheels, our plane went faster: fifty, sixty, seventy, airborne.

The SNB (Beechcraft) wasn't designed for quick climbing, so our ascent into the broken clouds was slow but steady. There was more than enough time to pick out all the landmarks of NATTC, including our barracks and mess hall. Soon Memphis was below us, looking more than ever the small town it really was in June 1951. Then, on our left there appeared the reason for our flight: the mighty Mississippi, gleaming in the strong afternoon sunlight.

We leveled off at 5,000 feet and turned on the APS-4 radar. The radar screen was all of two inches square, and I developed a lot of respect for the aircrewmen who had to operate this equipment in the last war. Had this operation continued much longer, I think I would have gone blind.

The exercise completely absorbed our attention, and we hardly noticed how chilly it had become. The flight line had been over a hundred degrees in the sun; our dungarees were soaked with sweat.

By the time we noticed the cold, we had already started to turn back, losing altitude in preparation for landing. Once on the ground with the hatch opened, the heat hit us like a fist.

Somebody had a camera and said we ought to record our first official naval flight. I don't have a copy of that snapshot; too much was going on those last few days in Memphis. I do remember that we wouldn't have fooled anyone into believing we were real airmen in our wrinkled, sweat-stained dungarees.

Deep down, though, I think we all felt differently. The long months of study and close order drill had finally meant something. We'd been airborne in a navy plane, and our names were in an official flight log. There were no wings to wear, but there'd be great stories to tell the freshmen and our girlfriends.

As our days in Memphis dwindled down, and the magic date edged closer, we became the envy of the newer students. I remembered how impressed I was when someone a dozen classes ahead of me told me he was studying multivibrators. It sounded like something out of a science fiction magazine. I imagined writing to some girl at home that I was working on multivibrators. Hell, if that didn't make her think I was an electronics genius, nothing would. In the end, the mysterious word turned out to be just another circuit, with the usual vacuum tubes, resistors, and condensers. Even radar revealed no surprises and was no more exciting than radio. Growing up in World War II, I remembered what a big deal it had been: the great secret weapon. Perhaps we were becoming blasé.

For the first time, we came to realize that most of these close friendships would be ended by graduation and new orders. These guys were our first real military buddies, and the parting would not be easy. Before graduation, however, everything on the base came to a grinding halt.

War or no war, the Cotton Carnival, an annual municipal festival, had to be celebrated. The pageant included a huge parade with elaborate floats, hundreds of coeds in long white gowns, and an amusement park that operated nearly around the clock. It was definitely Memphis's claim to fame, and "Boss Crump," the local political kingpin, was going to make certain its financial success was guaranteed by the navy. Since the admiral in charge of NATTC was named Stump, there was the inevitable linking of the two, and like some mythical law firm, they became commonly known as "Stump and Crump." There were thousands of tourists, mostly from nearby Mississippi and Arkansas, and it was standing room only.

I'd looked forward to taking Kate to the festivities, but she wasn't in any mood to celebrate. I'd just told her of my orders to Atlantic

Fleet Airborne Electronics School in Norfolk, crushing her hopes I'd be stationed in Millington. Out of this last school in Virginia, I could be sent anywhere, from Newfoundland to Trinidad, but the chances of going inland were almost zero. The only naval air stations away from the sea were manned by "weekend warriors" (reserve squadrons).

To raise Kate's spirits, I took her out to Millington, where there was an open house. Our afternoon was spent walking through my classrooms and out to the hangars, where I showed her the Beechcraft I'd just flown in. We ended up in my barracks drinking Cokes. Later, we sat alone in the lounge area, trying to make conversation.

Looking around, she said nursing school wasn't too far removed from our regimen. They also had strict hours, long classes, and they even stood watches, in the form of night ward duty. The girls lived communally, and the talk was mostly of boys, although the level of conversation was more emotional than physical. (I often wondered if they separated boys into "nice guys" and "wolves.")

The ride back to the hospital was endless. I guess we both knew it was good-bye, but neither of us wanted to admit it. Sharpened by loneliness, our relationship had gone a lot deeper than mere physical attraction. We were both so vulnerable that we had probably revealed more of ourselves to each other than we had to any other person. Sharing an absolute trust, we were totally at ease in each other's presence. It had been a memorable five months, but now we had to get on with our lives. A few months later, when I was in Norfolk, Kate sent me a long farewell letter saying that she'd become serious with a premed student. She thanked me for helping her get through a very difficult time. I guess I could have said the same thing.

The day our class shipped out, the navy pulled one last dirty trick. Some brilliant hospital corpsman trying to bring his paperwork up to date decided to give booster shots to nearly half the class. That would have been bad enough under normal circumstances, but we had to haul our seabags, weighing nearly seventy-five pounds, to the main gate. In addition, the regulation traveling uniform was woolen dress blues. Between the bag, the effects of the shots, and the heat of a Memphis July, bodies were strewn all along the path to the gate. Luckily, I missed the long arm of the Medical Corps, but the stupidity of the whole operation soured me and spoiled what should have been a momentous occasion.

Chapter 5

Virginia Interlude

OUR CLASS AND MEMPHIS PARTED WAYS 26 July 1951. It was almost a year to the day I was sworn in on lower Broadway, and a lot had happened to me and the world in those twelve months. I still hadn't seen a ship and I still didn't know what my final billet would be (there was still a final school to complete), but my course was set. The war in Korea had stabilized, and although we'd been badly mauled in the winter offensive by the Chinese, we were there to stay.

The navy had come a long way, too. The number of carriers had more than doubled, and all were incorporated with the latest advances in military technology. The armed forces would never again fall to such a low point of readiness. Sadly, this lesson had to be learned with blood.

Before the next school started in Norfolk, we were given ten days leave. I arrived home to find many missing faces: buddies gone to the army, navy, and air force and former girlfriends engaged or married. Still, it was heaven stretching out in my old bedroom again and raiding the refrigerator at will. I even went up to the Polo Grounds to see my team, the Giants, and Willie Mays rewarded my effort by hitting a home run. With the season more than half over, they'd finally put together a winning combination. Unfortunately, it appeared to be too late in the day to catch those high-flying Dodgers. Little did I dream what would happen in October.

My sisters' families were growing fast, and they spent all their free time looking at new houses. (Rita bought a place in Yorktown Heights, and Dot in Massapequa.) None of us had ever lived in our own home, but the whole country seemed to have caught the fever, and places like Levittown were booming.

My parents took me visiting relatives and wanted me to wear my uniform. Since this would have meant donning whites, I put up a battle and won. I was much more comfortable in slacks and a sport shirt (I was home after all). I smoothed their ruffled feathers by agreeing to wear my "blues" when the cooler weather came in. They also told me their days in our apartment were numbered. In less than a year, the world I'd known was coming apart at the seams.

I looked up one of my old girlfriends, but we were almost strangers. While I was away, I thought time had stood still, and I expected the world to be the same. In my mind, it was like walking out of a movie in the middle and returning the following week to pick up exactly where I left off. But the merry-go-round hadn't stopped, and I couldn't run fast enough to catch up. It was almost with a sense of relief that I boarded a plane and returned to Virginia, back to the more familiar ordered life of the navy.

Naval Air Station Norfolk was just a morsel in this huge complex, the largest base in the Atlantic Fleet. For the first time in my service career, I was housed in a brick barracks. Containing its own mess hall and laundry, it was home to over two hundred men. Now our bunks were laid out in quads, and I enjoyed a modicum of privacy. The rest of my classmates were scattered all round, and as students, we were in a distinct minority. The sailors sharing my space were older and already sporting "crows" on their arms. Their school days were over.

Breezy Point, the popular name for the air station, was set apart from the rest of the operating base. As a result, buses took us everywhere: the school, the post exchange, and the movies. N.O.B. (Naval Operating Base) Norfolk was so large that we had four different theaters to choose from.

Traveling these routes, we passed massive cranes and warehouses, machine shops and foundries, all serving a fleet that was just starting to flex its muscles. Behind the steel latticework of masts and radar assemblies, sleek grey ships silently moved up the channel. Here were carriers, cruisers, and destroyers. This, at last, was the real navy.

On the very first day of school, our class was separated into two types of electronic maintenance: patrol aircraft (multi-engine) and carrier-related equipment. Because of mission, size, and weight, the equipment was different, especially the radar. Continuing a praiseworthy naval air custom, we were given our choice: first come, first served. Most of my class opted for big planes, figuring their chances for flight pay would be greater. I let fate take its course and was assigned to tending single-engine aircraft. I wasn't much interested in flying anyway. (As it turned out, I got a lot more than I bargained for.)

The name of the school, Fleet Airborne Electronics Training Unit, Atlantic, was far more complicated than the course of study. It was known in navy parlance as FAETULANT, quite a mouthful. Those who made up these tongue twisters, must have been direct descendants of the New Deal. We were constantly bombarded by CINCLANT, (Commander in Chief, Atlantic), and had our planes serviced by NARU (Naval Air Repair Unit).

Our class was small, a dozen "green monsters" headed for what we thought would be a fighter or attack squadron. Essentially, the school was a continuation of Memphis, but narrowed to cover the specialized radio gear found on planes with folded wings. The classrooms were located in three long, low wooden buildings situated at the very tip of Breezy Point, in the center of everything.

The broad views into the bay were marvelous. All day, jets and props flew low over our roofs, rattling our windows and roaring their importance. Hampton Roads lived up to its name, with a variety of ships converging from nearly every point of the compass. It was hard to imagine that the *Merrimac* and the *Monitor* had changed the course of naval warfare on this very spot.

Since FAETULANT was the only school on the air station, and a tiny one at that, no mess facilities were provided. Students had to ride the grey bus back to the barracks. To compensate, we were allowed a two-hour lunch break. As most of the students and instructors had cars, we used the extra time to enjoy the sun and the scenery.

There was an archery range behind the school, and some afternoons the teachers would practice their skills with bows and arrows. They all wore green smocks to shield their "blues" from the blackboard chalk and on the range looked nothing like sailors. The standing joke when one of these petty officers was given new orders was to walk up to him and say, "Joe, turn in your smock and bow and arrow, you're through."

After a week, some of us decided to see what Norfolk was like. We'd heard all the horror stories about signs on the lawn announcing, "Sailors and dogs keep off." Rumor also had it that there was this noxious odor hanging over the whole area, resulting in its nefarious nickname, "Shit City."

Well, we never saw any of the signs, but the smell was all too real. Originating from a large fertilizer plant just outside of town, it was always there, no matter which way the wind was blowing, and no sailor ever forgot it.

East Main Street was a sea of white. Thousands of sweating swabbies shuffling from bar to bar. Each one was exactly like the last, except for the predictably exotic names: Archie's Place, Liberty Lounge, Singapore Sling, and Bali Hai. To break the monotony, every block held a small storefront church. These buildings had a

Morse code all their own: bar-bar-bar-mission-bar. You had to see it once, and once was enough. After this visit, I spent all my free hours on the base.

When I was eleven years old, an uncle gave me a copy of Fletcher Pratt's *The Navy: A History*. I was hooked. While my schoolmates followed the batting averages of Joe DiMaggio or Ted Williams, I devoured statistics on Bristol class destroyers, "treaty" cruisers, and North Caroiina class battleships. My bedroom walls were plastered with ship photos, and I remember falling asleep reading *The Bluejacket's Manual*. For my thirteenth birthday, my big present was *Jane's Fighting Ships*, 1942 edition.

For all this intense study, I'd only boarded one of the objects of my interest on one occasion when the fleet came into New York on Navy Day, 1945. Now, in Virginia, I was like an avid baseball fan who's never seen a game but is suddenly invited into the Yankee dugout.

My first excursion led me aboard the battleship *Wisconsin*, moored at one of the big ship piers. Over a thousand feet long, these docks could handle any vessel in the fleet. Once on board, I found friendly chiefs and whitehats, who were more than eager to show me their home. A gunner's mate led me into the thickly armored 16-inch main battery, and a quartermaster showed me the bridge. "Airedales" were rare creatures in the big gun navy. They were all ears when I told them about navigating the Mississippi using airborne radar. After the tour, which lasted over an hour, we all shared coffee in the galley. I'm sure most of them thought I was crazy to spend my liberty exploring a battleship when I could be having a drink on Main Street.

Other ships were there too: carriers with names like *Intrepid*, *Lexington*, *Ticonderoga* and *Bunker Hill*. I knew their stories well. Their hallowed decks were as sacred to me as the battlegrounds at Gettysburg or Valley Forge. Land battles are commemorated by granite monuments, but there's no place for a monument at sea. Only the immortal names remain, now taken by these ships.

To me, these vessels were more than a mere collection of steel hulls and parked planes. Like other national shrines, these great ships had taken on a spiritual dimension that transformed them into solemn places where the faithful came and brave deeds were remembered. When I walked the flight and hangar decks, in my mind's eye I could still see burning aircraft and the diving kamikazes. In a twist of history, these carriers had become as famous as the battles and ships they commemorated.

All this time, I'd been maintaining an active correspondence with family and friends. One of my old college buddies, Hal Atkins, had been in the ROTC and had gone into the army upon graduation. I wrote his mother for his address, and to my surprise learned he lived practically across the road. He was in the Army Transportation Corps and was assigned to the Hampton Roads Port of Embarkation. Most of the troops bound for Europe passed through here. Since there were no accommodations for military at the port, Hal was billeted at BOQ (Bachelor Officers Quarters) on the air station and was within sight of my barracks. He had just bought a secondhand Plymouth, and we decided to explore the region together.

Richmond was our first target, and we weren't disappointed. We must have looked odd together, he with the gold bars of a second lieutenant and me a bluejacket, but no one gave us a second look. Restaurants and hotels that might have rejected a sailor now warmly welcomed us. His uniform became our passport to the best watering places.

On one jaunt to Richmond, the local junior college invited us to a dance. Here we met Barbara and Jane. They had never been with anyone from New York, and probably half expected us to be carrying a gun. On our side, we had to listen very closely to understand those soft liquid tones that passed for language. Neither girl would have stopped traffic, but they were exotic in a way only out-of-town girls can be. We drove them home (Barbara was staying over), and Jane's parents, who were still up, invited us for Sunday dinner the next day. After a couple of long lingering kisses, we made our farewells. Hal and I both agreed that Richmond was the place to be.

Sunday at dinner, we were treated like long-lost brothers. Hal's courtly manners carried the day, and both sets of parents insisted we return and stay with them on our next visit. Driving back to our hotel, we couldn't decide whether we'd completely underestimated our charm or these nice people had found in us a convenient way to unload two eligible daughters. Back home, no one had yet put their hooks out for us. We might have expectations, but we hadn't finished college or established ourselves. These were the rules of the game. Give them some line before you "reel them in." Here in the birthplace of the Confederacy, we were simply prey.

Giving them the benefit of the doubt (they weren't really all that plain and the cooking was terrific), we returned a few weeks later. After showing us the homes of Madison and Monroe, Barbara and Jane directed us to what was probably the darkest spot in the state of Virginia. It wasn't long before we realized we could have carte blanche. There was a lot of heavy breathing and fogged windows, but somehow neither one of us took the Big Step. It might have been different had we been alone, I don't know. Hal and I had waited so long, we didn't want to waste it on just anyone. The Special Occasion required a Special Person. Eventually, we met those special people. What it boiled down to was this: everyone in the service was hungry, but while most were satisfied with a sandwich on the run, Hal and I belonged to a small group who were patiently waiting for a gourmet dinner. We were essentially one-gal guys.

Sometimes when I tell this story, people act as though we were some sort of freaks. In spite of all the folklore about wild sailors, however, we had plenty of company. Freedom of sexual behavior may have been the rule before World War II, when the navy's enlisted ranks were composed of the rough and ready, but with sailors now burdened with the weight of all that middle-class morality (and lack of experience), it just wasn't so.

It probably all came down to competition. For the average 18 or 19 year old, being placed in a position of put up or shut up with an experienced partner was more than he could handle. The opportunity for outright humiliation was just too great. You could lie about your sexual prowess in the barracks, but it was a lot different in front of the real thing. Most of those who did make it went with a group who were usually well fortified and couldn't remember too many of the details. It was a dollars and cents proposition, and the girl wasn't about to give you a refund if you passed out during the preliminaries. She'd no doubt tell you that you were marvelous. So long, next body.

Some of my classmates were cases in point. One, Ivan Gogoberich (not his real last name), was a giant of a man standing 6'3" and weighing at least two-fifty. Because of his wild hair and wilder expressions, he was known to everyone as the "Mad Russian." He never tired of telling all hands how good he was in bed. Multiple partners were his specialty.

Floyd, my Memphis buddy, told me they had gone to a highly recommended hotel (in Virginia Beach) in the hope of really scoring. It was all very simple, very businesslike. The desk clerk set you up for an appointed time, and you greased his palm. While they waited for the girls, they reinforced their courage at the bar. Floyd noticed Ivan had a bottle and was really knocking them down. In spite of the air-conditioning, he was sweating profusely. At last, the clerk told them they were "up," and they went into adjoining rooms.

Floyd's girl reminded him of a schoolteacher he'd once had a crush on, and it kept distracting him. He had a preconceived notion of what these "girls" were supposed to look like, and this sweet young thing just didn't fit the bill. However, any aura of innocence disappeared when she opened his whites. They soon got into the swing of things, and shortly he made his way back to the lounge.

The "Mad Russian" showed up sometime later, looking like a man who could hardly handle even one woman, much less two. At first he was quiet, but after a few drinks angrily related that, after all that effort, he was still unsullied. He discovered what untold numbers of men had learned before him: sex and alcohol (in large doses) don't mix.

His partner, whom he really could have gone for, tried every trick she knew, but he just couldn't perform. Disgusted, she finally called him "Ivan the Terrible." Floyd said he couldn't help laughing, and the more Gogoberich looked for sympathy, the funnier it got. Most sailors had wild stories about their amorous exploits, but we all knew the one about "Ivan the Terrible" was too cruelly true to have been invented.

The place you really couldn't miss was Petersburg, or so the story went. It was a WAC training command, and according to the latest hot dope, the girls were climbing the walls after six weeks of quarantine. All you had to do was appear in a navy uniform, and these female army types would swoon. The stories sounded so convincing we thought we had to give it a shot. It was also just far enough away from Richmond that we wouldn't run into our old friends.

As it turned out, the girls of Petersburg were the same lonely girls we'd seen everywhere, except they wore olive-drab. Neither particularly ravishing, nor ugly, they fell into that great middle ground. They had a little more bravado than the average female, but this may have had something to do with being in uniform and always traveling in a pack. I don't think I ever saw a WAC walking alone. We also wondered what their training consisted of. Did they have VD films, for example? It would be interesting to see how they handled *Don't Take a Chance* in reverse. After all, there had to be some horny women.

There was a big dance at the Enlisted Club the weekend we went up, and they were looking for warm bodies. Hal's uniform created a temporary road block, but he solved the problem by changing into some civies he'd brought along. Officers weren't supposed to fraternize with enlisted personnel, regardless of sex. Soon we were at a table with six WACs. The ratio of girls to guys was about five to one.

This was not to say all the "chesty" army types were ready to jump in the sack; they mostly wanted to talk and occasionally dance. These girls were just plain lonely, and the uniform didn't add or detract from whatever standards they'd carried with them from home. Most were from small towns in middle America, and were looking for a chance to travel and meet new people. The majority had adjusted easily to the service and viewed it as something akin to holding down a job in Washington.

Our experience proved that most of the tales about the WACS were untrue. As in any large group, I'm sure there were some predatory types, but for good or ill, we never encountered any. It was an experience, but not one to be repeated, and we returned to places where the women were at least more diverse.

One Saturday night, Hal's car was acting up, and we decided to return to Norfolk instead of remaining out in the hinterlands. It was after 1 A.M. when we drove through the main gate, and we both had trouble keeping our eyes open. Hal started to drive me to my barracks, but he suddenly stopped the car and said, "Jack, I just remembered I don't have a roommate. He left on Friday, and his place'll be vacant at least until Monday. Why not bunk with me tonight? I have some civies that'll fit you, and you can leave after breakfast." Always game for an adventure, I agreed. Besides, it would spare Hal the detour.

There was no one at the front desk as we walked up to his room. He'd given me his topcoat to put over my blues, and I stuffed my whitehat into my pocket. Bachelor Officer's Quarters looked nothing like our barracks: it was more like a country hotel. We were asleep in a minute, but I started to notice the big difference the moment I awakened.

To start, I didn't have to share this bathroom with 60 other bodies. When I began to straighten the bedclothes, Hal collapsed on the floor laughing. Old habits die hard. But the surprises were just beginning. At breakfast there wasn't even the hint of a line. The tables were covered in linen, and we ate off real plates with true silverware. A mess attendant gave us a menu, and everything was cooked to order. Hal signed for me; I was his guest.

While we were awaiting a second cup of coffee, three other officers stopped by to talk to him. It turned out Hal was rather unique: the only army officer in BOQ. He introduced me as a college friend and a radar officer (almost the truth). Later, one of the new arrivals asked me if I knew anything about early warning radar (he was scheduled to take a course later that month). Well, I raved on for about an hour, drawing diagrams all over the tablecloth. Hal said they looked mesmerized. We figured we were on a roll, and since I now knew half the complement of BOQ, we decided to stay for lunch. I hated to leave that afternoon, but I had to get back to the real world. Looking back, I figured I had had an experience that not one sailor in a million could duplicate. Talk about the Forbidden City; officers are far more cloistered than that. While I don't want to take anything away from them, the gulf separating us, was, to put it mildly, a bit wide. Did I say gulf? It was more like the Grand Canyon. A barrier this great made it nearly impossible for these officers to have any idea how we lived or what pressures we were under. Without that understanding the walls between us were only intensified. Some improvement could have easily been made in our living conditions. The chiefs had separate quarters; why not something in the middle for rated men? It always struck me as odd that those of us whom the navy had educated at a cost of untold thousands of dollars were billeted right alongside many who were barely literate. If they wanted us to become career men, they had a strange way of going about it. But it was all wishful thinking, the navy wasn't about to change. In spite of the differences, I could still look back on my adventure and smile. After all, I was king for a day.

Wherever we roamed that fall, Hal was an interesting study with women. He would ask a girl to dance, and within a few minutes, he'd have her relaxed and laughing. After I got past "Hi, come here often?" my conversational talents were few and punctuated by long, embarrassing silences. His technique was as simple as it was disarming: total honesty.

Ten seconds into the dance, he'd reveal he was nervous and ill at ease and appreciated that his partner probably felt the same way. Searching for words, he'd tell her he was a long way from home and very lonely. He thanked her for being kind enough to dance with him and said he hoped he wasn't stepping all over her feet (in reality, he was a terrific dancer). At this point he shut up. That was the cardinal rule. No matter how long the silence, he never uttered a word. Invariably, the girl started talking, and Hal became the good listener.

After a couple of dances, he'd compliment her on something most men wouldn't notice, like how she'd done her hair or how pretty she looked when she smiled. Now, all the girls, even the sad ones, look great when they smile, so it wasn't just flattery. The beauty of this approach was that it was all true. We were all insecure but were too afraid to admit it. The girls, no matter how sophisticated they might appear, shared this same anxiety.

Finding a man who was open about his feelings was a refreshing experience to these young women, and it soon had their sympathetic juices flowing. Hal's line never failed because it wasn't a line. Watching him, I learned more about the interplay of the sexes than I ever knew existed. I also knew I'd only glanced at the first page in a very long book. Of course, there were other methods.

Cameron George had the bunk below mine in our barracks. Cameron (no one ever called him anything else) was a most unusual sailor. In addition to quoting Shelley, Keats, and Byron, he was knowledgeable about classical music and played jazz piano in his spare time. Everything about him, from his uniform to his bunk, was spotless. His family owned a bank in Kentucky, and in spite of graduating from a fancy military school, he had opted for a stint as an enlisted man. He was also the only person in or out of the service that I ever heard pronounce the "g" in the word "fucking."

When I mentioned Hal's success with the girls, Cameron said that was all well and good, but far too time consuming. His modus operandi was more direct. He'd show up in a Catholic church late Saturday during confessions. He'd watch all the girls coming and going and settle on the one who'd spent the most time in the confessional. He'd engage her in conversation as she was leaving, and it was all downhill from there. He claimed he seldom missed, and looking at him, I didn't doubt it. With his Leslie Howard looks, Cameron could have made out in a convent.

The first member of our old gang from back home was going to be married on Labor Day. Since I had the long weekend free, I told Jim and Molly I'd be there to watch them tie the knot. Besides, Jim was a fellow swabbie, serving in minesweepers out of Charleston. Assuming there'd be thousands of cars on the roads for the holidays, I thought I'd save the fare and hitchhike. I'd done plenty of thumbing in Memphis and hardly had to wait more than five minutes between lifts. At 4 P.M. I was on the Hampton Roads ferry and picked up my second ride in an hour. It looked easy.

I was hoping to find a car going all the way through to New York, but I kept getting short runs of 25 to 35 miles. About 11:30 P.M., I'd made it to Wilmington, Delaware, and here my luck ran out.

These were the days before interstates, and there were no limited-access roads between Norfolk and New York. The New Jersey Turnpike wouldn't open until December, and the Delaware River had to be crossed by ferry at Pennsville. A farmer in a pickup finally gave me a ride after an hour's wait and dropped me on a truck road, Route 13, near Trenton.

It looked like the dark side of the moon: no houses, no diners, not even a billboard. Big trucks came by every few minutes, tearing up the road. By the time they saw me, they were gone. I wasn't the only one trying to get home early this weekend.

I started walking. At this point I'd have gladly paid for a train or bus if I'd seen one; I was shivering in my whites. After what seemed an eternity, I came to a traffic light. I stood there hoping to catch a car stopped at the signal, but the light never changed. It took me a while to figure out that the signal was triggered by a vehicle coming from the side road, and at this hour, there were no cars coming from what was probably a truck farm. I discovered the triggering device, a metal plate in the road, and when I'd see headlights in the distance, I'd jump wildly up and down to change the signal. No luck. I started walking again.

About 3 A.M., a car shot past me doing at least seventy, and I heard the squeal of brakes. I ran as fast as I could. I jumped in the car and thanked him for stopping before I even knew how far he was going. At this point, chilled to the bone, it made little difference.

Before he said a word, the driver handed me a pair of goggles. That's when I realized the car had no windshield! It was a '38 Ford, souped up. The young driver (whose name was something like Ace or Speedy) had driven nonstop from Nashville, and he was headed for Elizabeth, New Jersey, just the other side of the Holland Tunnel. He was functioning on coffee and "bennys." He said, "Keep me awake," and for the next two hours I told him every joke and story I knew. Even with the goggles, my face stung every time we passed a car or truck. I opened up my white hat and pulled it down over my ears and used a greasy blanket he had on the backseat to ward off the cold. At sixty miles an hour, I felt as though I was flying in an open cockpit.

The sun was just coming up as Elizabeth hove into view. We'd become such good friends that he drove me through the tunnel and dropped me at the subway entrance on Canal Street. I don't think I could have waited for another ride, regardless. He wanted to buy me breakfast, but I told him I had a wedding date and thanked him for saving my life. I'd had visions of standing on that road all weekend.

When he pulled away, I jumped into the nearest taxi. Before I could tell him my destination, the driver stared at me as if I'd just come from another planet. The expression on my face must have said it all because he pointed to his mirror. When I saw my image, I couldn't believe it: I looked as if I'd just stepped out of a coal mine. My face was completely coated with oily road dirt, and only the area around my eyes was light. My "whites," if you could still call them that, were wrinkled and stained. I had the appearance of a Bowery bum.

A couple of hours later, after a shower and an old-fashioned breakfast, I stood in the church watching Jim and Molly become man and wife. During the reception, a couple at my table started to tell me what a difficult time they'd had in traffic. I almost laughed in their faces.

My parents, after hearing of my odyssey, insisted on buying me a plane ticket back to Norfolk. Thus ended a weekend that was both ridiculous and sublime. I never hitchhiked in Virginia again.

The two-month FAETULANT course ended on the last day of September, and we all anxiously awaited our squadron assignments. Our careers were about to start in earnest. Most of the class went to two fighter squadrons in Jacksonville. Floyd and I, with two others, went to Composite Squadron 12, Quonset Point, Rhode Island.

Chapter 6

Rhode Island Reunion

My HIGH SCHOOL BUDDY DON ROLLER had enlisted in the navy in 1948 to study radio and communications. In those quieter days, one could predetermine his career by taking a test. Don had qualified and had gone to Aviation Electronics School.

Before the Korean War, Don would bring his buddies from VC-12 down to New York on weekends, and we'd all go out drinking and dancing. "Big Bob" Lipske, Chuck Knowles, and the Gleerup brothers were familiar faces. Now, when I walked into the electronics shop at Seaplane Hangar 2, it wasn't as a frightened newcomer, but as someone with plenty of friends. The million-to-one shot had come true.

Meanwhile, Don had been at sea in the USS *Oriskany*, which was returning home from a Med cruise. He had no idea I'd been assigned to his squadron, let alone that we'd be working together. We sprang a big surprise, and he almost fell over when he saw me.

Don had about six months remaining in the navy. Normally he would have been long gone, but the war had caused everyone's enlistment to be extended by one year. We caught up on old times, and every weekend we drove the 176 miles to New York in his 1948 Ford.

Don had been keeping company with Dot Johnson, probably the only girl he'd ever dated, and it was a foregone conclusion that they would get married. After a couple of lost weekends, hanging out with what was left of the old crowd at home, I started to double-date with Dot's girlfriend, Marianne Hockemeyer. I'd known Marianne and her family for a long time, and we'd gone to night college together. She was the proverbial girl next door. For years, I'd played in a marching band with her brothers, and when our gang was short of funds, we could usually be found at her house, freeloading cookies and coffee. Mrs. Hockemeyer was like a den mother to all of us.

Initially, I wasn't thinking in romantic terms, but I soon started to appreciate what I'd been missing. Here was a girl to lock onto. All

Author and Don Roller, Quonset Point, R.I., September 1951.

the while I thought I had known Marianne, when in truth I hadn't known her at all. It was like rediscovering a book you'd only glanced at, not realizing the riches buried inside. And, like a good book, she did not reveal all her charm in the first encounter. All this wasn't apparent on our first few dates, but I'm sure the chemistry was working. Fate was continuing to smile on me.

Composite Squadron 12 was an Airborne Early Warning (AEW)

unit composed of AD4Ws, popularly known as Douglas Skyraiders. I don't know how the navy derived the names for their planes— *Avenger, Panther, Devastator, Banshee*—but the *Skyraider* more than lived up to her title. She exuded power and confidence. The AD's lines said, "I'll get you there and I'll get you back," and for the most part she did. She was a big plane with a powerful engine. The "4W" had a wing span of 50 feet and an overall length of 38 feet, six inches. Standing 12 feet tall, she weighed in at 17,500 lbs. and could go up to 24,000 pounds if needed. This was a plane for all missions.

The squadron had World War II vintage TBMs (modified torpedo bombers) for most of its life and had just completed the transition to the Douglas aircraft when I reported aboard in September 1951. These TBMs were under-powered for the heavy radar payload, and, more importantly for the crewmen, they were not the easiest planes to evacuate if you ditched in the ocean.

Unlike most of its sister fighter or attack squadrons, VC-12 never went to sea as a unit. The main body consisted of about fifty aircraft and five hundred officers and men. Remaining at Quonset Point, VC-12 dispatched small teams to every carrier in the Atlantic Fleet. VC-11, our sister AEW squadron on the West Coast, performed the same function for the Pacific. Each team had three planes, with about five pilots and thirty enlisted men.

They were essentially self-sufficient and provided the carrier air group with a long range early warning and antisubmarine capability. The ship's "eyes" were extended two hundred miles to pick up an attacking force in plenty of time to launch a counter blow. Before this development, the fleet had to depend on shipboard radar, which had a relatively short range and was ineffective against low-flying aircraft. The bitter lessons learned off Okinawa in 1945 launched the study that led to single-engine, carrier-based AEW.

I wasn't thinking in these terms when I went up for my first familiarization flight. After the simple radar of our recent classroom days at Memphis and Norfolk, the array of switches, dials, and scopes of APS-20 (air pulse search) radar was staggering. It resembled something lifted from a science-fiction movie. Flipping those thirty switches over my head and finally pressing the red start button (which fired the radar) always gave me a kick. I found myself thinking that this was all a dream and it wasn't really me in the backseat of this aircraft.

On this flight, I was sitting next to a chief, observing the procedures. We were airborne only a few minutes when I heard a plane calling, "Mayday, Mayday. Request immediate landing instructions.

AD4W Douglas Skyraider, Composite Squadron 12, N.A.S. Quonset Point, R.I., October 1951.

No oil pressure." I looked out the small plexiglass bubble but couldn't see any other aircraft. I was about to ask the chief if he could see anything from his side, when I noticed he was as white as a sheet and frantically tightening the harness of his chute. By the time I realized that we were the plane in trouble, we were already on the ground, surrounded by crash trucks. It was finally determined that the oil pressure indicator had malfunctioned, but at the time I didn't understand the implications of what had nearly killed me. I was still, in the most eloquent of navy expressions, "fat, dumb, and happy."

Quonset Point was an ideal spot for a naval air station, jutting like a finger into Narragansett Bay. We were over water almost as soon as our wheels left the ground. As New York was 170 miles away and Boston about half that distance, the station offered a matchless opportunity for liberty. Providence, about 30 minutes by car, offered diversions closer to the base.

The views from the seaplane ramp just outside our hangar were spectacular. It wasn't hard to believe this had been a wealthy enclave before the government bought it in 1942 to develop a naval air station. Adjoining Quonset was Davisville, the largest SeaBee base.

There was never any mistaking who belonged where, since the Seabees were all World War II veterans and were no doubt master craftsmen.

In age, they could have passed for our fathers. They resembled, if nothing else, the tradesmen who used to come by to give our parents estimates for a boiler or a roof. Their chests were covered with ribbons: Asiatic-Pacific with battle stars, Victory Medals, Presidential Unit citations, and many Purple Hearts. In the summer, there was a picnic area, and even sailboats were available for those who wanted to prove they were real sailors. For someone from the Northeast, it could be the best of all service worlds.

The winters were something else entirely. The cutting wind off Narragansett Bay made working outdoors a miserable experience. You just couldn't find enough foul weather gear to make a difference. The Skyraiders' interiors doubled as deep freezers, and more than once the skin from our hands was left behind. To make matters worse, the equipment was always located in impossibly tight corners, causing the circulation in our legs to be cut off.

These experiences caused many airedales to volunteer for an October deployment. The cruises were six months in duration and returned when the Quonset winters had lost their bite. Southern Europe, although far from tropical, was a paradise compared to New England.

Chapter 7

Guppyland

COLD WEATHER BROUGHT AN ADDED DISCOMFORT: the necessity of donning exposure gear. The one-piece rubber outfit was more commonly known as a "poopy suit." It had fitted boots and elastic wrist and neck closures. In theory, if the suit didn't leak, one could stay alive in the cold water for 30 to 40 minutes. You fared a lot better if you could make it into your life raft, but that was easier said than done. In reality, the aircraft usually sank so quickly after a ditching that it was difficult to detach the raft from the parachute you were sitting on. Often, crewmen were suspended upside-down in a pitch black compartment rapidly filling with sea water. No one tarried under these conditions.

Underneath this miniature Goodyear Blimp, you wore a flight suit, two sets of winter underwear, and two pairs of socks. All this gear was topped off with a "Mae West" (rubber life jacket) loaded with flares, shark chaser, flashlight, knife, whistle, and dye-marker. Finally came the crash helmet, a close-fitting head protection not unlike that worn by profootball players. But this helmet had to withstand a lot more impact than anything dished out by the NFL. We didn't walk in this regalia, we waddled. More than anything else, we had an uncanny resemblance to the Michelin Tire Man.

Getting in one of these thermal body-bags demanded more than one set of hands and a generous amount of talcum powder. The sweating started long before the last clasps were fastened and continued until you were peeled out four hours later. Water temperatures around Quonset made wearing this gear a practical necessity from September until late June.

No one could be expected to stay aloft in a cold vibrating aircraft for four hours without some way of relieving himself. Enter the "relief tubes" (aptly named) for each member of the crew. The problem was trying to get your personal equipment to reach the tube through all the layers of clothing.

The cold weather only made things worse. Unless you were built like a stud horse, it was often a frustrating experience. Many of us just gritted our teeth and bore it. We tried to watch what we drank before going up, but the navy's long addiction to coffee didn't help.

One frigid Monday morning flying over Cape Cod, I was faced with a far more serious problem and one in which a relief tube offered no help. I tried to tough it out, but it soon became apparent that I wouldn't last out the flight, which still had three hours remaining. My fellow crewman said it was impossible to get out of an exposure suit in the air, but I had to give it a try. He didn't know I was prepared to cut myself out with my survival knife if it became necessary, simply because I couldn't even contemplate the alternative. We told the pilot to keep it level and I crawled up into the access tunnel. Somehow I got out and back into the suit without the knife and became something of a hero to the electronics shop. Our leading chief said if they ever made a movie about Houdini, I could play the role.

I'd always had a problem with airsickness, or at least that's what I thought it was. I'd usually lose my breakfast or lunch about an hour into the mission, after experiencing sweaty palms and waves of nausea. My efficiency as an air controller wasn't exactly enhanced by this. To compensate, I'd skip the meal before getting airborne. Then I'd just have dry heaves for two or three hours. I never felt guilty about accepting my flight pay.

Years later a doctor told me it was probably claustrophobia and that I could have achieved the same result riding in the back of a car with the blinds down. I never had the problem when we were on long navigational flights with unhooded windows.

Sometimes the flying could be fun. Operating over Long Island Sound, we'd look for snorkels from the submarines out of New London. Trying to locate those blips with all the boat traffic in warm weather or through the "sea return" in winter was a real challenge. ("Sea return" was a kind of white snow on the radar screen caused by the angle of the radar beam hitting the waves.) I had a tremendous respect for any controller who could plot a snorkel in those waters. It took hours of practice.

In the fall, there were cool crisp days when we'd rendezvous over Riverhead and fly low over the eastern end of Long Island. Autumn had left her mark on the land, changing scattered farms into a patchwork of brilliant decoration. The blue water sparkled, and for a moment one could imagine oneself over some South Sea isle, instead of New York. After watching the pleasure boats make their long lazy trails on Long Island Sound, we'd turn back to Point Judith and home.

A tone of quiet professionalism ran through VC-12. All the senior petty officers appeared overqualified. Many, like Bob, went on to become commissioned when the LDO (Limited Duty Officer) program was established a few years later.

Not that there weren't any characters; it wouldn't be the navy without them. One AC spent six months in the shop building a super-charger for his Buick. When he finally finished it, it wouldn't fit in the car. He'd flown a slew of missions off Hungnam during Christ-mas 1950, so no one bothered him.

Our division officer, Lt. Fantasia, had a mania for charts. He had graphs illustrating the percentage of planes up, planes down, sea time versus shore time, and God knows what else. The walls of his office were a veritable art gallery of zigs and zags. My buddy Don Roller put it best when he said, "Fantasia even has charts showing the progress of his charts."

None of us thought Clay, a taciturn Lincoln look-alike, had a sense of humor. One day, working on an AD in the hangar, he fooled us all. By accident, he discovered an antenna setting on our radar which would trigger the alarm of the adjoining squadron. He bided his time, and fifteen minutes before regular muster he set off their bell. Of course, everyone stopped working and fell in to be relieved. A very unhappy OOD (officer of the day) appeared, pointed at his watch, and raised his blood pressure a few notches. Clay pulled this trick for a solid week and no one caught on. The beleaguered squad-ron then had base maintenance rip out reams of wiring and replaced the alarm bell twice. The engineer's explanation was that it was caused by sonic boom.

Whenever a plane completed one of its periodic checks, usually every thirty hours, all departments had to test their gear while the aircraft was turning up on the apron. Our mechs would come into the shop to tell us that the plane was ready, and out we'd go. To check the radio, we'd climb up on the wing and plug our headset into a cockpit outlet. A quick call to the tower would tell us all was well. Some of the mechs enjoyed having a little fun at our expense. They'd rev up the engine to the point where we were literally hang-ing on by our fingernails. More than once, I lost my flight deck shoes during these fun and games.

In time, our turn would come. The electronics shop was the room-iest in the hangar, with wide aisles between the long work benches. We had a setup for every piece of equipment, including the massive APS-20 radar. The latter had a huge magnet, well hidden among the cables. When the mechanics came in to shoot the breeze over a cup of coffee, they'd usually ask if the gear was off before leaning back on the bench. They all had a healthy respect for electricity, especially the high voltage variety we specialized in.

Since all the mechs carried tools in their back pocket, it didn't take much skill to maneuver them close enough to the magnet so they were locked in. Someone would shout, "My God, someone left the power on. You'll be sterilized in twenty seconds!" In a flash, he'd be out of his dungarees and running back to the safety of his shop. It was no joking matter, though, if one forgot to remove his watch before working near that magnet. "Antimagnetic" meant nothing to those monsters.

Our radar was the only reason the squadron existed. It lent our department a purpose and direction not often found in other units. We had no guns, no rockets, no bombs. Here, ordnance took a backseat to electronics. The pen may not have been mightier than the sword, but in VC-12, surely the vacuum tube was.

The bulky radome, which made the Skyraider appear that it was about to deliver a baby AD, gave the squadron its trademark. Because of its resemblance to a well-known tropical fish, our aircraft were dubbed "guppies."

During the more extensive checks, 120-hour or 240-hour maintenance, the radome would be dropped. Although it looked like part of the fuselage, it was in fact a separate encumbrance composed of a composition of lightweight fiberglass and secured to the Skyraider by eight bolts. Once removed, it revealed a six-foot elliptical antenna that rotated 360 degrees.

Just forward of this dish, slightly behind the fire-wall, lay an inspection plate that provided access to the IFF (Identification Friend or Foe). This indispensable piece of equipment insured the safety of our aircraft when flying over our own forces. The IFF worked like radar, emitting a set of coded signals that identified the plane as friendly. Signals were changed daily in a combat zone, for security was paramount. If the codes fell into the hands of an enemy, the results could be devastating. To safeguard against this, destructors were built into the gear, allowing the pilot to destroy the IFF before bailing out or ditching.

These devices and the location of the equipment in the AD made the servicing of the APX-1 the most hated assignment in the division. Working through an opening barely two feet square, you had to balance the unit over your head in order to position it into its rack. Only your arms and upper torso fit inside, and once in, there was no way to pick up a tool or flashlight without completely removing yourself. The flashlight had to be wedged between your head and the plane, effectively immobilizing you for the installation period.

With sweat pouring into your eyes and the muscles of your upper body stretched to their limit, ten minutes seemed like ten hours.

Obviously, given the lack of any means of communication, this procedure was fraught with peril. Often a technician would get hung up when his dungarees or foul-weather jacket got snared inside the opening. All he could do was kick his feet and hope someone would notice. This happened to a hapless AT one morning, but all his kicking proved fruitless as everyone had gone to chow. After an hour of this torture, he emerged, cut and bruised and visibly shaken. He wanted to murder his assistant, who'd forgotten about him. Another time, Newberry remained so still while installing destructors, the metalsmiths spraying the landing gear didn't notice him and painted his dungaree trousers the sea-blue color of the plane.

I often wondered how much fun it was for our pilots to fly these modified dive bombers. In this configuration, the planes had a top speed of only 190 knots and usually flew much slower. I thought that compared to an attack AD, it must have been akin to driving a truck. All the pilots I met didn't find this a drawback. Although it looked ungainly, the radome had very little effect on the handling qualities of a Skyraider, and when it came to props, she was top of the line.

In the air, we developed a rapport with many officers who respected our ability as much as we respected theirs. To me, they were always the older brothers I never had. Flying this beautiful but deadly machine placed them, in my eyes, in the company of giants. With our very lives on the line, we had no argument with the navy's high standards. Only the best won the "gold."

These men in the cockpit were the steadiest in the fleet. No wild men here, trying to play "Top Gun." From the flight logs, it was easy to see the older men had nothing to prove. They'd sent plenty of enemy ships to the bottom in the last war, and there were more than enough Navy Crosses, DFCs, and Air Medals to go around. I felt secure in the backseat. Our pilots were as solid as the planes they flew in.

At the time, I didn't realize it, but this special rapport would indelibly change my attitude toward the navy. What I looked upon as normal behavior was, in reality, one of the distinct qualities of naval aviation. In General Service (nonaviation), officers were one step from God and expected to be treated as such. The enlisted man was little more than a serf, with about as many rights. One could rise up to the heights of the noncommissioned hierarchy with an unblemished record and then lose it in a wink merely by incurring the wrath of an officer. In a court-martial, the cards were pretty well stacked against the enlisted man.

In aviation, the officers were pilots first and brasshats second. Many openly shared our disdain for all the time-wasting nonsense we were put through. In the squadron, we were expected to be professional technicians: the rest of it was shelved for the most part. With each of our lives depending on the other, it was only logical. In later years, I discovered how lucky I was. Many of my buddies who had gone to sea in General Service had vivid memories of that caste system they had to live with. With few exceptions, they developed a deep-seated hatred of all officers, and that feeling hadn't mellowed much over the years. As I listened to their stories, it was painfully evident that for every Mister Roberts there were two Captain Queegs.

In the squadron, the men I worked with showed that we could perform far more efficiently if motivated by pride rather than fear. Both groups, officers and men, forged a bond of trust that carried over into everything they did. This was particularly true in the air. I developed such confidence I would sometimes forget where I was and become totally immersed in the sweep of the radar. The engine's roar was just so much background noise. But let that roar stop, and suddenly my heart pounded, as the dials on the altimeter and airspeed indicator started spinning the wrong way. It only took a second to realize we were changing fuel tanks, but in my early flights they were very long seconds indeed. I never quite got used to it.

For all this confidence, I never met an aircrewman who wasn't afraid of bailing out of an AD4W. Its aerodynamic instability (caused by the bulky radome) required the placement of two additional vertical stabilizers in the tail assembly. These knifelike fins stood directly behind the rear hatches. If we had to jump, it appeared the slipstream would carry us straight into the leading edge of this blade.

We searched the manuals in vain for any advice from the manufacturer. After a couple of conferences, we decided to go direct to the horse's mouth, the Douglas Corporation.

Lt. Fantasia, our maintenance officer, shared our concern (he flew too) and wrote to the manufacturer. They thanked us for our interest (an understatement if I ever heard one) and said they would let us know the results of their tests. In a few weeks, all the aircrewmen were called to a meeting, and a tech rep from the company explained they had performed experiments using dummies. Although the findings were inconclusive, they recommended diving out head first if we had to evacuate the aircraft. That way, if any part of the body made contact, it would be our leg, not our head. Very reassuring.

Two years later, in a remarkable coincidence, Lt. Fantasia had to bail out of a disabled Skyraider over Long Island Sound. He, the pilot, and another aircrewman all survived with little more than a cold dunking. I was in Korea at the time and often wondered if he went out head first.

In the three years I served in VC-12, the squadron's only fatality occurred in a night midair collision. Considering that there was always a minimum of three teams on board carriers, that was a record to be proud of.

Ground transportation was another story. Hardly a month passed without some grisly car crash. Weekends were the worst, with sailors driving at night in all kinds of weather. All hands, it seemed, stayed away till the last possible moment, timing it so they'd arrive just minutes before the Monday morning muster.

The road from the main gate to Route 3 was two miles long, straight as an arrow. Often, as we were landing after an afternoon flight, the cars below would be pulling *away* from us. The AD had a low landing speed, but it wasn't that low.

Too often I rode with real crazies. One nut, Russ, another AT, had a trick guaranteed to give you gray hair. Caught behind two slow drivers, he'd wait till the one in front of him started to pass on the left. Then, rolling his eyes back into his head, he'd floorboard it and pass both of them on the right shoulder, leaving them in a cloud of dust. He only asked $5 round trip to New York, but it was a thrill a minute. After a few rides with Russ, one felt guilty accepting hazardous duty pay for merely flying.

Louis M. was the other extreme. He was so absentminded, he'd get engrossed in conversation, edge up on the car in front of him, and tap bumpers. One never dozed off with him behind the wheel.

Of all the sailors I rode with, George Walls was the most interesting, if that was the proper word. George had gone to my high school in New York and had enlisted in the navy a few months before me. He personified the happy-go-lucky Irishman, but was rock solid when you needed him. In a short time, he would replace Don Roller as my best friend in VC-12.

George was happiest buying old cars for $100 or $200 and rebuilding them. One night, returning to Quonset from New York, he was doing 35 miles an hour in the right lane. A trooper moved in behind and tailed us for about 45 minutes. At the tollbooth, he pulled us over and made George get out of the car. The officer said that in eight years patrolling the parkway, he'd never seen a sailor driving that slowly. He was certain we were either drunk or driving a stolen car. Walls told him he was breaking in a new engine, but wait till next week.

Our most adventurous trip took place in a lashing rainstorm with his 1938 Pontiac. I think this car still had shades above the rear windows. They must have really conserved gas in those days, for this vehicle was ideally suited for far more interesting pastimes than mere transportation.

We started back to Rhode Island on Route 1, the original post road of colonial days. George wasn't too sure of this car, which had been built in Roosevelt's second term, so he took this slower road, filled with more cars and traffic lights, but also plenty of service stations. It was one of his better decisions that night.

On a particularly desolate stretch, blacker than black, with rain whipping across the road, the left rear tire went flat. Because the shoulder was a sea of mud, we could only pull part way off the road. Walls grabbed an ancient jack and attached it to the rear bumper. He handed me a flashlight and said to let him know when the wheel left the ground. He started to pump vigorously. Every minute, he'd stop and ask optimistically, "Is it up yet?" After the third inquiry, I directed the light beam to the bumper. The bar holding the bumper had moved up almost a foot into the left rear fender, but the wheel hadn't budged. The car's body was so rusted that the harder steel bar had gone right into the fender, like a hot knife through butter. The lunacy of what we were doing suddenly hit us, and we broke down laughing in the middle of the road. We were still there a half hour later when a heaven-sent tow truck found us and quickly resolved our problem.

Chapter 8

The Best-Kept Secret

VC-12 INTRODUCED ME INTO THE WORLD of aircrewmen. When most people think of naval aviation, they visualize lean young pilots streaking into the air from a pitching carrier deck. What would enlisted men be doing with wings?

After a little research, I discovered chiefs and whitehats were not only crewmen in the earliest biplanes, but actual pilots all through the thirties and World War II. In the latter conflict, most were commissioned.

During the disarmament years following the First World War, many Naval Academy men, lured by the adventure of flying, opted for Pensacola. Since the primary purpose of the Naval Academy was to provide officers to man the ships, the navy sharply restricted the number of graduates who could go on to flight training. In 1926, to fill this gap, Congress deemed that 30 percent of all pilots would be selected from the ranks of enlisted men.

Other than these enlisted pilots (NAPs), every naval aircraft (except fighters) had sailors who performed as radiomen, bombardiers, or gunners. On cruisers and battleships, they manned the radios and machine guns in the seaplanes used for observation. Here, every takeoff was a catapult shot, much as for today's jets. For putting their lives on the line, these ACs pocketed about $50 extra a month, the right to wear a set of silver wings, and the respect and envy of their shipmates. It was strictly voluntary, and nobody did it for the money. If the truth were known, most would have done it for nothing.

After the war, as the planes and the electronics became more sophisticated, the aircrewmen's role took on more importance. In some units, particularly airborne early warning and electronic countermeasures, the pilot's function was almost secondary to the mission.

For all this, the perks remained essentially the same. Often, after a four-hour stint over the radar scope, the aircrewman switched roles and changed from air controller to technician, servicing the very equipment he just operated. He shared the same cramped quarters with the rest of the crew, and the only place his opinion carried any weight was in the ready room or the backseat.

The pilots knew the value of aircrewmen, however, and strong bonds grew between the two groups. If his navigational receiver failed, the pilot knew he could always count on his radarman to locate the carrier, no matter how many times she had changed course.

The gap between ranks was seldom bridged in General Service, where almost all communication was made through chiefs. Naval aviation was a different story. Our direct dependence on each other in the air was one reason, and (at least in the Korean War) the educational level of the average aircrewmen was way above average.

Many had had some college, and those who held a degree wanted to limit their service to four years. This was no doubt the first time the navy had such an educated pool of talent not wearing the gold. The vast majority of flying officers respected our ability, and some socialization took place within the limits of discretion and common sense. The responsibilities shouldered by these lowly airdales were awesome, but the young men always rose to the occasion. The navy, I'm sure, acted reluctantly, but didn't have much choice. There weren't enough officers who were either available or interested in a career in air controlling, and the program had been developed to use enlisted men as early as 1946.

Most of us were cross-trained. Technicians were air controllers, and the operators pulled gear and performed bench checks. When it came to ATs, the navy got its money's worth.

It was in the nineteen-forties that aircrewmen first came into their own. Their contribution to victory is one of the best-kept secrets of World War II. Submariners, Seabees, Frogmen, PT sailors, and even weathermen in the Gobi Desert were all given their rightful recognition, but one looks in vain for any mention of these flying whitehats, either in celluloid or in print. On board the carriers, they manned the guns and radios in the backseats of Devastators, Avengers, Dauntlesses, and Helldivers. And how effective would the PBYs and PBMs (or even the blimps) have been without their enlisted crews?

In spite of this contribution, the press continued its conspiracy of silence. If they were mentioned at all, it was by last names or worse (Cmdr. Doe and Lt. So and So were lost with their crews). Their record pleads for a reversal of this attitude.

From the very opening attack on Pearl Harbor, aircrewmen put their lives on the line. Those crewmen in the backseat were just as astonished as their pilots when a routine flight from the USS *Enterprise* on the morning of 7 December 1941 rapidly found itself in the middle of a shooting war.

At 0615, *CV-6* commenced launching 18 SBD2s and 3s of Scouting 6 and Bombing 6. Their mission was to search ahead of the task force for 150 miles and then land at Ford Island in the middle of Pearl Harbor. As the men approached the base, the sky was full of antiaircraft bursts. Initially, they thought these were just more army maneuvers, but they were quickly jolted into action when bullet holes appeared in their wings and fuselages.

Ensign Perry Teaff's plane was one of the first to be hit, and his radioman Edgar Jinks RM 3/c unshipped his .30 cal. machine gun and engaged the Zero. Flying through intense AA (all of it friendly), Teaff miraculously brought his Dauntless into Ford Island with both he and his aircrewmen unscathed. Others were not so lucky.

Both Lt. Clarence Dickinson and Ensign John McCarthy tangled with many Zeros, coming out on the short end. McCarthy's SBD was set ablaze, and his radioman/gunner Mitchell Cohn RM 3/c was either dead or couldn't exit the diving aircraft.

McCarthy bailed out below 500 feet and broke a leg, but miraculously survived. Dickinson's plane was riddled by five Zeros, and his gunner, William Miller RM 1/c, was mortally wounded. Earlier, he had scored hits on one of the attackers before exhausting his ammunition. The pilot heard Miller say he'd been hit again before the plane went into a spin, and he told him to bail out. There was no reply, however. Dickinson made it out of his burning dive bomber and landed safely in a cane field. Ensign "Manny" Gonzalez flew into six Vals, thinking they were U.S. Army planes. He was heard on the radio at 0833, saying, "This is 6-B-3, an American plane. Do not shoot." Later he was heard instructing his radioman Leonard Kozelek RM 3/c to get out the rubber boat, but they were never seen again.

Ensign Ed Deacon, seeing Ford Island was a shambles, attempted to land at Hickam but was downed by more friendly fire. As he flew over Ft. Weaver, the site of a machine gun school, his plane was hit repeatedly; he was wounded in the thigh and his aircrewman, Audrey Coslett RM 3/c, received nearly fatal injuries. Coslett was hit in the right wrist, right shoulder, and neck. Deacon made a water landing just short of Hickam and was quickly picked up by a crash boat. Coslett survived.

Ensign Bill Roberts was luckier and landed his riddled aircraft at Hickam. His passenger, Don Jones AMM 1/c, was so incensed, he manned the single .30 cal. machine gun and fired at the strafers until his ammo was exhausted.

On the other side of Oahu at Kaneohe, aircrewmen and other airedales fought a losing battle to save the PBY patrol bombers of PatWing One. In two attacks, Japanese fighters destroyed or badly damaged every aircraft. Some men seized machine guns from the burning planes and fired back at the enemy. Chief Aviation Ordnanceman John Finn took a .50 cal. machine gun from one of the PBYs and set it up on a homemade steel stand he had fashioned for just such an eventuality. In spite of several painful wounds, he continued firing. Finn was later awarded the Medal of Honor. (Fifty years later, at a retrospective of the Japanese attack in Honolulu, I asked Finn what motivated him to repeatedly stand on an exposed runway and shoot it out with swarms of Zeros. "I just got damn mad," he replied laconically.)

The first few months of the war continued to thin the pathetically few surviving ACs from that historic *Enterprise* flight. Otis Dennis RM3/c and Harold Thomas RM1/c both perished with their pilots during the 1 February 1942 raid on the Marshalls. Ensign Perry Teaff crashed into the sea on takeoff before the Wake Island raid on 24 February 1942 and lost an eye, but his radioman Edgar Jinks went down with the plane.

Jack Leaming RM2/c was shot down over Marcus on 4 March and spent the rest of the war as a POW. (He was lucky; the Japanese executed many captured pilots and aircrewmen.)

All these men were lost, just from the 18 plane flight from *Enterprise*. The navy posthumously commended both William Miller RM1/c and Otis Dennis RM3/c for heroism by naming destroyer escorts DE-259 and DE-405 for them.

As a postscript to the December 7 attack, another aircrewman distinguished himself in a noncombat situation. William Roberts RM 2/c, flying in the backseat of an OS2U-3 piloted by Lt. J. B. Ginn, became one of America's earliest heroes. Nearing the end of a patrol, their plane crashed in the sea off Barbers Point. Roberts found the unconscious Ginn in the cockpit, trapped in the wreckage. After freeing the pilot, Roberts made repeated dives to free the rubber boat from its compartment under water. With the badly injured pilot, Roberts paddled the eight miles to Barbers Point, where the raft capsized in the surf. Pulling the pilot ashore and making him as comfortable as possible, he hiked inland to find help. Roberts was awarded the Navy Cross.

Other adventures not involving enemy action awaited two men who would have gladly passed up the honor. On 16 January 1942, just a few weeks after Pearl Harbor, a Torpedo 6 SBD that was low on fuel ditched after failing to find the *Enterprise*. An air search was made the next day, but the raft was not spotted.

The pilot, NAP Harold Dixon, and the aircrewmen, Tony Pastula and Gene Aldrich, had all survived the ditching. Although they were listed as missing in the trackless ocean, they embarked on what became a monumental struggle of men against the sea. Kept afloat by a fragile 8' × 4' rubber raft, they survived everything that nature could throw against them. For thirty-four days, they broiled under the equatorial sun and existed on rainwater and an occasional fish. After drifting a thousand miles, they landed on Puka Puka Island, just in front of a killer typhoon, ending the first such odyssey of this new war.

At Midway, the carnage among the torpedo bombers was horrific. The saga of *Torpedo 8* is well known. Like the gallant DEs off Samar in October 1944, they hold a special place in U.S. naval history. Pressing on in the face of almost certain death, these pilots and aircrewmen disproved once and for all the common Japanese belief that Americans were soft, but the price was high. All 15 TBDs of VT-8 were shot down. Fourteen out of fifteen pilots died. The mortality rate among the backseaters was 100 percent: fifteen out of fifteen.

The two other torpedo squadrons didn't fare much better, with twenty-seven out of thirty planes shot down. Radiomen/gunners from these groups shot down five Zeros, but twenty out of twenty-six aircrewmen were lost.

On occasion, other backseaters switched roles. On 31 August 1942, while making bombing runs on Japanese warships off Guadalcanal in an SBD-3, the pilot, Ensign E. A. Conzett, was badly wounded by a 20mm shell that lodged in his right leg. Seeing the aircraft veer wildly and assuming the pilot had been hit, the aircrewman, James Cules ARM 1/c, took over, using the rear controls. He successfully landed the plane at Henderson Field and carried the unconscious pilot to a group of marines, who then took him to sick bay. The next morning, Conzett was flown to Noumea, where the surgeons removed the projectile from his leg.

In *The BIG "E"*, Cmdr. Edward Stafford describes how critical the radiomen/gunners were to the survival of the dive-bombers. The action he describes took place in the battle of Santa Cruz on 26 October 1942. The dive-bombers had just left two enemy warships burning. Then the SBDs went down close to the white caps, slipping, jerking, twisting under the intense AA fire from the ships and repeated runs by the Zeros. With their mixture, throttles, and prop controls all pushed to maximum and their bombs gone, the pilots weaved and tried to cover each other. But Garlow and Williams (ACs) with their rear-facing .30 calibers held the only hope of getting the section back to base. Some Zeros got careless. One of the first to attack ceased firing too soon and banked away showing the plane's defenseless belly. Garlow stitched it thoroughly, and the fighter exploded into flame and rolled into the sea. A few minutes later Williams nailed one too, and after that the attacks were not pressed home so closely.

Every SBD of the sixteen-plane flight returned safely to the ship. They had shot down seven Zeros attempting interception and had left a carrier and a cruiser burning.

Perhaps one of the best tributes to aircrewmen came from a pilot from Torpedo 3 who was forced to ditch after a running battle with five Zeros. The following is an excerpt from Cmdr. Wilhelm Esders' USN article in the August 1990 issue of *The Hook*.

> Though our main weapon was the torpedo, radiomen/gunners in the rear seats were just as dedicated to fulfilling their mission as the pilots. They were not only well trained, but highly motivated, and shot their guns until they had no more ammunition or were incapable of carrying out their assignment.
>
> This happened to my gunner Mike Brazier. He was hit at least seven times with 7.7 mm. ammo. and twice with 20 mm. explosive projectiles. As if the small caliber wounds were not enough, the 20 mm. exploded, blowing away all the flesh on his legs between his knees and the ankles. Despite his enormous wounds, Mike somehow managed to change the coils in the radio receiver and helped me steer close to the task force, where we ditched.
>
> When I moved Mike from the sinking aircraft, I could see the large bones in each leg as I got him into the rubber raft. Of course, he bled to death. Yet this young man was still able to talk to me in the raft, expressing how badly he felt that he wasn't able to perform better or longer.

Buried in the archives of the Pacific war are other surprising facts. On 20 November 1943, when the "Blue Ghost," the USS *Lexington*, was making her initial contacts with the enemy, first blood was drawn not by a fighter pilot, but by radio/gunner William Hisler, who shot down a "Betty" from the backseat of his TBF.

George Bush, on his famous flight where he bailed out of his disabled plane and was picked up by a submarine, was also accompanied by aircrewmen. Lt. Ted White, taking the gunner's position, and Jack Delaney ARM 2/c, his regular radioman, were lost in this action.

Aircraft carriers weren't the only stage for these sailors in the sky. In the Philippines, the only naval aircraft were the PBYs of

Pat Wing Ten. Dwight Messimer's stirring book, In *the Hands of Fate*, gives equal recognition to the gallant radiomen and gunners who, with their pilots, fought a heartbreaking retreat through the islands.

> War came to these twin-engined seaplanes on the first day 8 Dec 1941 (7 Dec Hawaiian time). At Malalag Bay in Mindinao, the tender USS *Preston* lay at anchor with two of her aircraft moored near the beach. Six Zeros and seven bombers swooped down under the overcast and cut the planes to pieces. Both PBYs exploded, and burst into flames. On P-7 the pilot ENS Tills was killed instantly, and his radioman Al Layton RM 3/c jumped into the bay enveloped in flames. Badly burned, he survived.
>
> The next day in Luzon, "friendly fire" claimed P-21 returning from a Subic Bay patrol. Two aircrewmen were hit, Tom Marbry AMM 2/c in the knee, and Jim Gray RM 2/c in the groin. Gray survived, but Marbry died of shock and loss of blood five hours later. Things were evened up the next day 10 Dec. Lt. Harmon Utter's P-5 was attacked by Zeros and badly damaged. Standing in the bow, gunner NAP Payne returned the Japanese fire with his .30 cal. nose gun. The pilot watched the bullets pour into the enemy's cockpit and the Zero crashed in the sea.

The one-sided war was taking a heavy toll on Pat Wing Ten. PBYs were never designed to take on bombing missions without fighter escort, and by 13 December, the war being but five days old, the unit had lost ten of its twenty-eight aircraft. Four more were badly damaged and unable to fly. During the rest of December, the small force continued to be whittled down, and with the exception of three planes that made it to Java, the rest were lost. Three pilots and one-hundred forty enlisted men, including many aircrewmen, were captured on Bataan. Fewer than half survived the war. Seven pilots and four aircrewmen were honored by having destroyers named for them.

On the other side of the world, in conditions that couldn't have been more different, other radiomen/gunners fought an equally dangerous conflict. There were no enemy carriers or kamikazes, only submarines; but here the outcome was, if anything, more critical to final victory. Until the battle of the Atlantic was won, there could be no thought of landing and supplying an army on the continent of Europe.

From the pitching decks of CVEs (escort carriers), the Grumman Avengers, each with its two enlisted men, joined the Wildcats in breaking the back of the U-boat offensive. All during 1941 and 1942, the wolf pack tactics of ADM. Doenitz had nearly severed the lifeline from the New World to the Old. Landing on these tiny decks, about half the size of an Essex-class Pacific carrier, took a special act of courage. If you were unlucky enough to be shot or forced down, the icy waters of the Atlantic were far less hospitable to survivors awaiting rescue.

Elsewhere on this vast ocean, other crewmen manned the long-range patrol bombers and lighter-than-air craft. Mechanics, gunners, radio- and radarmen, they all performed their essential tasks, necessary to the successful completion of their missions. In the first year of the war, navy aircrewmen were probably dying at a greater rate proportionally than the members of any other branch of the naval service.

Yet (unbelievably) all this heroism was virtually ignored by the press and Hollywood. Unlike the infantry, these men had no Ernie Pyle. One would have thought the saga of enlisted sailors grappling with Zeros would have inspired countless newspaper and magazine articles, but except for footnotes, their exploits went unnoticed.

The Army Air Corps fared better. Colin Kelly's crew was idolized, and in *Thirty Seconds Over Tokyo*, Ted Lawson was unstinting in his praise for his gunner and radioman. Hollywood was quick to jump on the bandwagon. *Air Force*, an early war film, is a good example. This was the drama of a single B-17 that flew into the war on 7 December 1941 and continued on to the Philippines via Wake Island. It featured not the pilots, but the tail-gunner and crew chief. They were portrayed by John Garfield and Harry Carey. Now that's recognition. In *Winged Victory*, Moss Hart's prize-winning documentary, another noncom, Robert Walker, was given a leading role.

Naval aviation didn't get nearly the level of publicity rendered to its sister service, and when it did, it was usually fighter pilots who took center stage (*Wing and a Prayer, Flying Leathernecks*, etc.).

Within the air groups, things were different. The *Lexington, CV-16*, is typical of the carriers that took the war to Japan's doorstep in the last two years of the conflict. The records of Bombing 16 and Torpedo 16 list many awards for the action of 19 June 1944, but the price was high. Thirty-one aircrewmen were killed in action in these two squadrons. The very next day, as the battle of the Philippines Sea continued, Task Force 58 lost 16 pilots and 33 aircrewmen.

In the closing months of the war against Japan, flying whitehats took part in the destruction of its largest battleships (Yamato and Mushashi) and participated in bombing missions on the home islands. On 2 September 1945, when the enemy signed the surrender documents on the deck of USS *Missouri*, there were scores of backseaters in the thousand-plane flyover. Thus, in a symbolic joining of hands, these "sailors in the sky" came full circle with their gallant brothers who flew from the deck of the *Enterprise* on that fateful Sunday nearly four years before.

Chapter 9

Settling In

QUONSET HAD JUST STARTED TO FEEL LIKE HOME when in early December, I returned to Norfolk with three other technicians for Advanced Radar School. The course was only six weeks, but this move upset a groove I was becoming increasingly comfortable in, not the least of which was easy access to New York and Marianne.

By now, we'd strengthened the ties started three months earlier. The only advantage to this separation was that the school would close down completely for the holidays, and I'd have both Christmas and New Year's free instead of only one. I flew down with two sailors I hardly knew, Miller and Flynn. We soon became fast friends.

Pat Flynn lived in New Jersey and had never really grown up. He must have been his high school's comedian, and navy regulations did little to deter him. Chuck Miller, his partner, though not as wild as Pat, was willing to tag along down his path of destruction. Six inches shorter than Pat, he was the archetypical smiling Irishman and was Boston bred. I never tired of his pronunciation of the word *radaaar*, among others.

We were all billeted in the same brick barracks that had held me the previous summer. Among our fellow students were eight radio-men from the RAF. This was our initial exposure to foreign airmen. They created quite a stir the first night when they appeared in their grey flannel pajamas. Navy enlisted men only wore their skivvies when they hit the sack. For the sake of allied unity, neither of us commented on the other's sleeping apparel. Their English reserve made them appear more formal in our eyes, and it took a while to melt this away.

One night, at the EM club, a discussion started about the simi-larities between the Royal Navy's uniform and ours. The trousers, jumper, and flat hat were nearly identical. Chuck volunteered that the thirteen buttons on our trousers represented the original thir-teen colonies. I added that I'd heard the three white stripes on the jumper flap stood for Lord Nelson's three great victories. We'd all downed more than a few beers when one of the British aircrewmen asked if the two stars near the white stripes held any significance.

Now Pat Flynn liked our English guests as much as any of us, but deep down he was still an Irishman and couldn't resist this opportunity. Touching each star on my jumper for emphasis, he said, "The star on the left stands for the first time we beat the British navy, in 1776. The star on the right is for the second time, in 1812. And the room in between is for all the times we can do it again." The visitors took it good-naturedly, for Pat could say almost anything and get away with it. He was born with that gift.

In class, one of Pat's more notable contributions was to place a piece of cheese around a rectifier tube. Once the gear was turned on, the tube became red hot. The results were both predictable and devastating. He was also not above adding his own "troubles" to the radar to create confusing symptoms during trouble-shooting sessions. His technical ability was good enough to pull off these diversions without being discovered.

I joined Flynn on liberty almost every night. Among his more memorable escapades was the serenading of the Bachelor Officers Quarters with his favorite ditty, "I Once Knew a Sailor Before He Died." Another night, with Miller and me in tow, Flynn led the shore patrol in a wild chase through an amusement park closed for the winter. They finally gave up when we'd climbed halfway up a roller coaster. In the navy, Pat was a character in a sea of characters. The six weeks flew by.

APS-20 school ended in mid–February, and we returned to the frigid flight line at Quonset Point. With temperatures often in the single digits, we earned our flight "skins." Working on the ADs parked outside, we longed more than once for the warm classrooms of Norfolk. I took the test for AT3 and couldn't wait to get my "crow."

There was an opening on "night check," the evening work shift, and I jumped at it. Don Roller was already there, and as senior technician, he took good care of me.

If you were single and not living on the base, there were many advantages to night duty. You stood no watches, pulled no weekend duty (usually once a month), and had no reveille. We slept in a separate wing of the barracks, where blankets were taped around every window so the morning light wouldn't awaken us.

From the time we chose to rise until 1800, the day was ours. If one wanted to taste the delights of Providence or Westerly, he was free to do so. Our liberty cards stayed in our wallets. The only drawback revolved around breakfast. Small group that we were, the navy would not cook a special meal for us. Often as not, you'd sit down to chicken cacciatore when your stomach cried out for bacon and eggs.

Everyone in night check put out 100 percent. What we lacked in quantity, we made up in quality. Goofing off was unknown. Our job was to complete the unfinished work of the day force, whose members secured at 1500 (VC-12 was an early rising group). Night flying troubles were also our meat, so most of the time we had a full card.

Technically work ended for us at 0200, but there were times we'd continue well beyond that hour to complete a job or solve an intriguing trouble. We'd usually send the "brown baggers" (married men who carried their lunch in bags, much like school kids) home to their warm beds and, I hope, warm wives. If there was a big operation during the day, we'd come in early to determine the status of the more complicated jobs. It was easier to get the dope from the man on the job than to try to decipher the instructions left behind.

Occasionally officers, some quite senior, would come by to observe, and they often worked with us. For many, electronics was their hobby. Others wanted to learn more about early warning radar, the raison d'être of Composite Squadron 12. We'd have "three-stripers" crawling inside the tunnel in greens or blues until we found them a set of dungarees or an old flight suit.

Then there were the extra enlisted men who populated the shop most evenings. You were sure they'd never go near a plane. Their car radios and TVs, with names like Dumont, Philco, and Emerson, took up corners of the shop. We, of course, had schematics for just about every piece of equipment extant. This was only a small part of a thriving "cumshaw" (barter system) that was carried on throughout the squadron.

If one had car trouble, the mechanics handled it. No money changed hands unless parts were needed that couldn't be fashioned. In turn, their radios and TVs were our meat. Metalsmiths did minor body work on your car, electricians ran 220-volt lines for your dryer, and parachute riggers kept you from patronizing the local tailor. No one took much advantage, and within limits, the use of government equipment was tolerated. At any rate, we were improving our skills, and half the radios and TVs on the bench belonged to officers.

Running night check didn't require much discipline. Our main concern was getting all our planes "up." Man for man, we probably had the highest productivity in the unit. In all fairness, those who worked days had many more interruptions, with flying and musters. But it was still far easier to crap out in the backseat of an AD when you were one of sixty, rather than one of ten.

Evening chow in the navy is a light meal, so along about 2200 we'd be hungry enough for night rations. This box lunch type of food, consisting of sandwiches, hard boiled eggs, or a chicken leg, was the only concession the navy made to those who toiled after hours. We pretty much got the leftovers from dinner or the evening meal. If we knew a cook on duty, we might rate an apple pie or a large batch of cornbread, which I always thought of as cake. The galley was heavily staffed with Southerners, and the menus reflected this. Rice, black-eyed peas, and hominy grits were common in a place about as far east of the Mason-Dixon Line as you could get. The food was good. Not many meals were memorable, but cooking for hundreds is not the way of a gourmet chef. Very few sailors frequented the hamburger joints that were primarily designed for the civilian workers. More than once, pilots asked me to bring them a steak sandwich when their dining room fare left something to be desired. And they were paying for their chow.

One evening, after Don left, these night rations, or the lack of them, created a unforgettable row. Our new crew chief had been working on a plane with me some distance from the shop when the rations were delivered to the duty officer. Whoever counted heads forgot about us, and our department came up two short. The extra boxes were left with the ensign on duty. I guess the temptation was too great, and after half an hour he started to eat them. When we returned to the shop and discovered what had happened, the crew chief blew his stack. The ensign was caught with a partially eaten chicken breast in his hand, and our boss stormed out. He said, "I'm closing down, everybody out." The time was not quite 2330. Before extinguishing the lights, he went to the status blackboard and wrote in large block letters, "No fuckin' chow, no fuckin' work." I thought he was going to get hanged, but he only had a few months left in the squadron, and the navy was always sensitive about feeding its men, whatever the circumstances.

On a cold night in February, a returning aircraft from another squadron crashed into Naragansett Bay just short of the runway. The pilot got out uninjured but was unable to free his life raft before the plane sank. The crash boat picked him up in less than twenty minutes, but he died of exposure in the hospital an hour later. The water temperature was 29 degrees; the air 16. This tragedy was a shock to the aircrewmen who thought the exposure suits were foolproof.

As sobering as this was, there really wasn't anything we could do about it. As long as we wanted to fly, we had to accept the risks and depend on our pilot's skill to get us back in one piece. It was also infinitely safer than driving. A few weeks before, two sailors were killed instantly in a spectacular crash on Route 165. Their car hit a massive oak tree on a slight curve in the road. The road curved, but they didn't. Driving to New York, Don and I had often talked about that tree.

Chapter 10

A Medical Detour

WORKING NIGHTS LEFT ME with a lot of free time. On the average, I rose at 0900 and had coffee and a roll at the "gedunk" stand. Quonset Point was a modern complex, neatly laid out with two-story brick barracks and administrative buildings. It resembled a college campus more than a military base, and only the constant sound of aircraft revealed its true purpose.

There were ample facilities for athletics, including a large indoor swimming pool. A well-stocked PX adjoined the movie theatre, and the library could compete with any large branch in New York City. It was here I spent most of my afternoons in cold weather.

In college, I'd been an English and history major. The literature courses I'd completed ended with the Civil War, but I found it far easier to relate to writers of my own or my parent's generation than those of a century ago. In three months, I'd read all the Hemingway and Fitzgerald on the shelves.

A pilot gave me a copy of *The Web and the Rock* and introduced me to Thomas Wolfe: ten adjectives to every sentence (it seemed). After a while, one became mesmerized. Wolfe's books weren't read for plot, for in his case, "getting there" was all the fun. One weekend I was home with my parents, I mentioned how much I was enjoying this new book, and my Dad said he'd not only read all of Wolfe's books, but had actually known the man. While my father was attending Cooper Union in the early twenties to study art, Wolfe was a young teacher at NYU. On occasion, they'd talked over dinner at a local chop house. Wolfe hadn't yet published anything, but my father said you couldn't forget his formidable size or his command of the language. My dad made a number of sketches of him, and some turned up after Wolfe's death.

This was the first time I'd spoken to my father in a "man to man" way. As he reminisced about the days before he was married, I saw a side of him I never knew existed. I discovered I hardly knew him.

While I was growing up, my father was a forbidding figure. I was far too young to realize what the Depression was doing to him, but I knew he'd been out of steady work for years. It must have been devastating. Every time I saw him, he was either painting or reading, and I didn't want to disturb him. The few times we went out became treasured memories. By this point, he was slowly getting on his feet, but I'm sure the scars were still there.

While in the navy, I started a correspondence with my father that continued throughout my enlistment. We talked about books, history, and religion, and we shared things on paper that somehow we could never say face to face. Maybe it was just that old barrier that exists between parent and child; I don't know. Those few years of exchanging ideas and memories became far more important to me, however, than all the missed times of playing catch together or all the other things fathers are supposed to do with their sons.

One of the philosophies he instilled in me was "be your own man." Going against the grain sounds like a romantic and adventurous idea, but it can be terribly painful when you're young. My early interest in classical music instead of sports (I didn't become a dyed-in-the-wool Giant fan until I was 17) set me apart, and later in college (Catholic), I aroused the enmity of my fellow students by refusing to sign a petition trying to save Senator Joe McCarthy from being censured.

But most of all, this dialogue with my father brought me face to face with the most important part of our relationship. These letters were, in effect, chisels, chipping away at the shell that had separated us all these years. Growing up, my feeling towards him gradually changed. First it was fear, then respect, and finally (at this late stage) admiration. In no small measure, this affection sprang directly from my discovery that under all the thick layers of emotional insulation, here was a man just like me. And a man I deeply loved.

If you're in the navy, you're going to spend a certain amount of time at sea. That's a truism. There were a few exceptions, but they were very few and very exceptional. Two or three years on a destroyer or carrier (or a place like NAS. Coca Solo, Panama) and then back to a shore billet, probably Norfolk or San Diego. Obviously, what you did had a great deal to do with how long you'd spend where. There weren't too many niches ashore for boatswains and quartermasters.

Composite Squadron 12 was admirably fair. A chart containing every man's name in the electronics department hung in Lt. Fantasia's office. On it appeared the number of days you'd been in the squadron and the number of days you'd spent at sea. From that ratio came the all important statistic, percentage of sea time. It ruled your life.

Unless one volunteered for a carrier deployment or "cruise" (as they were known in those days), he wouldn't be tapped if there was someone in his grade with less sea time. You always knew where you stood. It gave you the priceless gift of being able to make plans, and this was especially important if you were married or had a steady girl.

After six months in the squadron, I was living on borrowed time. My percentage of sea time was zero. One day in March, I walked into the shop and there on the bulletin board was a neatly typed sheet with the heading "USS *Wasp*: Subject Cruise." Seven names were there, including mine.

In April, we'd be heading for the Mediterranean for six months, and Floyd and Pat Flynn would be working alongside me. It would be a super team. None of us had been out of the country, and we'd already served nearly half our enlistment. It was time.

Don Roller was leaving the navy and was all excited about his plans for the future. General Electric made our radar, APS-20, and like all smart government contractors, they were always on the lookout for sharp technicians. A tech rep from G.E. had set up an interview for Don in Syracuse shortly after he got discharged. If everything worked out, he'd start with them and marry the girl of his dreams, Dot Johnson. It was finally coming together for Don, and he deserved it. I was just sorry to be losing the best friend I had in the navy.

I requested ten days precruise leave, so I could have a real farewell party in New York with Don and say good-bye to Marianne. We'd been double-dating with Dot and Don on a regular basis since I'd returned from Norfolk in February.

Quonset Point had a blood bank program and, as an incentive, allotted two days off for each pint you gave. Technically, you weren't supposed to give more than once every four weeks, but no one kept close tabs. I'd given blood a week before, but in order to lengthen my leave, I let them take another pint on the morning I departed. I thought I was pretty smart.

Since Don had already left, and it was the middle of the week, I had no way of arranging a lift. I was heading for the bus to carry me to Providence and the train when a pilot asked me if I wanted a ride to Norwich. Norwich was about an hour from the base, and since it was only 1000 I'd have no difficulty getting lifts the rest of the way. After all, this wasn't Virginia, and hundreds of sailors thumbed successfully every weekend. I was right about getting picked up, but while I was waiting twenty minutes for my last ride on the Merritt Parkway, it started to rain and turn cold—typical April weather.

When I arrived in the Bronx, I was soaked and worn out. Not wanting to waste any of my leave sleeping, I showered, had dinner with the family, and was out on the town by seven o'clock. Marianne had night college classes, so I spent my first couple of evenings with some old buddies whom Uncle Sam hadn't corralled yet. After three days and nights of celebrating my newfound freedom, I came down with a beauty of a sore throat and fever. I'd forgotten about giving blood twice in one week, but it was coming back to haunt me. After bed rest and aspirin didn't help, my mother called in the family doctor, who immediately shot me full of penicillin. He said I'd be up and running in 36 hours. Thirty-six hours came and went, but I still felt punch-drunk, so back came the good doctor.

Dr. Rosenthal said he could take a whole battery of tests, but I'd be foolish to pay him when I was entitled to free medical care. He said he also thought I could find better ways to spend my leave than in bed alone. I agreed and called the duty officer at VC-12. His advice was to contact the nearest naval hospital, which happened to be St. Albans near Jamaica on Long Island, about 20 miles from my home.

Within an hour, a big gray Cadillac ambulance pulled up in front of my apartment, lights flashing and completely blocking traffic. They came upstairs with a rolling stretcher. I didn't want to get on this contraption, but they said it was regulations.

A crowd had gathered on the sidewalk, and I felt like an idiot. Once we'd driven away from my street, they pulled over and let me ride up front.

While looking for the parkway, they completely missed the entrance. When I told them they'd have to turn around, they just laughed and drove down the grassy slope right on to the main road, sirens wailing and lights flashing. The parkway traffic came to a screeching halt as they raced to the Whitestone Bridge. I wondered how these maniacs had missed getting into naval aviation.

The chief pharmacist at reception looked at my throat and said, "You'll be outta' here in 48 hours." I felt good. They bedded me down in what I later learned was the contagious ward, and in a few hours I'd slept my way into Easter Sunday 1952.

The next day I felt better, and my spirits really got a boost when Marianne and my parents arrived in the afternoon. The sun was warm, and I strolled the grounds, showing off my navy bathrobe. It looked like I'd soon be back in the whirl. I was glad I'd left most of my uniforms home.

After the visitors left, I had dinner and started to watch television with the handful of patients and the solitary hospital corpsman on duty. During the "Ed Sullivan Show," I began to feel very warm. I asked the corpsman if he'd mind taking my temperature. He said, "No problem" and stuck a thermometer in my mouth, not taking his eye off the TV screen. After a few moments, he read it and nearly jumped out of his seat. I asked what it was, and again he said, "No problem."

In no time, I was surrounded by two doctors (one very senior), two nurses, and more corpsmen. My bed was rolled into a corner, screens placed all around, and the mattress covered with a heavy rubber sheet. I was stripped and placed face down on the bed. One nurse commenced pouring the contents of a bottle of rubbing alcohol over me, as the other force-fed me tall glasses of ice water. I was told to drink and drink, and not stop. Not knowing what was happening to me, I was terrified. I wasn't some admiral, so I figured I was in deep trouble to be getting all this attention.

After an hour, I cooled down, and everyone looked considerably relieved. The doctors finally departed, but whenever I awakened during the night, there was a nurse and a corpsman next to my bed. It would be weeks before I discovered what happened. This was only after I got close to the ward doctor, who's name (oddly enough) was Dr. Ward.

Shortly before I was admitted, there had been three cases of spinal meningitis, two of which were fatal. The symptoms included an extremely high temperature that couldn't be broken. When the corpsman had taken mine, it was close to 106 degrees.

Although I'd survived the big night and my fever dropped to 101, I felt terrible. My throat was like raw meat, and I couldn't swallow without dissolving two aspirin on my tongue. For a month I existed on liquids; I lost 22 pounds.

Two weeks after being admitted, VC-12 temporarily detached me, not knowing if I was going to return to duty. All the contents of my locker at Quonset arrived, neatly packed in my seabag and two parachute bags. This upset me more than my medical condition, as the last thing I wanted was to leave the squadron. A nurse told me not to be concerned, as this procedure allowed the navy to transfer my pay records.

I was subjected to scores of blood tests, and soon discovered I had something with a long name—infectious mononucleosis. Before I had a chance to worry, I was comforted by two facts: it was rarely fatal and it was commonly known as the "kissing disease." I never learned whose kiss had laid me low, or if in fact it was one. Dr. Ward was more inclined to think the extra blood donation and my frantic social pace were the cause. He also cautioned me not to take this experience lightly.

Usually mono briefly disturbed the body's blood chemistry. After a few days of rest, you were as good as new. My situation, unfortunately, was far more involved. The infection had been particularly intense and had spread to my neck glands, liver, and spleen. It was going to take time, and rest was the only treatment. The doctor estimated my stay at about eight weeks. I was stunned. As it turned out, it was closer to four months before I returned to duty.

After my throat healed, life in St. Alban's improved immeasurably. I couldn't leave the hospital, but they made things as pleasant as possible. The food was as good as I'd ever eaten, in or out of the service. The hospital was something of a showcase, and VIPs were always coming or going. Some called it the "Bethesda of New York." The immense dining room was light and airy, and best of all we ate from china. The staff dined in a far corner, but ate the same food. I was on a special diet to regain the lost weight and rated a double malted at every lunch and dinner. It was a sacrifice, but I endured it.

There were movies nightly, and a couple of days a week we were treated to live entertainment: Louis Prima, Neal Hefti, and Vic Damone. On these occasions, the corpsmen would put us in wheelchairs so we'd all have front row places. We were told not to look too healthy or we'd be put in the rear. There was a huge library, and I resumed my journey through American literature, even squeezing in *The Caine Mutiny*, a big favorite at the hospital.

Marianne came over every few days, occasionally bringing my mother. Our family had no car, and the bus took over an hour. Thoughts of Marianne filled more and more of my lonely hours at the hospital, and fate was drawing us closer together. By early June, I was granted liberty, but had to be back on the grounds by 2200.

Every morning brought the dreaded blood test. It became the worst part of my hospital stay. A corpsman, usually the worst for wear from the night before, would awaken me at 0545. Without so much as a "good morning," he'd start sticking me with a needle, searching for a suitable vein. Mine were not too prominent, and the search would begin: jab, jab, jab, and finally success. After two weeks, I started to look like a drug addict. Coming out of the shower one afternoon, the senior nurse who was a "full lieutenant" in more ways than one, noticed the black welts on my arm. When I explained what happened, she said she'd take my blood from now on. She seemed to have a foolproof method for finding a good vein (maybe her proximity had an effect on my blood pressure), and the fact that she was cold sober didn't hurt.

One afternoon a few weeks after I was admitted, the quiet routine of the hospital was broken by the sound of many ambulances converging on the entrance. About eighty survivors of the destroyer *Hobson* were brought in. Some were burned, and some had broken bones. Others were suffering from fuel oil ingestion and exposure.

The USS *Hobson* was part of the escort for the aircraft carrier *Wasp*, the ship I should have been on. While engaged in night-flying exercises in the mid–Atlantic, the *Hobson*, a plane guard destroyer, either zigged when she should have zagged or estimated the distance too closely as the carrier turned into the wind to launch aircraft. The *Wasp*, 40,000 tons and moving at better than 20 knots, cut her in two. The *Hobson* sank in less than five minutes, carrying 188 men to their deaths. Neither the captain nor anyone on the bridge survived. No one knew for sure what had caused the navy's worst disaster since World War II.

The sailors being admitted to St. Alban's were the lucky ones. They were standing watches when the collision occurred. Anyone below decks didn't have a chance.

The *Wasp* lost sixty feet of her bow and returned to New York stern first after picking up the survivors. No one on board the carrier was hurt, but all were in a deep state of shock. My team from VC-12, with the rest of the air group, transferred to another CV in Norfolk and proceeded to the Mediterranean. The *Wasp* spent a month in Todd Shipyard in Brooklyn before rejoining the fleet.

Later I had a chance to talk to the survivors. It was a harrowing experience, but they had no qualms about returning to "tin cans." They loved the duty. They wouldn't fly off a carrier for all the money in the world.

Settling into the hospital routine, I began to notice patients who looked healthier than most men on active duty. They were awaiting medical discharges and were negotiating their disability before survey boards. Some claimed bad backs or other service-connected disabilities. In their spare time, most of this group lifted weights or chinned themselves from the curtain bars above the beds. I couldn't believe what was going on.

Dr. Ward told me I could get out on a "medical" if I wanted. He'd tell me how to go about it. I asked him if I could expect a full recovery with no after effects, and he said I'd be fine if I followed instructions. I told him I wanted nothing more than to be made well and returned to VC-12. My stock went up 100 percent. He arranged extra liberty and even a couple of overnights, which were unheard of. In World War II, he had served with the marines as a hospital corpsman on Pelileu and Okinawa. In 1951, he'd been recalled from his practice as a pediatrician.

I didn't want a medical discharge. After two years in the navy, I'd finally found my niche in the squadron and didn't want to be parted from the best friends I ever had. Besides, I hadn't even been to sea. Marianne agreed with my decision, but the "goldbricks" in the ward thought I'd gone off my rocker.

As July faded, my tests came in better with each passing day. I'd passed the exam for AT3 and was eager to return to the squadron with a crow on my sleeve. Later in the month, I bid farewell to St. Albans and took the train back to Quonset to resume the life I'd interrupted in April.

In the past five months, a few faces had gone and some new ones had taken their place. Mostly, it was old home week, and everyone in the shop welcomed me back. Soon, I was pulling receivers out of wheel wells and building new safety wire scars on my arms. I'd just reached the halfway point in my enlistment and was ready for sea. I wasn't kept waiting long. By August, my name appeared on a new list, "Subject Cruise: USS *Midway CVB-41*." We were to depart 25 August for northern Europe.

BOOK TWO

Chapter 11

Underway

Sᴛᴀɴᴅɪɴɢ ɪɴ ᴛʜᴇ ᴡᴀʀᴍᴛʜ ᴏғ ᴀɴ ᴀᴜɢᴜsᴛ sᴜɴ, I gazed up at the *Midway*. Towering over us, her massive side disappeared into the haze at the end of the dock. She appeared to be the largest ship I'd ever set eyes on. At 968 feet, only three other ships, all ocean liners, surpassed her length. Russ, of maniac driver fame, was standing next to me when I said, "Did you know this is the biggest thing in America that moves?" He said with a smile, "You obviously didn't see the bimbo Harmon had on Main Street last night."

Stepping across that gangway gave us no clue we were aboard ship. If anything, the *Midway* seemed more solid than the pier we'd just left. This feeling of being on some great immovable mass leads to many jokes about NAS (Naval Air Station) *Midway*.

Once we were bedded down and had secured our tool boxes and flight gear, this leviathan beckoned us. If we had not been traveling in groups, I'm sure some of us would have ended up as erstwhile Flying Dutchmen, roaming these passageways forever. We explored dozens of work and living spaces on five levels. The hangar deck, the largest enclosed area on any warship, was cavernous. It swallowed planes, machinery, stores and men; and if need be, the entire crew (over 4,000 officers and men) could be accommodated there. This was our meeting hall, our auditorium, our movie theatre. This giant deck and the open air one above it were what set the carrier apart from all other warships.

Surface combatants (destroyers, cruisers, and battleships) were essentially variations on a theme. They were floating gun platforms, their effectiveness limited to the range of their main battery. The *Midway*, on the other hand, could dispatch her "main battery," our air group, out hundreds of miles. She was the latest in a long line of aircraft carriers that had started with *Langley, CV-1*. In the opening days of the Pacific conflict, these ships had revolutionized sea warfare. Oddly, the *Midway*, with her huge distinctive square funnel, more resembled the first "real" carriers, the 1927 *Lexington* and *Saratoga* (*CVs 2* and *3*), than her immediate predecessors, the famous "Essexes." In less than ten years, she herself would be dwarfed by the Forrestal class, the first of the "super carriers." But that was down the road, and at least for now she was king of the hill.

The hangar deck was divided into three bays, or working areas. Giant steel doors could be closed in case of fire, and in reinforced conflagration stations the controls for these barriers were manned twenty-four hours a day. Each bay had its own elevator: forward and aft were centerline, the one amidships was deck edge. The latter was a real design inspiration. By being placed off to the side, it allowed planes to be moved between decks without disturbing the aircraft already in position on the flight deck. In a world where space was worth its weight in gold, this was no small achievement.

These lifts made everything ashore look puny by comparison. The famous elevator in Radio City Music Hall in New York, the one that could raise an entire symphony orchestra, had only two thirds the capacity of ours. The forward platform, when lowered all the way, made a perfect volleyball court. When engaged in real work, the entire air group of nearly ninety aircraft could be moved from topside to the hangar deck in less than an hour.

Our immediate interest was the aviation electronics shop. This is where we'd perform our radio maintenance and repair the radar. Once the ship was underway, it also served as a social room, supplying us with coffee at all hours and offering a haven from the brass.

Our berthing compartment, the nearest thing to a communal bedroom, was large and airy, boasting of three ports. Since the mess deck was only one level below, it was a perfect location. Our individual lockers were small in comparison to a shore base, but once our peacoats were stored in their own space, they handled all our personal gear with ease. VC-12's team of twenty-six men adjusted almost instantly to this new way of life. For about half of us, this would be our first taste of sea duty, and a ripple of excitement ran just beneath the surface.

We had two days in Norfolk waiting for the rest of the air group to arrive. This group (comprised of four squadrons of fighter and attack aircraft and four special teams, including VC-12) was always land based and only joined a carrier for an operational assignment. The people who made up the "ship's company," or regular crew, were known as "general service," to distinguish them from the airdales. Our pilots referred to seagoing officers as the "Blackshoe Navy," since only flying officers could sport brown shoes with their winter greens. I soon discovered there were really two navies, one seaborne and one airborne. Plenty of good-natured kidding went on between the two groups, but we got along hand-in-glove when air operations started. This, after all, was the only reason the *Midway* existed.

Since I had exhausted Norfolk's delights on previous visits, I decided to stay on board. I poked my head into every nook and cranny where I wasn't thrown out. Only the marines exercised this privilege, as they had a rather heavy card game going on under all that smoke. The officers section was also in this category. We were segregated, and this segregation was definitely not separate but equal.

In time, even the exploration of the *Midway* became tiresome (there's a limit to how many cables and cases one can walk over), and I ventured ashore to look at some other ships. Nearby, an ocean liner was getting her finishing touches after an overhaul. Visitors weren't permitted, but I could stand on an adjoining pier and admire her sweep and majesty. Liners had long been an extension of national pride, and my interest hadn't diminished one iota since I was a kid. Right after the war, when ocean travel boomed for over two decades, my friend Bruce and I would spend many Saturdays walking the decks on sailing day. Bruce, who had sparked my interest with brochures of the *Rex* and the *Normandie*, joined me on the *America*, the *Queen Elizabeth*, and even the venerable *Ile De France*. That was one advantage of living in New York City.

The *Newport News*, a heavy cruiser moored nearby, was being readied to join us in the Atlantic. I asked the OOD for permission to come aboard, and he readily assented. My flight jacket worked like magic on these ships. Heavy cruisers carried helicopters, but their tiny aircrew was lost in the thousand-plus complement. I should add that the wearing of aviation decor anywhere away from the air station was strictly nonreg, and roving masters-at-arms would quickly scoop you up if you ventured into any administrative facility. In the area next to ships readying for sea, I was just another body, and hundreds of sailors toiled under the hot sun in sweaty T-shirts. The heavy cruiser appeared much smaller than her nearly six-hundred foot length, and the spaces below decks were positively cramped. In spite of the warm welcome I'd received, I was glad to return to the wide open areas of *CVB-41*. The "Airedale Navy" was the one for me.

Early the next morning, the bullhorn announced, "Set the special sea detail." I moved up forward on the hangar deck. In the weak morning light, I watched the bo'suns moving lines and trying to keep warm in the chill breeze blowing in from the bay. It would be nearly two hours before we had to muster on the flight deck. Navy tradition requires all men not on duty to "fall in" on open decks when ships enter or leave port. This formation was known as "quarters." I became so fascinated with this panorama, I almost passed up breakfast.

By its very nature, a ship's departure borders on high drama. The slow, deliberate pace of this time-honored ritual has all the trappings of a grand opera. Once put in motion, it would be nearly impossible to stop. A ship waits for no one.

On the dockside below, the last equipment was being hoisted aboard. Knots of officers and men were making their emotional farewells to wives, children, and girlfriends. Another fifty or so spouses and offspring stood alone among the cables and crates. One of our last gangways was already being lifted by a giant crane, and the base band had just emerged from a bus. I didn't know anyone involved in these tearful partings, but it was difficult not to feel the vicarious pain of separation. A truck with last-minute supplies pulled up alongside, and a hastily formed working party was pressed into service unloading stores. I took advantage of this delay to go below and eat morning chow.

Returning to my perch, I found four tugs had taken up positions on the bow and stern to help move this 60,000-ton giant out into the stream. Brisk orders were being passed between the ships as the thick Manila hawsers took up the strain. Just as our last gangway and link to shore was lifted, a bugle sounded, and it was time to muster with the air group. Fortunately, we were facing outboard on the flight deck, so I had an unobstructed view of the proceedings. I wasn't disappointed.

As the last line parted, three long blasts from our whistle reverberated across the harbor. Bells jangled in the tug's pilothouses, and white water boiled up beneath their sterns. The tugs strained, but nothing happened. The *Midway* was like some huge beast coming out of hibernation: she was all dead weight. But with two powerful tugs pulling and two pushing, the inevitable happened. The *Midway* stirred. Slowly, ever so slowly, the distance from hull to the pier widened, first just a few inches, then foot by foot, until finally, open water appeared. Then, as if on cue, the band struck up "Anchors Aweigh."

As the flight deck cleared the pier, we could see the wives moving forward, pressing closer as if to give themselves more courage. The *Midway* would only be deployed for two months, but to these people, who saw little enough of their husbands and fathers, the separation was always painful. Tucked away, too, was that unspoken fear that this might be a final good-bye. They never forgot how dangerous carrier operations could be.

Once away from the pier, the tugs continued their pressure, but now a new sensation was felt for the first time. The great shaft had started turning, and ten decks up we experienced the first vibration. Not yet a pulse, or even a heartbeat, it was, perhaps, a murmur. This was the first stirring of the enormous power that the *Midway* held inside her vitals. Fully committed, her engines could generate 200,000 horsepower, capable of driving her massive hull 33 knots.

When we reached enough open water to maneuver, we bid our tugs farewell with a few more blasts, and our little friends moved over to the battleship *Wisconsin.* Soon she followed us into the stream. We all moved out toward Old Point Comfort and the open sea, stately ships in a steadily lengthening column. I could pick out my old school on Breezy Point, and wondered if Hal was around to see us go. The throb of the engines could now be felt way up on the flight deck, and the *Midway* was making her own breeze to cut the heat from the burning sun. The *Midway,* as if conscious of her task, began to tremble in earnest, her revolutions increasing with each passing minute. Like a bridal train, her wake billowed out, briefly changing the sea from blue-green to white. When the shoreline became hazy, we were released from quarters, and all hands went to work.

Since we had been aboard those extra two days, there was little for us to do. The air group was not involved with the running of the ship. Our only concern was the fighting efficiency of our aircraft. This would lead to a never-ending argument about who really did the work on board. In a way it was similar to the police and fire department. A cop coming off a tough eight-hour shift, where he was constantly on his feet and literally had to have eyes in back of his head, would gaze with envy on the firehouse. Here the firemen seemed to have not a care in the world. They sat around drinking coffee or watching TV. What the cop didn't see was the life-threatening three-hour warehouse blaze they'd fought in the predawn. One job had set hours, the other was performance on demand. And so it was on board.

Perhaps nothing brings home this wide difference more sharply than a famous Edward Steichen photograph illustrating an evening hangar deck scene on board the *Lexington* during World War II. In the foreground, airedales stripped to the waist are working on four TBMs. Just behind the first plane, a movie is being shown for hundreds of offduty officers and men.

VC-12's planes were ready to go, and all our gear had been stowed. Until flight operations commenced, we had no prescribed duties. I found a spot on a catwalk out of everyone's way and watched the ships head out toward the open sea.

There's a fantastic detached feeling that comes with boarding a ship. Perhaps it's that strange sensation of moving from one element to another. Earlier, some of us still harbored serious doubts that something this big could not only float, but move as well. Now that we were underway, there remained not a single unbeliever, since the *Midway* had become one with the sea. Soon she took on the familiar (and to some unfortunates, the deadly) rhythm of the ocean, rolling and pitching.

"Operation Mainbrace" was a major naval undertaking, the largest since the end of World War II. It would involve the British fleet, as well as forces from Norway. Our sister CVB (large battle carrier), the *F.D. Roosevelt (CVB-42)*, with her own air group, moved out right behind us, accompanied by the small carrier *Wright*. The *Wisconsin* was our only battleship, but there were the heavy cruisers *Newport News* and *Des Moines*. Smaller, but no less important, came the destroyers, the task force's first line of defense against submarines. Finally, and equally necessary, were the oilers, whose life blood sustained us. Like the driver of a car crossing the desert, every captain always kept one eye on his fuel bunkers. In heavy weather or when engaged in combat, one doesn't always have the opportunity to refuel at sea. The destroyers were particularly vulnerable because of their limited capacity and high consumption.

The two air groups in our armada comprised over two hundred planes. Later, in European waters, two British flat-tops and a fourth American carrier, the *Wasp*, would join us. The battleship *Vanguard*, the U.K.'s only BB, and her screen would complete this awesome display of modern sea power. The pièce de résistance would be an amphibious assault on the coast of Norway. British and American marines would join forces for this part of "Mainbrace."

Historically, this task force was breaking new ground. The Pacific had always been the traditional bailiwick of the big carriers. In the battle of the Atlantic, it was carriers, albeit CVEs (escort type), that eventually turned the tide against the U-boats, but aside from a few incidents, large flat-tops stayed in warmer waters. In May 1941, it was carrier aircraft launched from the HMS *Ark Royal* that found and disabled the *Bismark*, enabling the heavy units of the British Home Fleet to close and eventually sink her. Later in the war, the USS *Ranger (CV-4)* made a daring raid on German bases in Norway and also provided air cover for our invasion of North Africa.

All this information about our upcoming operation was relayed to us by the captain, as the *Midway* met the first Atlantic swells. We were now at our cruising speed, and as I looked below the catwalk, I could see a ring of foam hissing along the ship's flanks. I spent the balance of the afternoon basking in the warm sun and watching the taxpayer's money being spent in a good cause. Any doubts I might have had about remaining in the navy after my hospital stay receded with the shoreline.

As I stood on that flight deck, I suddenly realized that I was accomplishing far more than just going to sea for the first time. What was happening was nothing less than the fulfillment of all my childhood fantasies. How many times had I imagined myself in the real navy, standing on deck as my ship conquered her first deep ocean swells. And now it was all real. This was no book, no movie, that would snap me back to the physical world when I closed the cover or left the theatre: it was the dream come true.

At the time I didn't know it, but the flight deck would become the perfect place to think and dream and sort things out in the two years ahead. I must have stood there for close to an hour. I didn't want to talk with anyone. Sweet solitude is what I wanted, and that's what I got. Besides, even if I'd had the inclination, never in a million years could I have mustered up the courage to reveal my feelings to anyone else on board. I'm sure the rest of the crew were thinking about the wives and girlfriends they'd left behind.

At last I was alone. The crew had obviously gone to chow, but in my reverie I hardly noticed. I was hungry enough, and yet I didn't want to break this spell. In reality, the actual encounter was everything I'd long imagined it would be. As I grew older, I discovered this was the rare exception and not the norm. Finally my stomach won out, and I headed for the mess deck. Strangely, I had an inner satisfaction that couldn't have been matched by the finest dinner in the world.

Nothing prepared me for the vast immensity of the ocean. Up to now, my total maritime experience had been a few trips up the Hudson River and a two-hour ride to the Jersey shore on the venerable *Sandy Hook*. This was the first time I'd been out of sight of land.

The *Midway* appeared tremendous when we were standing next to her on the pier in Norfolk, but now it would be our whole world until we reached port. After a week at sea, it started to feel restrictive (confining would be too strong a word). Part of the problem was that I didn't have the run of the ship. Only the skipper and executive officer did. Everyone was involved with their own division. I, of course, was in the air group, and that gave me more territory than most. I had the flight deck, hangar deck, electronics shop, the ready room, and all the spaces open to the whole crew. That included the mess deck, library, and the barbershop.

Chances were I'd never set foot on the bridge or the engine room and all those working areas in between which were so vital in the running of this 60,000-ton floating airfield. I'd have loved to drop by the printing shop, the laundry, or the galley (where 12,000 meals were prepared daily), but it just wasn't done.

Members of the ship's company were fiercely territorial, and each division coveted its privacy (a rarity on board). Every compartment was considered "turf," and outsiders weren't welcome. Entrée was only permitted to guests, and since I didn't know anyone outside the air group, that didn't include me. Later, on the carrier *Lake Champlain*, I'd break that barrier, but for the time being, I'd only rub shoulders with airedales.

Air operations were on the next day's menu, and I was scheduled to fly with Russ. Our pilot would be Lt. Rayburn.

Chapter 12

First Carrier Flight

ONE'S FIRST CARRIER TAKEOFF, like one's first kiss, is never forgotten. My feelings were hard to describe. I welcomed this chance to join the airborne elite, but at the same time I was slightly terror-stricken at the thought of flying off this moving platform. And that was only the half of it: the real kicker was landing.

Our ready room was crowded and noisy the next morning, with pilots and crewmen changing into flight suits, exposure gear, and Mae Wests. Up front, a teletype chattered away, giving updated weather conditions and radio frequencies and identifying which carrier had a ready deck in the event of an emergency. In the days of "straight deck" CVs, we could either launch or recover, but not do both simultaneously, hence the need for another landing area.

Russ and Hickman kidded me about how long an AD (Skyraider) floats and told me the sharks were friendly in these waters. I joked back, but I probably looked as numb as I felt. The teletype printed one sentence three times: "Pilots man your planes." My nervousness disappeared as we moved topside. As we moved through the passageways, I noticed the looks of awe from the ship's company flattened out against the bulkheads. I couldn't believe I was really doing this. Russ said, "Jack, this is where the navy starts getting a return on all that money she spent on you." As we moved into the blinding sunlight, I half expected all the pilots to break into a dead run for the planes. When I mentioned this, our pilot, Lt. Rayburn, smiled and said, "They only run in the movies, Jack."

The first two jets, F9F Panthers, were already positioned on the catapults. On our Skyraider, the plane captain helped Lt. Rayburn with his chute, as Russ and I crawled into the rear compartment. Russ leaned over to check my seat belt and shoulder harness for snugness and gave me a big wink.

Props started slowly turning and then leapt into life with a cloud of exhaust. Our plane captain stood off to the right and gave us the "thumbs up" signal, indicating "all clear." There was a high-pitched whine, and our engine roared into life. From my bubble window, I could see the jets taxiing forward, but because of the sharp angle, I was unable to see them being catapulted. Our plane captain pulled the chocks, and a "yellow shirt" directed us forward. We moved up in a rocking motion toward the island.

When the last jet had become airborne, the heat barrier was recessed and it was time for the props to take the spotlight. First came the F4Us, Corsairs of World War II fame. As soon as they went full power, the tail lifted off the deck, and the fuselage went completely horizontal. As the *Midway* was cutting through the Atlantic at close to 30 knots and into the teeth of a stiff ocean breeze, these planes were airborne almost instantly.

Now it was our turn. We moved up into position just opposite the "island." The *Midway*'s "vultures row" (catwalks on the island) was packed with officers and men, engrossed in this always exciting ballet of planes and men. I could clearly observe the flight deck officer giving his signals to our pilot. He looked like a conductor inspiring his orchestra as he rocked his arm in a waving motion asking for more power. Finally, he raised his right arm as he braced his body against the 40-mile wind. Lt. Rayburn went full throttle, and as the director's arm and body bent towards the bow, he released the brakes and started our run. Almost instantly, I felt our AD's tail rise. Power flowed through the plane and into every joint of my body. I could almost feel the adrenaline coursing through my veins, tuning every nerve ending and joining my body to the Skyraider as if we were one. In a few seconds, the air-speed indicator was over forty, then sixty, and we were up.

As we banked sharply to the right, I had a spectacular view of the *Midway*'s starboard bow cutting through the seas with a "bone in her teeth." The flight deck was now nearly empty, with only three props taxiing up to the launching spot.

When I looked out at the ships below, my fear vanished. I managed to pry the fingers of my right hand away from the overhead bar, and to my amazement, the plane continued to fly straight and level without my help! The task force planes were leaving their long white trails on this incredibly blue sea as we climbed to 5,500 feet and went to work. I hated to close the leather shade and darken the interior, but once the radar was fired up, we had a different, but almost as interesting, view. We could "see" 100 miles.

It was easy to pick out the *Wisconsin*, *Midway*, and *F.D.R.* because the APS-20 radar performed beautifully. After an hour, Russ turned the plotting over to me, and I started to track air targets on my repeater scope: APS-31. The "sea return" wasn't too bad, and since there were no pleasure boats or private planes, it was far easier than performing the same exercise over Long Island Sound.

We flew around the perimeter of the task force, about one hundred miles from the center. Other than a few fishing trawlers and two small freighters, the sea was empty. We were a long way from the usual shipping lanes. The skies within our radar range were also free of any air targets other than our own planes. The Atlantic stretched flat and clear right to the horizon.

For three hours we flew in fifty-mile legs, high enough that we could track every ship. Just as we were nearing the end of our last box circle, other aircraft appeared on the scope. They were the vanguard of our air group, returning home. We secured the radar and joined them. From ten miles out, the *Midway* was a speck. At five miles, she still looked like a model in a pond. Now we had to land on that model.

As we approached within four miles and started our "final," I could see other props in the landing pattern, and one which had just touched down. All the jets were safely aboard. Their flying time was considerably shorter than ours.

Russ checked Lt. Rayburn off for landing: "Flaps down, wheels down, hook down, mixture full rich." We tightened our shoulder harnesses until we couldn't move an inch. Glancing across Russ's body, I could see the port side of the *Midway*. No longer a model, she loomed big and menacing against the darkening sky. Our altitude was 500 feet, our air-speed 115.

When the gray hull disappeared, we banked sharply to the left and started dropping. Our air speed fell to 95. Now I could see the ship's wake very close. In a split second, the flight deck appeared and bang, we were down. Our heads snapped forward for an instant as our hook caught a wire. Safe and sound. All the tension drained from my body as we taxied forward to make room for the planes behind us.

I was a little wobbly stepping down to the flight deck. It was a bit like getting off a roller coaster. But in a few seconds, I experienced a spontaneous feeling of elation. I couldn't wait to do this again.

Carrier flying was far more exciting than operating over land. For some reason I could never fathom, my problems with airsickness disappeared. I also had this strange feeling of indestructibility. It was as though we could always land on the water if anything went wrong. Fortunately, I never had to test my theory.

Back in the ready room, Russ added to my euphoria by compli-

First carrier takeoff, September 1952, Atlantic, USS Midway.

menting my radar skills in front of the team pilots and crewmen. I started to say something but stuttered so badly I couldn't get a word out. Everybody roared, and Lt. Rayburn slapped my back as he walked by. Now for the first time, I felt I was part of the inner circle. It was one of the happiest moments of my life.

Flight operations were carried out for the next three days as we sailed closer to the British Isles. I flew every day, volunteering to replace a chief who had a bad head cold. Because of my long hospital stay, I was an unknown quantity to most of these people, and I wanted to prove I could carry my weight.

In the electronics shop just below the hangar deck, the same camaraderie existed. Here there were no pilots, and we shared the space with many ATs from sister squadrons. We all pulled our "checks" on receivers, altimeters, and sometimes the radar. It was our good fortune never to have to manhandle any of the major pieces of equipment down to the lower deck. On a rolling ship, guiding an eighty-pound rectifier timer down three steep ladders isn't exactly fun and games.

This was also our gathering place when we weren't working on an aircraft or engaged in flight operations. Light and airy, it was far more comfortable than any compartment. For one thing, we had benches to sit on. In the berthing spaces, you either stretched out on your rack or sat on the cold, hard, steel deck. Considering the

Midway was our last word in technology, it struck me as odd that with the thousand and one items in the ship's inventory, no one thought about providing a few places to rest our weary butts. Aside from the library, and of course the head, almost everyone stretched out on the steel deck. So the shop became a place to read mail, swap stories, or drink coffee.

Every working space in USS *Midway* had its own coffee pot. One could literally have a "cuppa Joe" anytime of the day or night. An army may travel on its stomach, but the navy definitely moved with the coffee bean.

Being an AT3, in the midst of all these top-rated technicians, placed me near the bottom rung of the social strata. It became my duty one morning to make the coffee. A First Class gave me a crash course on producing a really good cup. These were connoisseurs after all, and only the best would do. He showed me how to fill the percolator up to the line (and a little more) with the contents of the bag. Now I was directed to the head for the water. I found a cold spigot and brought the water up to the prescribed point inside the pot. By the time I'd plugged in the urn, sailors were already clamoring for their "life's blood." Soon it was ready, and I was eager to see the results of my first effort. The AT1 told me, "Whatever you do, don't make it too weak," so I put in two more spoonfuls than called for.

Three cups were poured in quick succession and then all hell broke loose. Everyone spit their coffee across the deck. It didn't take me more than a few moments to realize that I'd made my first pot of coffee with salt water! The unmarked spigot I'd used was for hosing down the deck. I was never again tapped to make the morning brew.

One of the radiomen from a sister squadron kept pretty much to himself. He was part of a countermeasure unit where all the technicians were expected to fly. Electronic Countermeasures, or ECM, were teams whose main function was to jam enemy radar. They also flew Skyraiders. Oddly, "Pappy," who'd been in the navy over twelve years, didn't fly. He'd taken the train down to Norfolk from Atlantic City, where the squadron was based. Most of the other aircrewmen thought he was an oddball, and some thought he had no guts. We were soon to learn how wrong we were.

Just before the *Midway* reached her first port of call, the captain called for a full-dress inspection (dress blues with service ribbons). Most of us, except those who'd been in World War II, sported a Good Conduct Medal or National Defense Service ribbon. Not exactly Audie Murphy. Pappy showed up with two-and-a-half rows, including two Purple Hearts, an Air Medal, a Presidential Unit Citation, and a Pacific Campaign with seven battle stars.

Our senior chief, who knew him back in the forties, said Pappy had been a radioman-gunner on a Douglas Devastator in the USS *Enterprise* during the early carrier battles of the South Pacific. During one action, Pappy's pilot had made two dry runs on a Jap carrier while planes fell all round them, and their wings were shredded by flak. The radioman wet his pants each time the plane made a new run, but no one joked when they landed. The pilot was bleeding badly, and Pappy had shrapnel wounds in his legs and back. Later in 1943, when most of his squadron had been killed or wounded, he went into the hospital and never flew again.

Since flying is voluntary, the navy honored his wishes. He was finishing out his twenty years as a "wingless" airedale.

One morning, while standing on a long chow line (were they ever anything else?), we discovered some other "airedales." They never paid any attention to ship's orders or announcements and flew around whenever they wanted. Our newly discovered guests were a family of sparrows, who were using the *Midway* for a temporary home as we moved across the Atlantic. Their nest was built up high on the hangar deck, just above a drain. The crew looked at them with endless fascination.

Ashore, these men would scarcely glance at birds. Now, finding them so far from their usual world peaked everyone's interest. We wondered if they had planned this trip, perhaps returning to the land of their ancestors. Soon, it became a ritual for every crewmember joining that line to check the nest. It gave us something to break the monotony and generated a lot of wagering. Would our little guests stay with us all the way to Scotland or fly away someday unannounced? Later, I saw one flying above the flight deck and worried that she couldn't keep up with the ship's speed. But she made a few sweeps and other maneuvers that would put our hottest pilots to shame and returned to the hangar deck and her nest. The family thrived on the food droppings from scores of men, and it seemed everyone in the crew left a donation for our guests.

The task force had been engaged in air operations for nearly six days, her planes making hundreds of launches and recoveries without incident. On the seventh day, tragedy struck, not once but three times.

Two Corsairs from the carrier *Wright* collided in midair. One pilot parachuted and was picked up by the chopper. The other, the squadron commander, went down with his plane. About an hour later, an F2H Banshee jet from the *F.D. Roosevelt* experienced a malfunctioning catapult and was shot directly into the sea. The aircraft disappeared and sank in 2,000 fathoms. Nothing came to the surface.

If this wasn't enough for one day, two radiomen on one of our destroyers were badly burned when an electrical panel exploded while they were testing it. I watched them being transferred by high-line to the *Midway* (we had a fully equipped hospital). After being stabilized, they were flown off the next morning to a burn center in Scotland. The *Roosevelt*, down to one working catapult, was detached and proceeded to the Clyde for repairs.

Russ and I stood down from flight ops so the others could get their time in. On these off days, we'd sit on a catwalk above the flight deck to watch the recoveries. It was never dull. The Panthers and Banshees were stirring to see coming in for their "controlled crashes." The physical and mental coordination these flyers exhibited was beyond my comprehension.

A pilot must adjust for many variables to place a 10-ton aircraft on a plot the size of an average home site. These men who land at a speed of 120 knots on a deck that's not only moving forward but also pitching are indeed a breed apart.

If he's low and slow, a pilot will hit the ramp and disintegrate in a fireball. If he's high and fast, he could easily miss all the arresting wires and the steel barriers. In either case, he'll usually wind up killing himself and his crew (and often many others). On occasion, an errant pilot has come close to wiping out not only a squadron, but the ship itself.

In a world where mediocrity was the norm, and huge sums were paid to singers who couldn't carry a tune, it was refreshing to see the skill of these men played out day after day. More than anything else, it restored one's faith in such unpopular beliefs as hard work, intense pride, and love of country.

Pilots weren't the only ones risking their necks. Below decks, it was easy to forget you were on an aircraft carrier. The passageways, compartments, and engineering spaces were exact facsimiles of those on cruisers or battleships. Only our top two decks set us apart. The flight deck, when empty, gave no hint as to its true purpose. It resembled, if nothing else, a huge open-air theatre. This analogy was not exaggerated. The area was truly a naked stage, awaiting a set and a group of players. In this case, the stage was the exclusive domain of airdales and the planes they flew and serviced.

From a distance, the launching and recovery of an air group doesn't appear too difficult. The planes are catapulted or roll down and fly away. Looks simple? It isn't. First, there's the limited space to consider. On land, airports are usually built way out in the boon-docks. There's plenty of room for all the planes to park, taxi, take off and land. Thousands and thousands of square feet, acres and acres.

F9F Panther landing on the USS Midway, *September 1952.*

On board a carrier, the situation resembles that infamous stateroom in the Marx Brothers' *A Night at the Opera* or an indoor parking garage. Space is at a premium; that's why navy planes have wings that fold. It doesn't matter how modern the ship or its aircraft are; on some level, carrier aviation is just a clumsy, primitive undertaking. It involves a great deal of stuff: stuff that weighs a lot, costs a fortune, and has to be moved around, often at the most inopportune time.

I should explain that there are two types of aviation personnel: ship-based (or general service) and those assigned to the air group. Members of the ship's company watch over the equipment that's permanently attached to the carrier, like catapults and arresting gear. The air group airedales take care of the planes. Although the two groups toil on different levels and rarely rub shoulders, their efforts all aim for the same result—getting the maximum number of planes in the air for each mission.

During launches and recoveries, the flight deck is the most dangerous place in the navy. The airedales to whom this is home not only need eyes in back of their head, but must also be also blessed with the proverbial nine lives of a cat. This innocent-looking stage could turn into a vicious killer when the bugle sounded "flight quarters."

Whirling props could lop off an arm or worse, or jet intakes might suck you into a thousand spinning razor blades. Other times, one could be blown over the side by jet blast or be decapitated by a broken arresting cable. These horrors, and more, all occurred during my two operational cruises.

When the command "start engines" was given, each pilot looked for the thumbs-up signal from his plane captain. This signified "all clear." Once the engines had warmed, other airdales crawled under the wings to remove the wooden chocks that held the plane in place. If the pilot in the plane ahead gunned the engine the airdale could easily be blown away by the slipstream. Once the aircraft had commenced launching, other airmen, wearing yellow shirts, directed the taxiing jets and props forward. The jets moved to the catapults. It was here that the most hazardous work took place.

Some of the catapult crew, all ABs (aviation bosun's mates), attached a steel bridle, or launch bar, to the undercarriage. In turn, the bar was attached to the catapult, which was powered by tremendous hydraulic pressure from deep below decks. This device effectively became the sling shot that propelled the ten-ton Skyraider or Panther into the sky in a couple of seconds. Just before their planes were launched, the pilots turned up full power and put pressure on the hold-back bolt. At this point, the AB crawled under the landing gear to make certain the bar was set securely into the catapult slide. To be lying under this screaming and vibrating twenty thousand pounds of airplane was one of the most terrifying experiences I could imagine. When it came to displaying courage, these ABs were in a class all their own. They accepted these heart-stopping hazards as all in a days' work.

When the air group had come home to roost, it was time to refuel them and "respot" the deck. Aircraft that were crowded into the forward part of the flight deck were towed back in the same sequence they'd be launched on the next operation. While minor repairs were performed on the flight deck (during the recovery), planes with more serious problems were taken below on the forward or deck-edge elevators. It was critical that all the planes be gassed, armed, and respotted for takeoff as quickly as possible. In combat, this could mean the difference between victory and defeat.

A carrier is never more vulnerable than when she's rearming and refueling her air group. One hit, no matter how small, in the middle of all those bombs, rockets, and gasoline would turn the flight deck into an inferno. This is exactly what happened in the battle of Midway when our dive-bombers found the Japanese in the midst of changing bombs to torpedos. On our side, the *Wasp* was torpedoed while refueling her aircraft, and the resulting fire finished her.

The more involved maintenance was done in the cavernous hangar deck. In separate bays, everything from a 30-hour check to an engine change was handled by the aviation community. During flight operations this could mean working round-the-clock, and every airedale wanted his plane in an "up" status. Often after working close to midnight (being kept up by an ornery radar), we'd walk past a group of mechs toiling on work stands around an engine. The ship's company, having watched a movie in another bay, would by now be long sacked out. Russ and I both agreed that, no matter how hairy the flying got, neither of us would ever change places with those brave men on the deck. To confirm our judgment, one day a Corsair landing on the *Wright* caught a wire that immediately parted. The stress on the cable (which can almost instantly stop a 10-ton aircraft hurtling in at 100 mph) was hard to imagine. When the wire snapped, it lashed back and cut a rubber-necking off-duty yeoman in two.

Chapter 13

First Port

On the long, lazy afternoons when I wasn't involved in flight operations, the great ocean beckoned. There were times when one could almost forget that he was afloat on this strange element, but not for very long. A mighty carrier we might be, but in the Atlantic's scheme of things, we were just so much driftwood. The *Midway* creaked and groaned as she took each long swell, and we learned to sway with every roll.

At first glance, this endless summer sea always appeared the same, but upon closer examination it was undeniably different. Not only the shape of the waves, but the color and direction changed with the wind and the sun. As our prow drove through these waters, even the sound varied in pitch and intensity. Perhaps Debussy described it best when his music "spoke" about the "dialogue of the wind and the waves."

In the middle of the Atlantic, those who were observant saw another phenomenon: the Sargasso Sea. The *Midway* appeared to be sailing through an endless patch of sea grass. Actually it wasn't "sea" grass at all, but plant life carried out into the middle of the ocean by the action of the Gulf Stream.

Each wave meeting the bow stirred my imagination. One could concentrate here like nowhere else. On land, a walk would sort out your problems, for movement was just the catalyst needed to stimulate the brain. Here, the sea would provide the action.

My thoughts revolved around Marianne. The more I analyzed our close relationship, the more I realized that this was the girl with whom I wanted to share my life. I'd never felt this way about anyone else. The feeling was both exhilarating and terrifying. This girl, whom I'd seemingly known forever and used to look upon as a third sister, had taken on an entirely new dimension. She was a treasure, and I worried that someone else would wake up to this fact, someone far closer to the scene.

I started to pour out my feelings in long, emotional letters that probably stunned her. We had, after all, never talked in quite these terms. Letters allowed one to say things that were difficult, if not impossible, to say in person. I wanted to stake my claim in the clearest manner possible, and until I could do so face to face, the written word would have to do. I knew I was taking a chance because all my life my philosophy had been "don't come on too strong," and I wondered if I'd frighten her away. No matter how close you get to a woman, there's no guarantee she won't back off when you pop the big question. Having made my own mind up, I had to know if she felt the same way. As they used to say in the navy, it was a calculated risk, but it had to be taken. As I sealed the letter, there was an announcement about liberty in Scotland, my first port of call.

The Plan of the Day, the ship's official directive, announced that we'd be entering the Firth of Clyde early the next morning. We were to remain two days, ample time for a couple of excursions. Excitement ran high because for most of us, this would be our first time on foreign soil.

In every traveler's heart, there's a special place for that first exotic sight. Whatever happens in the rest of his journeys, nothing ever comes close to that initial experience.

The navigation division told us the sun would rise at 0542, so I set my body clock. Like going to the head in the middle of the night without awakening, setting our body clock was another trick we learned in the navy. Don't ask me how it works, it just does. Just before going to sleep, you "tell" your body you want to wake up at a certain time, and you do, to within a few minutes. Most watchstanders will tell you they rarely had to shake their relief. They were already awake.

Five-thirty found me heading up the ladder to the flight deck. I couldn't wait for my first look at the Old World.

The task force had formed a single line for entering the firth (a Scottish word meaning narrow arm of the sea), and we were following the battleship *Wisconsin*. Astern of us, I could pick out a cruiser and a carrier, but it was still too dark in the west to identify them. As we entered this gap, the *Midway* was close enough to shore for me to see some people playing golf. I remember how astonished I was that anyone would be engaged in a sport (or anything else) at this hour. It was barely 0530.

The sky was brightening, and it was going to be perfect weather—not a cloud in sight. Scotland was incredibly green, so it was obvious that this was not your average day. The brightening light revealed more cottages, with smoke curling from every chimney. These huddled stone buildings spoke more of the eighteenth century than the twentieth, and the scene was like a page out of Dickens. As the sun burned away the morning mist, distant hills came into focus, and we moved well into the firth.

The *Midway* dropped her hook off Greenock in one of the loveliest harbors in the world. In the changing morning light, the line of hills in the far reaches of the estuary were turning from dark shadow to bright shades of green, bringing everything into sharper focus. The whitewashed shops and homes of this ancient seaport stood out vividly against the blue-green waters of the Clyde.

I caught the tail end of breakfast and quickly changed into dress blues for entering port. By the time we'd assembled with the rest of the air group, all the ships had taken their places in the anchorage. The *F.D.R.*'s spot had been taken by the USS *Wasp*, which had proceeded independently from the States. For the first time, we saw the heavy units from the British fleet: the battleship *Vanguard* and the carrier *Illustrious*. Shortly after we anchored, in a custom as old as Nelson, the sounds of gunfire echoed across the water as ship after ship exchanged salutes. Our band struck up "God Save the Queen" and our national anthem, and soon the formalities were complete. Now all hands were ready for the serious business: liberty. Our bo'suns handled the impatient shore party with dispatch, and in no time our happy group had quickly boarded trains for Glasgow.

For this writer, the passenger coach held far more fascination than the outside streets. It was straight out of Hitchcock's *The Lady Vanishes*, with individual compartment doors that opened on to the platform. Unlike American railroads, accommodations occupied only one side. The remaining space was taken up by a narrow passageway that allowed us to move about while the train was moving. Hickman, one of our ATs, was from Mobile, Alabama, and his drawl flowed like molasses. He shared a coach with a middle-aged Scottish woman, and I would have given anything to be the proverbial fly on that wall.

Glasgow was a dingy old port city. It was not highly rated in the travel books, but for us it was Paris, Rome, and London all rolled into one. We'd expected an austere and taciturn populace, but instead found a generous and fun-loving people who charmed us at every turn. We were the first American servicemen they'd seen since the last war, and they pulled out all the stops. We were fussed over wherever we went. The stores held little, the restaurants even less, but there were 18-karat smiles beaming from every face. It took us six tries to locate an eatery that even had eggs, and once inside, we had our collars yanked by waitresses who had the rosiest red cheeks I'd ever seen. It turned out to be an old Scottish good luck gesture.

The war had been over for more than seven years, but not much had changed in the British Isles. Rationing was still the order of the day, and a severe regimen of austerity gripped every facet of life. Most of us were unprepared for this surprise, and it left us shaken and disillusioned. It hardly seemed fair that a country that had stood alone against Hitler while we rearmed, and was on the winning side to boot, should be in these straits. We obviously had a great deal to learn about economics and winning wars.

Later, in a bar near the docks, Russ made a big hit playing dominos with a group of old-timers. He showed he could beat the best of them, and they loved it. I tried my hand at darts and didn't fare nearly as well. We couldn't pay for a drink all afternoon. This was also the best Scotch I'd tasted. I was no connoisseur, but it was my father's drink, and I had a pretty good foundation from which to judge it. We shopped for ties, linen handkerchiefs, and argyle socks, and I bought two tartan berets with their characteristic pompoms. Children tagged along wherever we went, and the only way we could lose them was to throw a handful of ha'pennys in the air and run like hell.

That evening, we all went downtown to a huge dance hall, which soon had to close its doors because of the crowds. The music was quaint by our standards, but there was no lack of partners. I could listen to that burr all night. Packed like sardines, one didn't have to know the first thing about dancing; you just held on to your partner and the moving crush of humanity did the rest. After an hour of this, about a dozen of us broke out of the steaming dance hall and went for some drinks before heading back to the station.

We found ourselves escorted by a like number of lassies who didn't want to see us leave. In a nearby café, we had beer and sandwiches and discovered what it was like to live under these conditions. The girls, all about sixteen or seventeen, explained the harsh rigors of this austerity. Oranges and grapefruit, in fact all fresh fruit, were rarely found in the stores. Shoes were worn and resoled until the sides rotted away. A couple of samples were quickly produced, and we could see it was all too true. They refused money but asked us to bring some fruit for their younger brothers and sisters when we returned tomorrow.

Sobering as this was, we all returned to the ship in various stages of a high, only partially caused by the national drink. The whole day had been pure enchantment. Nobody felt like sleeping, so we sat up for a few hours talking and smoking, trying to wear off all that restless energy.

The next day's liberty took us to Edinburgh, and although the city was brighter and more prosperous, our visit didn't have nearly the bite that the first day had (nothing ever did). The capital was a lot more prosperous, at least on the surface, and we had a chance to discover that a Scottish tea was anything but tea and comprised nearly a complete meal.

Later back in Glasgow we met our young friends from the night before and created a mini lend-lease. Their mothers and younger siblings joined them at the station, and we had to almost fight our way back to the train. Had we had the time, I'm sure they would have carried us home to have a meal. Besides all the fruit we could carry, we had loaded up on Hershey bars and gum from the ship's store. We hadn't forgotten the refrain that had followed us clear across Glasgow the day before, "Any gum chum?" The "wee girls" wouldn't let us go and ran alongside our train waving wildly until they finally could no longer keep pace.

Early the next morning, under a light drizzle, we weighed anchor and headed out into the gray Atlantic. Our fleet was twice the size of the one that had departed Norfolk two weeks before. The *Midway* pointed her bow toward Norway and the Arctic Ocean, and Operation Mainbrace commenced with general drills for all hands.

On board a carrier, the aircrewmen have no General Quarters station except to fly or stand by in the Ready Room. We did plenty of both. I flew five ASW ops (antisubmarine flights) during the exercises that lasted about ten days. I was hoping to be catapulted on one of the launches, but there was always more than enough wind across the flight deck. It was more like a gale at times. On those days, we were airborne long before we reached the end of the deck. The seas were running ten to fifteen feet, so the flight deck officer had to time the launch with the rise of the bow. I'm sure the pilots had their hands full adjusting for the pitching stern when lining up for touch-down, but they made it appear routine. All our recoveries were flaw-less. The air group didn't even have a barrier crash.

As we gradually moved into our steaming formation, the destroy-ers raced about, showing off their speed and maneuverability as if they were some preening athletes. The *Midway* didn't handle like a destroyer; nothing else did. But she possessed a far better quality: she had authority. Perfectly suited for her job as flagship, the *Midway* made every man onboard immensely proud just to be part of her crew.

Just as we joined up with the other ships, a chopper came aboard. Out stepped Vice-Admiral Felix Stump, who was going to fly his three-star flag on the *Midway*. Things had come full circle. Admiral Stump had commanded NATTC Memphis when I first arrived there two years earlier. Looking at his face as he left the helicopter, I had the distinct feeling that he was as happy to be on board as I was.

Three days later, marines from the U.S. and the U.K. landed on the coast of Norway. Our air group provided air cover, but VC-12 wasn't involved. NATO wanted to show the Russians that regardless of how quick and devastating a surprise attack they could mount against one of their neighbors, they'd still have to contend with a carrier task force. And this force could dispatch hundreds of planes out in retaliation, many armed with nuclear weapons. But our real ace-in-the-hole was the tactical advantage of being able to move our floating airfields around at will.

Our navigation department made us aware of a more spectacular show a lot closer to home. The *Midway* had sailed far enough north for us to view one of the most glorious sky shows extant: the Northern Lights, or aurora borealis. Since the flight deck is kept dark to preserve the night vision of those on the bridge, we had perfect conditions. Hundreds of officers and men gazed up at the luminous night sky, standing silently in awe of the heavens. We were lucky; soon clouds moved in.

After this night, the weather deteriorated to where almost all flying ceased. Only the British, who were either very brave or very foolhardy, launched aircraft in these terrible conditions. Nearing the Arctic Circle, about eighty miles from the coast, we plowed into a full-fledged gale. The ocean was now more than making up for the smooth passage we'd experienced on our eastbound leg. Green water rode over the bow and at times climbed to the flight deck, breaking into a thousand needles that searched out every open patch of skin. Aircraft were secured with triple tie-downs. These were steel cables strung from the wheels and fuselage to padeyes in the flight deck. Plane captains put their lives on the line as they constantly checked these moorings for slack. One could literally lean into the wind, and I saw maintenance people crawl from tie-down to tie-down to keep from being blown over the side.

At this latitude, the days were much shorter than we'd ever known. Once the pale sun came close to the horizon, the Arctic night would rush down on us, broken only by the blinkers in the task force conversing in the darkness. With our Skyraiders grounded, card games flourished in the compartment and the smoke grew thick. As a crewman, I was entitled to use the rear of the Ready Room, where nonstop movies were being shown. When my eyeballs had enough, I'd retreat to my bunk to write letters. Other times, I'd find a protected perch to watch the sea.

The wild ocean inspired terror, awe, and wonderment, and in spite of the cold, I was hypnotized by it. What filled my vision was sheer chaos. Without rhyme or reason, the giant waves surged and tumbled in confusion, whipped into a frenzy by the howling gale. Never in my life had I been this close to the cutting edge of nature. The destroyers were having a particularly hard time maintaining course and speed in the huge swells. They'd bury their bows into mountainous waves up to the base of their bridge, and as they shook free, tons of green water cascaded from the upper deck over the sides. At times, the whole forward part of one of these ships was exposed, revealing its glistening red underside.

It was an exhilarating, yet sobering, sight to see the ocean humble our mighty task force. At the same time, it made me more than grateful to be riding on a 60,000-ton platform instead of a frail destroyer. In this maelstrom, though, no ship ever seemed quite big enough.

As the storm increased in fury, we were driven straight into its eye. The *Midway*'s world had shrunk to a circle of a couple of miles, and she was pounded by huge waves that rose up like cliffs in our path. In the wild wind, the tops of the wave crests were flattened and whipped to a froth. Our carrier was taking solid body blows, but like a boxer, she shook them off and surged on, never changing her course.

The night we crossed the Arctic Circle, the tempestuous seas took on a new ferocity. As a safety measure, we strapped ourselves into our racks. It was a long drop from the top bunk to a steel deck that had little give. The *Midway*'s plates and girders groaned with every big one, and we could hear loose gear rumbling on the deck above us.

Around midnight, some of the locker doors started to break loose, and rivulets of Acqua Velva after-shave lotion coursed their way across the compartment. No one ventured out to secure these doors. We wedged ourselves into our racks and cheered the storm on.

The forced air ventilation soon picked up the strong odor of the Acqua Velva and filled our space (and most of the carrier) with a scent more appropriate to a boudoir than a warship. Most of the Acqua Velva was used to obtain that special shoe shine for which sailors are famous. I finally fell asleep, only to be awakened by a tremendous crash of breaking glass above us. Nearby, a massive cupboard holding innumerable pieces of crockery had ripped loose from its bulkhead and crashed to the deck. It was becoming a night to remember.

Snug in our compartment, we felt as if we were riding some giant elevator. The aft, our end, would rise up and balance itself uneasily on the top. After a few seconds, down we'd go, shaking violently, as our screws dug in, thrusting us forward into the night. Strapped in my rack, I said a silent prayer for my fellow sailors, the real sailors, on the destroyers. They earned their sea-pay that night.

One of the more remarkable side effects of all this turmoil was that no one in our team became seasick. We were all too busy just holding on for dear life to think about our stomachs. So, with the waves pounding and the beams creaking, we drifted off into an uneasy slumber, lulled by the steady rhythm and nearly intoxicated by the strong aroma of all that after-shave sloshing around below us.

Less than ten years before, in these same frigid waters, the last clash of European battleships had taken place. On that December night in 1943, the German battleship *Scharnhorst* met her end under the 14-inch guns of the Royal Navy's *Duke of York*. Over 2,000 men perished. This final Atlantic meeting between these behemoths had been nearly ignored, pushed off the front pages by all the other war news. More easily recalled were the protracted struggles of the Murmansk convoys. Thousands of merchant and naval seamen died trying to supply the Russian armies, who were locked in a death grip with the Wehrmacht on a thousand-mile front. For nearly three long years, these convoys had to face all the naked might the Luftwaffe and the U-boats could throw against them. Mountainous waves and zero-zero fog made these the cruelest seas in the world. More than once, the Allied freighters and tankers entered Murmansk with fewer than half the ships they'd started with.

The next morning the seas calmed. We discovered our task force had indeed been in a blow. None of the ships had been spared. The *Midway*, because of her size, had fared relatively well. The carrier *Wright* had four aircraft severely damaged when they broke their moorings on the hangar deck. Our destroyers suffered damage in varying degrees, mostly to antennas and deck gear.

But the *Midway* hadn't escaped unscathed. On the port side, a 50-foot motor boat boom composed of solid oak and banded with broad steel rings had simply disappeared. This enormous pole had been welded into the side with a reinforced hinge, but it was gone.

The navy gave us a lasting remembrance of this northern adventure in the form of the Royal Order of the Bluenose. While not as well known as the Golden Dragon or Royal Shellback, it was at least a certificate we could frame to prove to the folks back home that we'd really been out on the bounding main. On 30 September 1952, at 66 degrees, 10 minutes, on the Arctic Circle, all hands were initiated.

The sun broke through late in the afternoon, and air defense exercises were held. First, one of our planes flew by towing a target sleeve. I was up on deck checking out one of our receivers and didn't hear the word passed. I was about thirty feet from the five-inch gun mounts when they opened up. I think I jumped ten feet into the air. I was half-deaf for a couple of days.

Later, six British jets from the *Illustrious* came streaking out of the sun doing better than five hundred knots. Approaching at wave height, they were gone before we heard them. It was a frightening demonstration of the new age we'd entered. We desperately needed something much more sophisticated than five-inch 50s to stop those babies. After that, our Early Warning Radar was looked upon with greater respect.

The excitement of this "air attack" had hardly subsided when another bolt came out of the blue, this one much more pleasant. Instead of sailing to Plymouth, the *Midway* proceeded to Cherbourg, France, for four days, and a tour to Paris was arranged for five hundred men.

Chapter 14

Weekend in Paris

I WAS AMONG THE FIRST TO FORK OVER MY $35, thinking the tour would soon be sold out. Later, I was astonished to learn that only four hundred men had signed on. The other 3500 men apparently felt the wine and women in Paris weren't worth the eight-hour rail journey. What they wanted could be found a lot closer to the ship. C'est la vie.

During the next few days, we sailed south, and finally we approached the upper reaches of the English Channel. The weather remained clear, and for the first time in weeks, sea birds followed our wake, escorting us closer to land. In the evening before she reached port, the *Midway* reduced her speed to insure our arrival in daylight. During dinner, everyone eagerly looked forward to the next day.

Afterwards, I went up into one of the catwalks off the hangar deck and was stunned at how quiet it was. Nearly alone on a dark noiseless sea, we seemed to be almost drifting without power. Looking out, I could see but one small light in the distance, and it appeared to be another ship traveling in the same direction. As we entered the throat of the channel, traffic dramatically increased in the form of lighters, trawlers, and coasters, filling the night with looming shadows and causing our navigation department to work overtime. Some of these tiny vessels acted as if they wanted us to hit them. It reminded me of the small dog, big dog, routine.

I climbed up to the flight deck and walked all the way forward. When my night vision returned, I could see lights coming from land on both sides of the ship: England on the right, France on the left. I tried to burn this image into my memory. It was my first evening landfall, and to top it off, I was looking at two countries I'd never seen before.

"Pretty sight, isn't it Jack?" I jumped at the unexpected break in the silence. I quickly recognized the voice of Chief Somerall in the darkness. "It sure wasn't this calm the last time I sailed here eight years ago. I was on the battleship *Nevada* covering the invasion force on D-Day, June 1944. Boy, was I scared! It was my first time in combat. We didn't know what the Germans might throw at us. There were all kinds of wild stories about secret weapons and poison gas and everyone not on watch was up on deck."

Somerall offered me a cigarette, and we both lit up. "You think this task force is big? You should have seen the stuff we had back then. At least five battlewagons, about a dozen cruisers, and loads of destroyers. And big as we were, we were lost in the hundreds of transports, LSTs, and God knows what. There were so many ships, there was a joke goin' around that said you could board a vessel in Plymouth and walk clear across the channel to France. All night long, waves of planes flew overhead, all heading east toward France. The roar went on for hours."

We finished our cigarettes, and then he went below. I pondered what it must have been like to be approaching that shore on that historic night. His conversation just added another dimension to what was already an overcharged experience.

I thought of the thousands of British and French troops who used this body of water as an escape route after being nearly pushed into the sea off Dunkirk (perhaps it was that city's lights I saw twinkling off our port side). I wondered if any of those beleaguered soldiers ever thought, even in their wildest dreams, that almost four years to the day, they would return to France with a force unimaginable in those dark days of 1940.

I found it difficult to sleep that night. In a few hours I'd be in France. Although Scotland would always hold a special place, it wasn't all that foreign. Even their spoken tongue had a vague resemblance to English. But France was different. Now all those pages from my French textbooks were going to come to life, and I could hardly wait.

Cherbourg harbor didn't look particularly unusual, but the stark wreckage of some half-sunken ships was a grim reminder that the war hadn't ended that long ago. The town itself, or what I could see of it, resembled nothing I'd ever seen in any book. Row upon row of concrete block buildings rose up behind the dock area. I later discovered that the bombardment had been so severe that there was nothing left to rebuild. They just erected blocks of modern flats on empty land. It may have been efficient and up-to-date, but it didn't strike a chord in my memory. I'd have to wait for the train to take us inland to see the real France of my dreams.

As the ancient rolling stock of the French National Railroad eased out of the maritime terminal, a carnival atmosphere took over

the train. Most of us couldn't believe this was real and half expected
the duty P.O. to come in and call reveille. This poor kid from the
Bronx pinched himself a few times to make sure.

The Norman countryside didn't look that much different from
Scotland. A little flatter, a lot more cows, but surely as green, if not
more so. Every once in a while we'd notice some war damage, but far
less than we expected. Although the entire train had been chartered
by American Express, we still made several stops on the eight-hour
journey to the capital. We figured the travel people had some sort of
arrangement with the station caterers. At each stop, enterprising
vendors covered every open window, offering wine, fruit, cold meats,
long fresh loaves of crusty bread, and the best cheese I'd ever tasted.
I had been raised on Kraft American, so it was no contest. By the
third stop, the wine had taken its toll, and we felt as though we were
floating to Paris; indeed, many of us were.

At last the steam train came to a weary halt in the huge confines
of Gare St. Lazare. Out poured streams of bluejackets, eager to make
the most of their seventy-two hours. Buses labeled with the names
of our hotels were soon filled, and we started the last leg of our journey across the city into the Left Bank.

Even in the early twilight, enough could be seen through the
grimy windows to cause our pulses to quicken. Images from *French
Grammar I* and geography textbooks sprang to mind, making me impatient to get out and really experience this City of Light.

Most of the other whitehats shared my feelings, but there was a
hard core who couldn't have cared less. Paris might have been Any-
town. What they were looking for, wine and women (and maybe a little song), they didn't have to travel 250 miles for. The trip was $35
inclusive: transport, two nights in a hotel with bath and breakfast,
and a tour of the city and Versailles. As great a deal as it was, I'm
sure American Express wasn't losing a dime.

I shared a small suite in the Imperator, an ancient hotel on the
Left Bank, with Tom Hickman, an AT, and Pete, a stocky mech. The
Imperator looked like a Hollywood set for a Paris hotel of the twenties. Potted plants and decrepit couches filled the lobby. But the
centerpiece, the jewel, was a tiny cage elevator that rose directly
from the middle of the room into the dark recesses above.

About eight-thirty, the three of us headed out on the town. Armed
with the concierge's recommendation, Hickman and I made for Les
Halles across the river. Here we'd have dinner and absorb the real
flavor of Paris. Pete struck out for a different kind of flavor, and we
didn't see him for the rest of the evening.

It was Friday night; the streets were crowded. Young couples walked arm in arm, and shoppers lingered in front of well-lit store windows. We noticed immediately how little motor traffic there was. Except for some prewar taxis, cars were almost nonexistent. Hickman and I hopped into one of those old Renault taxis, and I half expected to see Jean Gabin behind the wheel. My high school French elicited a raised eyebrow, but it got us to the brasserie.

We probably ordered all the "wrong" things from the tourist menu, but I do remember a terrific flaming crepe that ended the meal. We were the only sailors in the bistro, and our uniforms brought us more attention than usual. The French were fighting in Algeria and Indochina to preserve what remained of their shrinking empire, so the military weren't that out of place in this Paris of October 1952. No one bought us drinks as in Glasgow, but three English-speaking natives came over to converse. As we were leaving, a couple at one table raised their glasses and shouted, "Vive America!"

I had a city map, and since it was a beautiful night, we decided to walk back to our hotel. We had to admit Les Halles really had atmosphere. It might have been midday instead of nearly midnight. We discovered we were in the center of the main market of Paris. Every foodstuff, bottle of wine, and all the fixings were processed through here. More than once we had to detour around a husky butcher man-handling a side of beef.

The streets were thronged with tourists, workers, and couples walking arm in arm. They paused every few hundred feet to savor a long lingering kiss, oblivious to the world around them. It was just like a movie.

Back at the Imperator, Hickman took half of a large double bed, while I sacked out in the sitting room on what resembled a long chaise lounge. Like all good sailors, we fell asleep immediately. It had been a long day.

The next thing I remembered was Hickman shaking me awake. I couldn't read my watch, but the weak light of dawn was peeking around the drapes on the double French windows. (What else?) He said he'd awakened to the sound of moaning, and Pete hadn't been to bed all night. We followed the sounds to the bathroom, and there, stretched out in a tub that could have easily accommodated all of us, was Pete. He was obviously in some pain, but gradually spilled out his sad tale.

Pete had met this blonde at a bar in Pigalle and after almost no preliminaries had bedded down in a flea-bag across the street. He was a good sailor, so upon returning to the hotel, he remembered to take a "pro" (a strong germicide). Unfortunately, he had waited until he was lying in this steamy tub, and he promptly passed out. The long-term effect of this "preventive maintenance" was devastating and finally cut through his drunken stupor. Poor Pete. He was going to be out of action for the foreseeable future. Even the simple act of relieving himself would bring tears to his eyes. We helped him into bed, and after a few swigs of Cognac, he was out again. Hickman and I went back to bed and resumed those dreams Pete had so rudely interrupted.

The next morning we ordered breakfast in the room for Pete. He was in no condition for a city tour. Hickman and I went below in that great elevator to the dining room for petit déjeuner. Like everything else that weekend, it was an experience, no bacon and eggs here. The French were not big on breakfast and opened their eyes with a café filter and croissants. A café filter resembled a miniature percolator drip pot, and that's exactly what it was. The pot was positioned over a cup, and the coffee slowly dripped, dripped, dripped. I asked the waiter how long it took to fill the cup, and he said, without missing a beat, "Anywhere from three minutes to three days, Monsieur."

Our bus was only half full of bleary-eyed swabbies. Evidently, many had followed Pete's crimson path or were just plain hung over. Our tour hit all the highlights: the Arc de Triomphe, and the Champs-Elysées on the Right Bank, then the Eiffel Tower, the Invalides, and Ecole Militaire on the Left Bank. Notre Dame dominated a small island between the two banks.

The Indian summer sun enabled us to eat outdoors, and we reveled in dining European-style. Our afternoon was free, so armed with a street map of Paris, I struck out on my own. I explored Place de la Concorde and the Tuilleries before finishing my solo tour in the Louvre. I'd always wanted to see the Winged Victory of Samothrace. Unlike too many sights first seen on the pages of a history book, this one didn't disappoint me. I probably sat there for fifteen minutes.

That Saturday evening, a large group from the *Midway* went to the Casino de Paris for dinner and a nightclub show. The comedians were bilingual, and the biggest laughs came from the English version. There were some original settings, but they weren't going to put Radio City out of business. Their show girls, however, were shapely and pretty. Best of all (from the sailor's viewpoint), these Rockettes had only one costume for every two dancers.

I got up at 7 A.M. Sunday morning and quietly bathed and shaved. Hickman and Pete were snoring loudly. Pete had come back strong after spending most of Saturday in bed. He found that he could forget the pain after a few drinks, but he lived a celibate life for the remainder of the weekend.

I tiptoed out and had my café filter alone in the big dining room.

My waiter couldn't believe that someone from our group would be up this early. I walked in the bracing morning air toward the river and the fulfillment of another dream: Mass at Notre Dame. The brilliant sunlight etched these ancient stones in sharp detail, and the streets, while nearly deserted, had a squeaky clean smell rarely associated with cities. Blue-clad street cleaners were the solitary occupants of every "rue" I passed. Wielding long tapered brooms fashioned from branches, they resembled characters I remembered from an illustrated set of Dickens my mother had read to me when I was five years old.

But not everyone was asleep. Every block or two, I'd pass a fortunate local carrying some of those long loaves of crusty bread. The aroma made my mouth water. I made a mental note to pick up one after church.

I ran into two pilots from VC-33 just outside the cathedral, and the three of us occupied a pew near the main altar. We all put 200-franc notes in the collection basket. Everyone else dropped a coin. At 360 francs to the dollar, we could afford to be generous. It was a memorable mass in historic surroundings, and we all stayed for the Benediction. As we headed toward the bright sunlight, organ music poured out, deep and resonating, and filled every corner of the church. We passed under the great rose window, hardly noticing the crowd, each one of us lost in the moment. We wanted this to last.

Sunday afternoon's schedule called for a group tour to Versailles, but I opted to spend the last few hours in Paris alone. I strolled along the river under the falling leaves, passing still more lovers walking with arms entwined. For the first time, I felt the sharp pangs of loneliness. How I wished I had Marianne here to share all this. I made a vow that someday we'd come back together. There was no Trevi Fountain, but I threw a few francs in the Seine.

I rode the elevator to the top of the Eiffel Tower and then took the long walk back to the hotel. In the approaching dusk, I made my way through back streets watching young men playing boules and old men smoking their tiny cigarettes. On every corner, vendors sold fresh oysters. The stores were all closed, but I enjoyed looking at the window displays. One can usually learn more about a country from its shops than from a hundred guide books. There were almost none of the modern appliances we had at home and the clothing was almost nondescript, but the food was something else entirely. It seemed as though every other shop featured delicacies that would tempt a saint. Most of them were strange to my limited palate (and would remain so for a long time), but I marveled at both the variety and the ingenuity that brought about their creation. These people had raised eating to an art form. All the imagination that was lacking in the other consumer goods was funneled into things for the table.

About a mile from the Imperator, I boarded the Metro for a couple of stops, just to see how it stacked up against the IRT. The Metro won.

In the hotel, awaiting our bus, we decided to have a farewell drink. Someone had the noble idea of leaving all our loose francs for the waiters and chambermaids. The young girls were ecstatic, but my waiter pointed to the cigarette packs sticking out of our pockets. If it was all the same to us, he'd rather have a few Chesterfields. I still had a carton in my bag, so I gave him the pack. I thought he was going to kiss me. On the train, we got 400 francs a pack, more than enough to buy the remainder of our souvenirs in Cherbourg the next morning. It was better than a 10 to 1 exchange.

A lot of wine and cheese changed hands on the slow journey back to the ship. It started out as a replay of Friday, but by now the sun had set and since most of us were sated, we slept a good deal of the way.

Back on board, I found a pile of mail on my rack. I raced through the envelopes looking for that "big" letter from Marianne. It was there. She'd been surprised at first by the serious tone of my message, but in the end she felt the same way about me. I probably shouted more loudly than I expected, and the guys thought I was crazy. Russ walked by on the way to the shower and said, "What happened Jack? Your girlfriend have her period or something?"

I was too excited to sleep. This long-awaited news coming off a Paris weekend had set my heart working overtime. I went up to the flight deck. It was nearly midnight, but many other sailors had the same idea. We sat on the wings of the parked planes and gazed at the lights of Cherbourg twinkling across the harbor.

The next day, steaming west in the English Channel, we got a bonus. The towering liner *Queen Mary*, inbound to Cherbourg, passed us less than a mile away. Passengers and crew of both ships lined the rails to witness a meeting that would probably never happen again. We, with our two sisters (the *F.D.R.* and the *Coral Sea*), were the largest carriers in the world. The *Queen Mary* and her (almost) sister *Queen Elizabeth* topped the scales as the reigning ocean liners. We met each other at a combined speed of better than 50 miles an hour.

The *Midway* anchored off Plymouth, England, for six hours. No liberty. After that frenzied weekend, most of us couldn't have mustered much enthusiasm regardless. Three of our aircraft that had landed on the *F.D. Roosevelt* were lighted out and taken aboard by crane. The *F.D.R.* (CVB-42) had gone on to the "Med" after her cata-pult repairs.

Our voyage home was uneventful. The *Midway*'s P.A. system was hooked up to the ship's radio, and as we sailed into the sun every afternoon, we were serenaded by the voices of Patti Page, Joni James, and Eddie Fisher. Some of the hit songs were particularly appropri-ate to what we were doing on this ship—"Far Away Places," "Harbor Lights," and "Cruising Down the River."

Chapter 15

Getting to Know You

WHAT ARE COMMONLY CALLED TOILETS or bathrooms at home are known in the navy as heads. Aside from their obvious functions, they also serve as reading rooms, smoking rooms, and in some cases, a place to answer letters. Everyone would leave the hometown paper he'd received in the mail for all hands to read. As a result, we had a rare chance to absorb a taste of small-town America.

For someone who grew up thinking milk came from a bottle, I was fascinated by the dailies from the South and the Plains states. Here was an intimate window on a world I hardly knew existed. These were farming towns that had changed little in the last thirty years. The news was all about hogs and soybeans and corn. Full-page ads trumpeted the latest tractor or threshing machine. Half the paper covered grange meetings and church suppers, and local high school sports elbowed out the professionals. There was scarcely a mention of world events, and major league baseball coverage merely consisted of yesterday's line scores and standings.

Being raised at the center of national news on all levels, I found these places hard to believe in 1952. It was as if they were completely insulated from all that was happening in the outside world. At the time, I wasn't smart enough to realize that being born, growing up, falling in love, and raising a family were the really important events in life, and people liked to read about them. Their newspapers reflected these homey stories that touched on individuals and families, rather than the more notable or notorious fringes of society we read about in New York. Here was just one facet of the broadening experience of the navy. I had held a few jobs before enlisting, but I'd never met anyone who wasn't from either the Bronx, Brooklyn, or Manhattan. Now I rubbed shoulders with Californians, Georgians, Hoosiers, and Kansans. Most came from small towns, smaller than the enrollment of my high school (2,500) or, more to the point, the complement of the USS *Midway*.

Much to my surprise, I soon discovered that New York wasn't high on the list of places most of them wanted to live. Most of these sailors were suspicious of any big city, as though the people in it were somehow tainted. To those who'd never been there, it was hard to explain that New York was really a group of loosely connected neighborhoods, and each in its own way was every bit as provincial as any prairie town in Nebraska. We didn't frequent nightclubs or live in skyscrapers. We looked forward to going to Radio City once a year, and a date in Times Square was a major event.

The *Midway* was, in fact, a floating cross-section of America, so I could travel the country without leaving the ship. I learned more about the people and places of America than if I'd driven coast to coast a dozen times. The tourist glances at many sights, but sees little. How often does he meet a native, except as a waiter or bellman?

This exchange of ideas, fears, and set notions was a perfect way to send all my illusions to the cleaners. Some came back starched and pressed. Some didn't come back at all.

One of the more startling revelations was that there were so many Protestants. My neighborhood in New York City was split pretty evenly between Irish, Italian, Jewish, and German. My family had mostly German roots but had been in America well over a hundred years. For the most part, my friends were first generation and were almost all Catholic. I'd gone to Catholic schools right through college. I might add that we were also segregated by sex. I didn't sit next to a girl in class until I was eighteen.

German and Jew, Irish and Italian: we all mixed well. Only Protestants were in short supply. In the navy, of course, they were a distinct majority, and it took some getting used to. Cross-section New York City was definitely not cross-section U.S.A. I didn't think about it at the time, but the same thing was happening in reverse. There were swabbies from Georgia and Alabama who'd never laid eyes on a "fish eater."

By 1952, the navy had been desegregated for about four years. Before Truman's presidential order, the only blacks in the navy were found in the galley or serving the officers in the wardroom. Now, they were sprinkled about, one or two in every division. Except for a few hardnoses, all hands accepted them on the same basis they accepted everybody else: you were OK as long as you carried your weight in the workload.

There was a lot of good-natured kidding among all of us, and whether you were Irish, Jewish, or Italian, a New Yorker or a Redneck, you came in for your share. But for some reason, no one ever kidded Greer, our solitary black. Perhaps we felt he had enough bullshit to contend with in the outside world where he had no protection. Then, too, none of us had enough familiarity with the black community to make a remark that was funny without being hurtful.

Also attached to this social adjustment was a strong sympathy for these people. As enlisted men, we understood far better than most Americans, the experience of being discriminated against and treated like dirt. And not being able to do a damn thing about it.

All these exchanges aside, ninety-nine percent of the talk revolved around girls, girls, girls. It was only natural on a ship with over 4,000 men whose median age was probably nineteen. We may have had a tremendous collective knowledge about gunnery, engineering, navigation, and electronics, but we sure didn't know much about women.

Tom Hickman volunteered that maybe that was our problem. The navy had provided us with manuals for everything from hand tools to loran, but when it came to women, it was strictly do it yourself. And this do-it-yourself method was leading to frustration, broken relationships, and divorce. What we desperately needed was a *Bluejacket's Manual* for the opposite sex.

Every whitehat had some off-the-wall theory about how to turn "nice" girls on, but it never worked. The prevailing belief was that they were just as horny as we were, and all you had to do was find that magic button. Every sailor was looking for girls who would "go all the way." Clay, who everyone knew was a virgin (like most of us), was asked, "Didn't you ever meet a broad who'd go all the way?" Clay looked at his questioner for a moment and said, scratching his head, "All the way? Shit, I never met one who could even find the bus terminal." They kept searching for the impossible dream: the nice girl who'd jump in the sack on the first date.

Of course, a few of the guys had figured this out for themselves. They'd learned, for example, that a girl is a creature apart. Having an older sister helped. Some of us "oldies" (I was nearly twenty-three) tried to explain that women had to worry about their reputations far more than we did. Especially in a small town, once a girl was labeled "easy," her chances for meeting a good prospect for marriage were few indeed.

It appeared everyone on the team had some input for this new book. This new *Bluejacket's Manual* would have to be both general and concise. It would have to answer, among other questions, why girls didn't go to the head alone like we did and instead formed a convoy every time they had to powder their nose. If another swabbie or two accompanied us to the men's room for no apparent reason, we might get a little nervous. And why did so many of them lead us on when they had no intention of finishing what they started? We had a special label for these hellish creatures, for they were teasers of the worst kind. All of us had lifted too many car bumpers after those sessions.

The manual would also have to verse us in the labyrinthine ways of the romantic small talk in which the girls reveled. They all wanted to be romanced hour after hour before dispensing any of their hoarded favors, and sailors just didn't have that much time. And what about the occasions you'd catch them doing something idiotic, but instead of admitting they were wrong, they'd turn the tables and come up with the goods on you. They could catalog this stuff right down to the hour and the day and leave you speechless.

But, in spite of all the gripes, most of us would admit we wouldn't want it any other way. These soft delights were infinitely more sensitive and emotionally complicated than we were. If you thought about it at all, that's what made them so damn desirable. One day I heard an old chief lecturing a group of young mechs, and he put the whole thing into perspective. "This engine," he said, "is like a woman. If you don't treat it right, it'll make your life miserable."

As the *Midway* neared Norfolk, I had a chance to do some serious thinking. The past two months had sorted out many loose ends, and for the first time I felt I was on the right track. Professionally, I'd completed my first carrier assignment and found I could hold up my end. Other than my coffee-making fiasco, my ability in the shop or in the air had been accepted. All that training had paid off.

Emotionally, I'd reached a turning point too. I had the right girl, and she felt the same way about me. We could start making plans, and now at last I could think about a life after the navy. Before Marianne, there was no motivation to look down the road. There were too many new places and challenges to ponder the future. Now I had the perfect mate.

I was nearly two years beyond that magical bench mark of 21, but better late than never. To paraphrase St. Paul, I'd left behind "the things of a child" and had turned the first, and surely the most important, corner of my life.

Chapter 16

Prelude to Korea

AUTUMN 1952 WAS THE BEST SEASON OF MY LIFE. I returned to Night Check and enjoyed every weekend in New York. Marianne monopolized my time, and we became "locked in." Soon we were referred to as "Jack and Marianne" (like ham n' eggs), and in the weeks before Christmas we were inseparable. Our most surprising discovery was that, even after ten years, we knew relatively little about each other.

New York was our oyster, and we squeezed it dry. We saw *South Pacific*, *The King and I*, *Of Thee I Sing*, and even attended the Ballet Russe. Among other events, a highlight was seeing Toscanini at Carnegie Hall. After watching the skaters at Rockefeller Center, we'd usually head for a French bistro, where we shared a boeuf bourguignon and a bottle of Beaujolais (I'd learned something from the last cruise). One chilly night after a movie, we stood in Times Square and watched the election returns proclaim Eisenhower as our new president. On 8 November, our friends Dot and Don Roller (late of VC-12) tied the knot, and we were Best Man and Maid of Honor. It was a happy time.

With the new year came new orders: a "qual cruise" to Guantanamo Bay, Cuba. These short jaunts out to sea were mounted to qualify pilots in carrier takeoffs and landings. They were usually ten days in duration. The ATs were strictly employed as technicians—no flying with untrained pilots.

We sailed out of Mayport, Florida, in early January on the battle carrier USS *F.D. Roosevelt (CVB-42)*, a sister of the *Midway*. The name *F.D. Roosevelt* intrigued me. Weren't carriers supposed to be named for famous ships and battles? Why was this one named after a president? I started to do some reading and discovered that if an exception had to be made, F.D.R. was the perfect choice.

From a biography, I found he was not only instrumental in rebuilding the navy in the early thirties, but was a major force in creating

With Marianne, October 1952.

our 16-inch battleline way back in 1914, when he served as Assistant Secretary of the Navy under Woodrow Wilson. When the constraints of the Great Depression starved our military budgets, Roosevelt made sure the navy had its share. He so favored the Senior Service that his actions were an embarrassment to his administration. All the vessels that held the line against the Japanese in the early days of the war and the massive new construction that brought us victory were laid down during his four terms. After obtaining a fuller understanding of what he meant to our branch, I often thought he should have been called the "Father of the Modern American Navy." Even eight years after his death, every ship I ever served in or with was shaped by his vision.

The weather in the Caribbean was a marked improvement over Quonset Point, where the ground was already under five inches of snow. We didn't do any flying, the work was light (no radar was in use), and the tropical air raised everyone's spirits. The pilots came round and round, day after day, and after a while not even the rubbernecks bothered to climb up into the "island." One warm starlit evening, after our operations had been completed, we were sitting in the catwalk drinking Cokes. A few miles away, the *Coral Sea* was engaged in night "quals." Then in an instant, the dark night was shattered by an explosion and brilliant fireball. A flyer had misjudged the deck and caught the leading edge. His jet disintegrated, and he simply vanished. One minute we were enjoying a quiet night under the stars, the next we were witness to violent death and destruction. It was a sharp reminder of what a deadly game this could be.

Back in Rhode Island, I knew that my two short cruises wouldn't keep me from being a prime candidate for an extended "Med" trip. In preparation for this, I was sent to a school for a new UHF receiver that was about to replace the venerable ARC-1. This was naval air's first piece of new radio equipment since World War II, and it was a quantum leap forward.

Two new teams were being formed for April departures, and my name was on one of them. Our carrier was to be the *Coral Sea* or the *Wasp*; final assignments would be made later. It was a good crew. Chief Talley, one of our best technicians, would head the AEW crew. "Trigger" Kinney AT1 and George Walls AT2 would work with me. Among the controllers were Jacques Dupre (about to make chief), Calley, Winslow, and Bill Munroe. Bill, our newest man, was not long away from the football fields of Columbia, where he'd made first string. Most of the mechs and metalsmiths were old-timers, and I knew just about everyone. The pilots, on the other hand, were an unknown quantity, except for Lt. "Preacher" Williams, with whom I'd often flown. He had come up through the ranks, but he didn't let those two silver bars on his collar stifle his warm personality. Lt. Herman, our team leader, wore the Navy Cross and two D.F.C.s along with a ton of Air Medals. As a torpedo bomber pilot in 1944, he put two "fish" into Japanese carriers in the battle of the Philippine Sea.

We even had an oddity. Lt. Overton was an electronics officer who'd been recalled from the reserve. Essentially, he duplicated our airborne duties, but was paid much more for it. He seemed like a fish out of water and rarely engaged in small talk with us as the other officers did.

In early February came electrifying news. A new carrier, USS *Lake Champlain* (CVA-39), had just come out of mothballs at Newport News, Virginia, and was headed for Korea. Our team leader, Lt. Herman, switched assignments, and we would join Air Group 4. The *Lake Champlain* would be the second Atlantic Fleet carrier to go to the Pacific, and CAG-4 would comprise the third air group to change oceans since the war started nearly three years ago. The USS *Leyte*, returning from Europe after a "Med" cruise, was deployed through the Panama Canal and saw some of the heaviest fighting in that summer and fall of 1950. The *Bon Homme Richard* carried an east coast air group in 1952. VC-12 had teams on both ships.

In the middle of this uproar, I was completing the squadron course to be designated an aircrewman. Those who'd volunteered for the program were vigorously trained, not only in radar interpretation and all the new language needed to vector aircraft, but also in Morse code, blinker, and ship and aircraft identification. We studied for this after completing our regular maintenance duties.

In VC-12, one did not have to be a designated AC (aircrewman) to pull down flight pay. There was more than enough money to go around. Most of us took the course as a matter of pride in ourselves and in the squadron. After passing the test, we were given a diploma at an appropriate ceremony in the hangar and were awarded a set of silver wings. On 11 February 1953, I was one very proud airedale.

Lt. Herman let it be known that this team would be composed entirely of volunteers. Those who chose not to go would join another carrier in the Mediterranean. Soon we were besieged with offers of $75 to $100 from people wanting to take our place. No one left the original group. This would be the voyage of a lifetime.

In March, our three ADs were chosen and repainted with the designations 701, 702, and 703. All departments checked and re-checked every piece of gear and started to gather the spares for our tool boxes. Because we were the only carrier-based planes with our type of radar, we had to make certain we didn't get caught short at sea. Initially, we had all the time in the world, but soon every minute seemed precious.

Although we were to be granted ten days leave before we shoved off, those last remaining weekends took on a special meaning. I toyed with the idea of getting married, but my parents discouraged it. No one would forget that golden spring just before we sailed.

When the last of the leave-takers returned, I found that two of my shipmates had tied the knot. One would have a baby before we returned to the States. I remarked that he certainly didn't waste any time, having a baby in ten months. Little did I dream I'd better his record the following year.

I'd only been back to Rhode Island a few days when I felt the ter-rible pain of separation; there'd be no more weekends for the rest of 1953. My best instincts told me I was crazy to leave Marianne for eight months while I was on the other side of the world. We should have at least gotten engaged. When I told this to Lt. Williams, he said, "If you've got the right girl, she'll wait. If not, ten rings won't make any difference." It was good advice.

Two weeks before we departed, all the pilots and aircrewmen went out to a pistol and rifle range behind the station ordnance shack. Here, a chief aviation ordnanceman demonstrated the fine points of firing a .38 caliber pistol. All flying personnel had to carry sidearms while engaged in flight ops in the war zone. I found the choice of weapon odd. Having served in the National Guard for three years, I'd qualified in everything from the BAR (automatic rifle) to the .50

caliber machine gun, including the .45 pistol, M1, and carbine. But I'd never fired a .38.

The old chief said the best thing he could tell us about this pistol was to throw it as far away as we could if we were forced down. Against troops with automatic weapons, it was worse than useless: more good advice.

Our planes, meanwhile, were being upgraded with the installation of the new radio receiver, ARC-31. Engineers and technicians from O and R (overhaul and repair) changed the antennas, the wiring, and the power racks over a three-day period. We were occupied elsewhere because installation was not within our province (as it developed, we should have paid more attention). In any event, there was little we could have done even if we had wanted to. Our time had run out.

All our pilots and Mr. Overton flew down to Norfolk in our three Skyraiders. The rest of us followed in an R4D (navy transport). Upon arrival at Breezy Point, trucks carried us to Pier Seven, Naval Operating Base, the same berth I'd sailed from the previous August. There, on a sunny cool day in early April, we got our first glimpse at what would be our home for the next eight months: USS *Lake Champlain (CVA-39)*.

Chapter 17

The *Champ*

THE *LAKE CHAMPLAIN* WAS ABOUT EIGHTY FEET SHORTER than the *Midway* and the *F.D. Roosevelt*, but standing on the pier you'd never notice it. From the tip of her clipper bow right down to where her side disappeared from view, she was an awesome beauty. Without her brood of planes, one would never guess she was an engine of destruction. *CVA-39* was one of the famous Essex class carriers that had destroyed Japan's fleet and brought the war to her front door.

The *Lake Champlain* herself had seen no combat. The atomic bomb was dropped just as she was completing her shakedown cruise in 1945. Pressed into service as a troop transport, she joined Operation Magic Carpet, carrying our happy soldiers home from Europe. On one of her runs from Cape Spartel, near Gibraltar, to the Chesapeake Bay buoy off Hampton Roads, she cranked out an incredible average speed of 32.048 knots (over 37 miles per hour), eclipsing the *Queen Mary*'s Blue Riband record. This mark, though unofficial (only liners were eligible to compete for the Blue Riband), stood until the summer of 1952, when it was broken by the SS *United States* on her historic maiden voyage.

After the troops had been returned, the *Champ* was placed in the reserve fleet and mothballed, seemingly a prelude to the scrap yard. Fate decreed otherwise, and here she was, awaiting her second air group and first combat deployment.

VC-12 was bedded down in an airy compartment just below the hangar deck, a little forward of the island. Since there was little for us to do, we left our gear lying on our racks and went ashore to the movies or the EM Club. The ship was in the process of being onloaded, and anyone not so engaged was just in the way. A few members of the team stayed behind, much to their later regret.

That evening, while most of us were drinking beer or enjoying the flicks, all hell broke loose. The fighter and attack squadrons

Lake Champlain, CVA-39.

came aboard, and our berthing space was one of the first to be req-
uisitioned. As they outranked us, there was no argument. The four
poor souls who'd remained on board were pressed into service and
had to move all the gear of thirty men up to the hangar deck, where
it was unceremoniously dumped among some jets.

When the lucky segment of the team returned on board sometime around midnight, they walked into indescribable chaos. Some
sleepy lieutenant from the Operations Department was solicited by
one of our chiefs, but the best he could do at this hour was issue us
some cots. So Team 44 spent its first night on board sleeping under
the wings of three F9F Panthers. We were promised another compartment as soon as "things sorted themselves out."

With first light, the ship came awake, and we found our "bedroom" invaded by a chow line. I stowed my gear in the electronics
shop. At least I didn't have to worry about half the crew using my
seabag as a souvenir stand. Two days later, we were reassigned to a
compartment in what was literally the bowels of the ship, directly
above where they heated the oil for the boilers. It was just below the
waterline. We immediately tagged it "Dante's Inferno." A few of us

were having second thoughts about having signed on for this trip. That old navy saying about not volunteering for anything was turning out to be all too true.

Moored at the next pier were three APAs (Attack Transports). One of them was the *New Kent,* the ship Marianne's brother Carl was on. I stopped by over the weekend, but Carl wasn't on board. After looking over the APA, I was glad I was an airedale, cots and all.

At sometime in our lives, we've all had the dreadful experience of packing up all our personal gear and moving from one place to another. On other occasions, we've had to get ready for a long trip, worrying that we have forgotten to take something vital. Multiply this by three thousand, and you have some idea what a carrier looks like while preparations are being made for a voyage two-thirds of the way around the globe.

Pier Seven was a sea of packing crates loaded with spare parts, canned goods, light bulbs, fire-extinguishing foam, cigarettes, and those easy-to-forget items like rubber bands and toilet paper. The latter caused a real storage problem, for we wouldn't have access to a U.S. naval depot for nearly six weeks, and our final complement was over 3,800 officers and men. For the Supply Department, this had to be a logistical nightmare, but they more than rose to the occasion.

All that final, frantic weekend, conveyer belts moved carton after carton onto the hangar deck, and forklift trucks hauled them God knows where. Giant steel hatch covers had been removed, revealing a cutaway view of the lower decks. Gazing down into this abyss, one could start to grasp for the first time the tremendous size and complexity of this floating airfield. When it seemed all the spaces below couldn't accommodate one more box or barrel, there were still hundreds of bushels of potatoes and apples stacked on the deck. These were finally crammed into overheads and gun tubs or were lashed along the catwalks. In the planning of the menus, these fruits and vegetables would be used first. For a while, apples were available on demand, but the novelty soon wore off.

Some fraying of tempers was inevitable as the nearly one thousand men of the air group were gradually absorbed into the everyday routine of the ship. The ship's company had only been aboard since October (when the *Champ* was recommissioned), and the bulk of these people were just becoming familiar with a ship still reverberating to the sound of air hammers and riveting guns. Many, too, were just out of boot camp. Crowded themselves and constantly picking their way over snaking power cables, they now had to contend with a horde of strangers who spoke a different language and wore little wings on their ratings. The permanent crew were some-thing akin to the townspeople of a tropical resort who have to suffer a swarm of tourists every winter. The town probably couldn't survive without them, but you'd have a hard time convincing the natives.

At times, this "them and us" attitude carried all the way to the top. Old-timers who'd served in prewar flat-tops like the *Yorktown*, *Lexington*, and *Enterprise* told of their air groups being treated like so many poor relations. Flight operations were curtailed at night be-cause they interfered with the movies, and the Operations Depart-ment was constantly groaning about the oil droppings on the flight and hangar decks. Later, when all CV skippers wore wings, this changed, but I'm sure there was still some resentment among the more traditional navy ratings. Once I remember being chewed out by an Engineering Lieutenant Commander while I was filling canteens for the pilots and aircrewmen before a flight. He thought it was a waste of water.

In time, most of this friction broke down under the knowledge that we were literally and figuratively in the same boat. Occasionally, though, we still had to remind a few officers and men that this was after all, an aircraft carrier. Ironically, my first new friends on the cruise turned out to be from the ship's company.

On 18 April, we departed Norfolk, but *CVA-39* sailed south in-stead of east. On this detour to Florida, we carried a bunch of con-gressmen and VIPs on a seagoing junket. This side trip met with uni-versal disapproval, for our first days and nights away from home were wasted. If we were to undertake this great voyage, then let it begin. If we were to be parted from wives and sweethearts, then let it count for something. Let's get on with it, we thought.

The *Lake Champlain* finally got underway for good at 0800 on 26 April 1953. I thought of the *Midway*'s departure eight months be-fore. A similar pathetic band of wives stood on the pier, clutching babies and waving, until the tugs nosed us out into the stream. There was no band to see us off this time, and our company would only be the *Coral Sea (CVA-43)* and four destroyers. It was a far cry from the train of ships that escorted the *Midway* across the Atlantic. The familiar Virginia landmarks passed in review, until the final chan-nel buoy disappeared into the haze. It was to be our last link to home for eight months.

Before we rendezvoused with our escorting destroyers (DDs), we had one more chore to complete—filling our tanks with high octane aviation fuel. Late in the afternoon our tanker, lying low in the water, appeared out of the mist and grew larger every minute. About half our crew lined the catwalks and railings as the distance narrowed, and a strong breeze started blowing at right angles to the ship. As we bore down on the slower-moving oiler, this wind almost ended our voyage before it started.

A steering maneuver was ordered to bring the *Lake Champlain* along the port side of the tanker, gradually reducing speed until the vessels were running parallel, about 100 feet apart. At this point, lines would be run across and the big fueling hoses connected.

As we approached to about three hundred yards off the tanker's stern, our wheel was turned to bring us alongside. Nothing happened. The *Lake Champlain* continued to bear down on the oiler at the same angle. The wind blowing from our port quarter was carrying us too far to the right. The carrier, three times taller than the oiler, was acting like a giant sail, rendering the rudder (at this low speed) nearly useless.

Our collision alarm sounded as the tanker's stern disappeared beneath the forward overhang of the flight deck. Our hull shuddered as the sound of shrieking metal cut the air, and the engines were reversed. In the arc of a descending pitch, the extreme end of our forward catwalk sliced into the stack and cabins of the hapless oiler. Luckily, the accommodations were empty as all hands were on duty. On the next rising wave, the ships parted. Now we started a completely new approach, this time much more conservative. I couldn't see our bridge, but we had a bird's-eye view of the other, and I never saw people move so fast in all my life. We could imagine how they must have felt watching this monster bearing down on them, all the while sitting on six million gallons of high octane gasoline.

None of us even wanted to speculate on what would have happened had the gasoline ignited. We had eighty gassed aircraft on board, and they would have gone off like so many firecrackers. Our magazines were loaded with bombs, rockets, and ammo. It would have been the USS *Franklin* all over again, only worse. (The carrier *Franklin* was bombed just off the coast of Japan in March 1945 as she was launching aircraft and the resulting holocaust cost well over a thousand casualties.) We were a sober crew when the tanker departed licking her wounds, and when the Catholic chaplain announced that a Rosary would be said on the fantail that evening, he did a land office business.

As the oiler disappeared below the horizon, we settled into a routine that, except for a few ports of call, would remain monotonously unbroken until we reached Japan nearly two months later. *CVA-39* would cross the equator, span twenty time zones, three oceans, countless seas and gulfs, and even traverse the Suez Canal, but the ship's daily pattern would not vary. It was a time-tested regimen of

work and watches and sleep that the navy had been perfecting since
the days of sail. Once immersed in this nautical time capsule, Monday could be Friday and April might be June. In some parts of the
ship, like the boiler rooms, night could be day.

The *Lake Champlain* was sailing east instead of west for a very
good reason. She could not fit through the Panama Canal. As originally built she could, along with her other Essex class sisters. When
modernized, however, not only her tonnage increased, but also her
waist (or beam), in the form of torpedo blisters. This bulk added just
enough "fat" to make the transit impossible. All the CVs commissioned after World War II were the same. Strategically, it was thought
that we had enough carriers to protect both oceans, unlike the early
days of the Pacific War, when flat-tops were frantically shuttled back
and forth.

Although cut off from land, we were a complete American community, self-sufficient in almost every way. The *Champ* had its own
police and fire department and a hospital that would be the envy of
many a small town. Our radio station kept us abreast of world events
and filled our off-hours with the likes of Patti Page and Nat King Cole.
The ship's paper, *The Champ*, was a weekly. It featured many photographs and was read from cover to cover. (Later, its editor, John
Williford, would become one of my closest friends.) The *CVA-39*'s chefs
could boast about serving 10,000 meals daily, and although there
were the usual complaints, I never saw anyone eat elsewhere.

Rounding out this floating village was a fresh-water plant, a
laundry, two churches, a library, and our very own shoemaker. Did
I forget anything? Oh yes, I think we had an airport.

Among the things that were missing were women. Here we resembled a monastery—all male and serving under similar vows: obe-
dience and chastity (at least at sea).

There were other things we lacked, and some of them wouldn't
become apparent right away. None of us would be able to get behind
the wheel of a car for eight months, and for those who enjoyed a
drink after work, it soon became only a fond memory. The navy had
been officially dry since 1912. If so much as a bottle of beer was
found in our quarters, the full weight of naval justice would fall on
us like we'd just sold some radar secret to the Russkies. On the
other hand, when I delivered messages to pilot's staterooms, I was
occasionally offered a welcome Scotch or Bourbon. After watching
sailors ashore, I never questioned the wisdom of the navy's policy. I
felt a great deal more secure in the air knowing that everyone who
performed maintenance on my plane was at least cold sober.

Like all towns, we were composed of neighborhoods, and each

compartment resembled a street, with one big exception: these neighbors knew almost everything about each other. There weren't any doors or curtains to close.

The enlisted men literally rubbed shoulders (and other things) in their crowded quarters. Comfort held a low priority when it came to designing a fighting ship. Living spaces were squeezed anywhere there was room and often where there wasn't. Our bedroom/living room was fifteen feet wide, twenty-five feet long, and eight feet high. To twenty-eight men, this was home.

We slept on steel racks that held stretched canvas like a sail. On this canvas was a two-inch mattress (not exactly a Beautyrest). Usually, there were three racks fitted from deck to overhead, with the space in between measuring about twenty inches. If the man above you was in the two-hundred pound range, he would often sag down into your "air space." Rolling over was then a cooperative measure. Pipes and electrical cables ran close to the overhead, and one learned early on not to sit up too quickly. Stories abounded of sailors knocking themselves senseless while responding to General Quarters in darkened berthing spaces.

Only a fortunate few had compartments with portholes. To ensure watertight integrity, most warship hulls had the fewest possible openings. The air we breathed was blower-fed, moving through ducts that twisted and turned before angling down to the various decks, where the air at last arrived in a lukewarm flow. When a division was assigned to a living space, the bunk next to the air register was a treasured spot. Sadly for that individual, things usually turned out far differently than he planned. Within a few days, everyone in close proximity to a duct would have cut openings into it, funneling a stream of air in their direction. When this diminished breeze finally made it to the register, there was hardly enough force to blow out a candle. It was a case of the biblical prophecy come true: "The first shall be last, and the last shall be first."

More ingenious types placed elaborately rigged fans over their racks to bathe themselves in a steady flow of air. In our compartment, one aircrewman (who was not exactly a favorite) hung two fans fore and aft of his rack and figured he had the nearest thing to air-conditioning. His Rube Goldberg invention became an exercise in futility however, as everyone going up the ladder to the head tilted the fans away from him.

Air operations commenced our third day out. Considering that this group of airdales was brand new to the ship, the launches and recoveries went as smoothly as if we'd been working together for months. The flight and hangar deck crews had hundreds of hours of drills behind them, and their officers and P.O.'s had spent years in carriers, many of them in combat.

Every division of the ship had many recruits fresh from boot camp, along with a large complement of reservists. Some of the latter were recalled veterans like Lt. Overton. These people weren't strangers to sea duty, and many had experienced the ordeal of battle. The majority, however, were young men who'd joined the Naval Reserve to avoid the draft. These were the so-called "weekend warriors."

Air Group Four was comprised of all "regulars," as the navy required a four-year enlistment to qualify for a service school.

Later, my friendship with John Robben, the Catholic chaplain's assistant, drew me into a circle of the ship's company almost exclusively made up of these weekend warriors. College graduates for the most part, they drifted into jobs where they were altogether overqualified. Not desiring to be commissioned or extend their two-year tour of duty, they spent their time shuffling papers and keeping out of everyone's way. None even tried to make "seaman," the grade above apprentice, and they wore their two lowly white stripes with a sort of reverse pride. This unique streak of orneriness was probably what attracted me to them in the first place.

Chapter 18

Death at Sea

THOSE FIRST FEW DAYS OUT OF NORFOLK became, for many, a harsh period of adjustment. About half the complement had never been on the ocean before, and the motion of a ship at sea takes some getting used to. Fortunately, King Neptune smiled on us, and our transit across the Atlantic was smooth. My problem was not the movement of my new home, but finding my way about in the endless companionways and unfamiliar spaces.

The *Champ* was laid out a lot differently from the *F.D.R.* or the *Midway*, and more than once I found myself in a dead end while trying to move along a corridor. Part of the problem was caused by the modernization of a ship coming out of mothballs. Adding all this new radar and fire-control equipment into what was essentially the same size hull, resulted all too often in an alteration of the original layout. And even for those who'd been to sea before, there was still a break-in period required to rid ourselves of our landlubber habits.

It was even tougher for the married men, who lost the comfort of being able to reach out in the middle of the night and feel something soft and warm next to them. But I guess the biggest loss was one of freedom. For most of the next eight months, none of us could take a walk longer than the distance of the flight deck or hop in our cars and just go out for a drive. We were locked in just as surely as if we were in a penitentiary, and as a result, there weren't too many happy faces as those first long days and nights passed. Our youth only made it more painful when it came to putting the length of our deployment into context. When you're in your teens or twenties, eight months can seem like eight years, so the time stretched interminably. Two of the men in our team had just been married during those last few weeks before we sailed, and I didn't envy them. I, at least, didn't know what I was missing. But, like all things in the navy, we got used to the *Champ*. We had no choice.

While all of us were settling into our new home, *CVA-39* had been eating up the miles, moving steadily eastward. Ten days out of Norfolk, the Atlas mountains of Morocco appeared off our starboard bow, and our first ocean was behind us. As we neared Gibraltar, the captain's private plane (an SNJ) was brought up to the flight deck. Because it was a tiny aircraft, six men had to put their weight on the wings to keep it from being blown over the side in the strong wind. Captain Mundorff climbed aboard, and as soon as the sailors let go, the little plane rose almost vertically, like a helicopter. He flew to the "Rock," arriving a few hours before us.

We anchored in the shadow of this historic bastion, but there was no liberty. While we were waiting for our skipper to return, however, there was a mail-call, which resulted in some smiling faces on the chow line that night. Six hours later, the USS *Coral Sea* left us to join the Sixth Fleet, and we moved out into the Mediterranean in the company of our four destroyers, heading for Greece.

Early the next morning under a warm sun, flight operations commenced. Kinney and I shared the backseat of 701, scheduled for an ASW op (antisubmarine flight). The first dozen jets had been "catted" off, and we started to taxi forward. Suddenly, word came from the Air Boss to stop all engines. After the props stopped turning, Kinney opened his hatch and looked aft. He said something had happened to one of the aircraft behind us, but all he could see was a crowd of flight deck personnel. Sooner than we expected, we had our answer. A wire stretcher was carried past us, bearing the mangled body of a green-shirted figure soaked in blood. The bearers and a corpsman holding a large compress were also covered in blood, and a gory trail extended back the length of three planes. I didn't know the human body could hold that much. A flight deck crewman had walked into a whirling prop.

As we shuffled slowly back to the ready room, we passed three pilots retching violently in the catwalk. They were unlucky enough to have witnessed the full effects of this terrible accident. The luckless sailor had lost a third of his skull, and bright red blood spurted with every heart beat. Incredibly, he still lived.

The ship was brought to a stop about two hundred miles from Italy, and two specialists were flown in. A five-hour operation ensued, and all activity ceased as a hushed stillness gripped the ship. Only the sound of the blowers could be heard over the whispers of the crew. For the men of the *Lake Champlain*, it turned into a death watch. I'd never been on a silent ship in the middle of the sea before, and it was an eerie feeling. Shortly after noon, the airman died without regaining consciousness. Later, after an impressive memorial service attended by the entire crew, the story came out.

John Casster, SA, had been in the engine room. He didn't like working below decks and volunteered for duty with the flight deck team. His job involved pulling the chocks from beneath the planes before they taxied forward. While moving from one side of the plane to the other, he either turned the wrong way or was blown by the slipstream into the aircraft behind. He had been in the navy just six months. We didn't know it at the time, but he'd be just the first of nine men who wouldn't return to the States.

The memorial service did more than just honor the memory of a brave man. In one dramatic stroke, it united every sailor on board. Before Casster's death, I thought of myself first as a member of VC-12 and second as a part of the air group. Now, I was welded completely into the ship's company, and the *Lake Champlain* took precedence over all other units in my loyalty. Suddenly, those men in the chow line were no longer nameless faces; they were shipmates. On that sad morning when we all remembered a fallen comrade, we stood as one for the first time. When the last strains of taps echoed and died on the hangar deck, so did any illusion that this was a pleasure cruise. In our heart of hearts, each one of us said, "This could have been me."

As the revolutions increased to normal speed, the rising breeze acted as a tonic, washing away the heavy depression that hung over the ship. The timing of our first liberty port couldn't have been better. Three days after the accident, *CVA-39* dropped her hook off Piraeus, the port of Athens.

Chapter 19

First Liberty

For MANY ON BOARD, ATHENS WOULD BE their first foreign port, and they eagerly looked forward to getting ashore. This ancient cradle of democracy stood out clearly in the sharp morning air, although it was still more than twenty miles away. The unfamiliar Greek national anthem was played as honors were rendered. The formalities over, a tide of white-uniformed sailors poured aboard a landing ship tank, which easily accommodated the first liberty party. Ashore, we blended with the architecture of not only present-day Athens, but also the city of Homer and Pericles.

This capital, the most prosperous center of the country, was still desperately poor. Shop windows were bare, and most of the people appeared to be concerned only about making it to tomorrow. Nevertheless, everyone was genuinely glad to see us, and a quick barter soon sprang up. Since the drachma was almost worthless, cigarettes became the coin of the realm. There wasn't much to buy other than a few dolls and handicrafts, but there was no end of things to see.

We took a tour of the Acropolis, the Archaeological Museum, and the Royal Palace, where we watched the changing of the guard. Their honor guard wore skirts, but they revealed legs of pure concrete. After a few Chesterfields, the ice was broken, and they were happy to pose for photographs. Later, I met a young soldier who wanted to practice his English, and for the price of lunch I had a five-hour tour of the "real" city.

George was a self-taught man. His father had been killed in the civil war that ravaged the country in 1946. The following year, Truman, in order to keep Greece from falling into the Communist orbit, asked Congress for $400 million in economic aid, a lot of money at that time. Unfortunately, the native bureaucracy was so corrupt that we had to manage the program ourselves, in reality setting up a government within a government. This triggered what became known as the "Truman Doctrine." It also created a peacetime precedent of aiding any country trying to preserve its freedom. Few realized it at the time, but all of us in the task force heading east were the direct result of that policy. To these olive-skinned natives of the Mediterranean who never saw an American soldier or tank, the regular appearance of the carriers of the Sixth Fleet lent a tangible reality to our European commitment.

As evening approached and liberty wound down, we all drifted back to Piraeus. I said good-bye to George and gave him the last of my cigarettes and drachmae. While awaiting the landing craft, I witnessed a phenomenon that would be repeated in every liberty port more than halfway round the world.

The U.S. Navy had been stopping here regularly for the last seven years. Sailors being sailors, many hadn't ventured far beyond the first bar, where the ouzo had laid them low. Now all these limp bodies had to be rounded up and returned to their respective ships. The natives knew this routine better than we did, so by 5 P.M. all the choice tables adjoining the fleet landing were taken. They were looking for a good show, and they got it.

The shore patrol had a couple of army trucks at their disposal, and each returned bearing 15 to 20 sailors in various stages of paralysis. A few could walk with help, but most had to be carried. Many toted huge artifacts that they were convinced they couldn't live without. Large fur hats were the rage, and some swabbies had traded parts of their uniform when they ran out of money and cigarettes. The dockside scene soon took on the trappings of a full-scale costume party, and more than one skirt ballooned under a regulation jumper.

Cheers rose from the tables as each motley group slid from the trucks. The biggest roar greeted a pilot leading a goat on a tether, which had to be gently but firmly removed from his grip. The LST was packed with heaving sailors, but all agreed Athens was just what the doctor ordered after two long weeks at sea. The *Lake Champlain* remained for three days, allowing all hands to savor the glories of Greece.

Early the next morning, when we were underway, the familiar sound of flight quarters rang throughout the ship and I took off with Mr. Quinn for a four hour op. About an hour out, a cluster of small mountainous islands appeared, breaking the endless, sun-drenched Aegean Sea. They were easily the most beautiful islands I'd ever seen. With hardly a sign of human life, they appeared to have been just created by God and dropped into the sea. Mr. Quinn brought our AD-4W down to 500 feet, and soon we saw shepherds tending their flocks. All of them waved at us as we skimmed the valleys and rocky cliffs. When we finally turned back towards the *Champ*, we were both sorry to leave such an idyllic sight. Most of the time, our radar duties required us to fly over unbroken stretches of ocean for hours on end.

As we sailed south through the incredibly cobalt Aegean, spring changed to early summer, and the mercury took a sudden leap upward. Around us, ships of every size, shape, and nationality appeared, all steaming in one direction: the Suez Canal.

Our carrier and four destroyers passed thirty odd tankers and freighters waiting to enter the canal. It was strictly one-way traffic, and groups of merchantmen sailed in convoys. At the halfway point was Great Bitter Lake, which acted as a siding because there was no night navigation. The *Lake Champlain* had priority since we had a schedule to keep, and the British and French (who controlled the canal) were among those fighting in Korea with the UN forces.

With the *Champ* in the van, our force of five warships moved slowly across the flat desert, taking on the illusion of some seaborne caravan straight out of the Arabian Nights. The Suez Canal, it turned out, was nothing more than 108 miles of monotonous ditch connecting the Mediterranean to the Red Sea. In this cloudless sky, the heat was straight from hell. Our flight deck measured 115 degrees in the sun (there was no shade). With the exception of a few air-conditioned spaces (where enlisted men seldom roamed), the rest of the ship was over 100 degrees. Our five-knot speed scarcely ruffled the flag on the mast, and holiday routine reigned as we inched our way across the desert. We later learned that we were the largest ship to transit the canal.

Every officer and man who was not on duty packed the catwalks, flight deck, and the upper level of the island structure. Some brave souls even ventured out on the mainmast crossbar which held the radar and radio antennas. They could probably see 50 miles. The views offered many contrasts. On the port side looking forward, the land was green. There were date palms and tall grass, and on occasion a tiny village, where long-masted dhows nested against rickety piers. The canal was two hundred feet wide, and as our beam was half that, we posed no threat to these ancient sailboats.

Slightly inland, telegraph poles punctuated a highway carrying camels and a few motorized vehicles. All the camel drivers stopped and waved. They were no doubt inwardly cursing the fact that there was no way of trading with us.

The view from the other side of the ship couldn't have been more different. There the silent and barren desert stretched to the horizon, and no building or living thing broke the unending plain. Those

Suez Canal, 14 May 1953, en route to Port Said.

who remembered their geography knew that this was just the beginning of the great Sahara that rolled clear across the continent to the
Atlantic. Early in the evening, we dropped our pilot at Suez, where
he boarded a ship heading north. For the first time in many hours,
we could see water on all sides as we moved out into the Red Sea.
We started to crank up 18 knots, and along with it came a welcome
breeze.

Chapter 20

A New World

THAT 108 MILES OF THE SUEZ CANAL was far more than a conduit between two bodies of water. It ushered us into a time change every bit as dramatic as Alice's looking glass. The *Lake Champlain* had entered a new world.

It was a world much older than Europe, and far older than America. A place where Christianity was almost unknown and what we called Western civilization had little impact on daily life. Suddenly, the rules had changed.

It was nearly dusk the next day when we approached Aden, on the coast of Arabia. This would be a refueling stop. The town, a handful of whitewashed buildings, was miniscule, and any thought of liberty was out of the question, since even a fragment of our crew would have overwhelmed them. In spite of this, Aden held our interest.

The port boasted an underwater system of pipelines which ingeniously fueled each ship, not unlike a bay in a service station. Getting into position required some fancy ship-handling, and the captain (an old airedale himself) utilized the power of the air group to line up his command. Twenty Skyraiders were lashed down forward, in two rows of ten, each facing inboard. A similar group was placed aft. Their props effectively took the place of our ship's propellers, and by turning up different combinations, the captain could maneuver the bow and stern without forward motion. The energy of the props turned the ship like a pinwheel, hence the name "Operation Pinwheel." It was definitely a crowd-pleaser, and all hands enjoyed the show; all hands that is, except those who had to maintain those aircraft engines. Some of the ship's company quipped, "Well, they finally found a use for the air group."

Our tanks filled, we moved from the superheated Red Sea into the tropical Indian Ocean. The humidity soared, and a sheet of dew painted everything. All the creases in our clothing disappeared, and along with them our good natures. But there were rewards, too.

Platoons of flying fish broke the surface of the flat blue sea, gliding out at right angles from the bow wave, their silver wings glistening in the sun. Best of all was the sky's daily parting shot: sunsets that grew and grew, until the eye couldn't absorb any more. These were so spectacular they left many of us speechless.

By now, Chaplain Kelly's rosary on the fantail (following evening chow) had become for many a daily ritual. It was a place to meet shipmates one would never have seen in the normal course of events. Here officers and chiefs, airdales and seamen, all rubbed shoulders, their differences forgotten. The darkening sky, the feeling of being alone hundreds of miles from land, all led to talk of home and family. This long voyage had only just begun, and already the specter of loneliness was evident in a lot of eyes.

But for everyone who was lonely and unhappy, there appeared to be an equal number who were relatively content. The navy had an expression that said, "You look like you found a home." This, for many of my shipmates, was painfully true. While I'd grown up during the Depression and had seen my family endure hard times, it was still a family, with more than enough love and affection to go around. New York City, where I was raised, was also a place of unlimited opportunity, with a variety of jobs and easy access to good public education.

This wasn't the case for many on board. Some were born in small towns in the South or grew up on farms where they had almost no options. More to the point, scores were victims of broken homes or had been abused by alcoholic fathers. Most were mired in "nothing" jobs. A disproportionate number of swabbies came from the poor sections of Alabama, Georgia, and Mississippi. They joined the navy, not for travel or adventure, but for sheer survival.

While the "chickenshit" and long periods of separation were sometimes galling, the navy was their only ticket out of the mines and farms and away from dead-end jobs like sweeping floors. Many admitted the navy was the first place they enjoyed indoor plumbing, and for others, the chow served in the mess deck bordered on the exotic. Their contentment was founded on substantially more than just good food and regular paydays. Now, they'd been given something denied them in their former lives, a feeling of self-worth and personal esteem. For the first time they felt wanted. That's no small accomplishment for an eighteen year old who's been ignored by his parents and hounded by the local sheriff, as one of our mechs had been. For this group, the navy became the "great escape."

Overall, the aviation community appeared to have the bigger slice of this "good life." For openers, everyone in it was a graduate of a service school. Working around aircraft was demanding, with no margin for error. We were envied by the rest of the crew, and our profession had a highly respected and well-paying counterpart in civilian life: the airline industry. For the majority who were spending just four years, it was an unparalleled chance to master a technical trade.

Within a few months of leaving my last school, I was tackling advanced radar problems a civilian technician wouldn't see for years. The navy wasn't shy about pushing you into more challenging work, and it expected you to rise to the occasion. You learned a lot, and you learned fast. You had to.

In college, you might say to yourself, "I won't take this course, I'm no good at math or science, or whatever." Here, there was no second guessing. If the navy thought you could do it, you did it and usually surprised yourself in the process. When I woke up one day and realized I was repairing radios and radar and it was a deadly serious business, I was stunned. I couldn't believe this had all happened in just a few short months.

I wasn't good with my hands, but I found electronics more cerebral than manual. It was also totally new ground. I was constantly surprising myself with my ability. Once broken down into logical steps, trouble-shooting a receiver was not that difficult, and it could be a hell of a lot of fun. I never used my electronic skills after I left the service, but plenty of my buddies did. The training wasn't wasted, however, and later on my navy background came to my aid in many subtle ways. After bouncing around with three different employers in two years, I fell into a situation where I was pretty much on my own: no set hours and little supervision. You got paid on exactly what you produced. It was sink or swim (a good navy analogy).

The service never taught me anything about selling, but the work habits I'd formed made all the difference in that first tough year. "Don't Give up the Ship" and "Any job worth doing, is a job worth doing well" may be navy clichés, but the attitudes they generated made all the difference.

For many of my fellow whitehats, there was no civilian life to return to, and they had truly found a home. Very few were married. The navy, in essence, became their mother and father and, in some cases, their wife.

Among the things that attracted this group was a routine that had varied little since John Paul Jones or Admiral Farragut. Bells and bugles replaced clocks. The horizon was no longer filled with wheat fields or apartments. Now it was the sea—always the same, yet in its own way always different. This regular, ordered life held great appeal. You knew when you were going to stand your watch, and what weekend you had the duty. This continuity, this indelible line of tradition, was so strong, a sailor from the first *Lexington* (1930s) could have been transplanted in time to the hangar deck of the *Champ* and would have felt at home. We wore the same dungarees and dress blues, and the ship's routine had barely altered.

The navy cherished her old customs the way the French loved their old stones. Ships still fired salutes much as they did in the days of John Paul Jones, and the same piccolo-pitched bos'n pipe called hands to quarters. The loudspeaker never announced, "It's OK to smoke now." Instead, it intoned, "The smoking lamp is lighted in all authorized spaces." Smoking lamps went out with sailing ships.

One wasn't ordered to "report," you were told to "lay up to the quarter deck." Disciplinary action was meted out at "Captain's Mast," although chances are it took place in his air-conditioned cabin.

These pronouncements had an almost biblical cadence and were couched in eighteenth-century language: "Keep silence about the decks" or "All hands turn to." If you didn't like change, you'd love the navy. The whole place had the comfort of an old set of slippers, and as far as I was concerned, that was one of the best things about it.

While the chance of staying on one ship or duty station for more than two years was rare, there was a closeness among your shipmates that had no parallel in civilian life. The other paradox was privacy. Communal living was tough on those who were used to their own room because the barracks or compartment offered little privacy. It was just the opposite when it came to your private life, however. No one particularly cared what you did on liberty, as long as you didn't get arrested. You could chase women and get roaring drunk, but if you could stand and salute the OOD on the quarterdeck, no one noticed. There were no nosy neighbors (or wives or parents) wondering where you'd been. Under all those regulations and crowded living conditions, this singular freedom was the one most cherished and remembered, so the lure attracted many.

Among the new people I met during those sessions on the fantail was John Robben, the chaplain's assistant. We became fast friends. John kept a journal; I sent my remembrances home to Marianne in long letters, probably boring the poor girl half to death. Through Robben, I met John Williford, the editor of the *Champ*, the ship's newspaper. In time, we were joined by Rich Murphy and Danny Klein from Chicago. Both had a lively sense of humor, and Danny, a World War II veteran, added a little maturity to our circle. John Williford remarked that with Danny being a Jew, our circle resembled that

typical Hollywood bomber crew or infantry squad, where every eth-
nic group had to be represented.

These new friends would form my inner circle. Our common
interests would link us until we arrived back in Mayport nearly eight
months later. The two other Johns, Robben and Williford, shared my
joy of reading and writing, and Robben had also gone to Fordham
University, my alma mater. Danny Klein and Rich Murphy were simply enjoyed for themselves and their unique sense of humor.

Of course, I was still closely bound to George Walls, Bill Munroe,
and other members of my team from VC-12. One group did not
detract from the other, but they rarely mixed. I enjoyed what was
essentially a two-tiered friendship. There was probably some common ground they could have both explored, but somehow it never
seemed worth the trouble. I was happy with the arrangement.

Of the four in the inner circle, John Robben became my closest
friend. We were the same age, and we were both from New York.
John was a far deeper student of American writing and introduced
me to the finer points of writers like Hemingway and Fitzgerald. On
the other hand, sharing the perils of flying from a pitching carrier
deck placed George and Bill into an inner circle with me that was all
their own.

Danny Klein had one of the most unusual jobs on board. He was
solely in charge of the care and maintenance of the *Champ*'s four
Coke machines. With nothing else to drink, except flat-tasting water
from our evaporators, these machines were real moral boosters.
Over a million Cokes were consumed during the cruise, and as
sailors were always trying new ways to beat the machines, Danny
was kept running day and night. As we moved closer to the equator,
the demand almost overpowered the supply.

Every morning after we entered the Indian Ocean, the great sun
ballooned over the horizon, bringing a sullen heat that was inescapable. The sea lay flat and formless, finally joining the building cumu-
lus clouds that held the promise of a welcome afternoon shower.

Our constant sweating made the air in our fetid compartment
resemble that of an unemptied hamper. To alleviate this loathsome
condition, a new routine was instituted that was called, simply
enough, "air bedding." Each division in turn would remove the sweat-
stained canvas pieces from their racks and clean them. I had visions
of scrubbing them with a long-handled brush, but the navy (God
bless her) came up with a simpler and far less painful method.

As we stood at the end of the lowered deck-edge elevator, we
were handed long lines. After fastening these lines securely to an
eyelet in our bedding, we lowered these strips of canvas over the

side. Someone remarked that we looked as if we were flying kites in the ocean. The turbulence of the rushing sea worked miracles, and in a few minutes all the stains were removed. A few hours under the tropic sun not only bleached them, but gave them that clothesline scent our mothers cherished on laundry day. The scores of sailors all tending their lines reminded Bill Munroe of a fishing pier. "I wonder what the hell the fish are thinking, looking up at all these fart sacks trailing alongside. You know Jack, when you think of it, that might be a pretty good title for a book about this cruise, *Fart Sacks in the Sea.*" It broke us up.

Working in this tropical heat and humidity also resulted in a big run on the showers. Soon the crew was using fresh water in prodigious amounts and severely taxing the capacity of our evaporators. Our boilers used half the water to generate steam to run the ship, and the laundry and galleys gulped most of the rest. Enter "water hours."

The time slots that we could take a shower were sharply regulated. We were also restricted to taking what is known as a "Navy shower," and guards were posted to see that the rules were enforced (a Navy shower, incidentally, involved wetting down for a few seconds, turning the water off, lathering up, and finally rinsing for a few more seconds). The times were limited to an hour before breakfast, an hour after work, and an hour before lights out.

One hot day, just before flight operations, this rationing resulted in what I like to think of as "the great battle of the water fountain." Canteens were part of our airborne equipment, and every fighter or attack pilot's plane captain made sure he had an ample water supply before takeoff. A plexiglass canopy greatly intensified the sun's rays, and the high altitude dehydrated you. In VC-12 and VC-33 (the two teams with aircrewmen), one of us was usually delegated to make sure we all had enough to drink.

I took the three containers to a nearby water fountain in the passageway. I'd almost finished my chore when I was grabbed from behind, and the canteen I was filling fell to the deck. Before I could identify my assailant, I heard this voice screaming, "You're on report! You're on report! I'll show you what it means to waste water. Give me your name and division, and you can bet your sweet ass I'll be there when you're standing in front of the captain." For the moment I was speechless. Turning, I saw a scrawny, khaki-clad figure with the gold leaves of a Lieutenant Commander. He was the Engineering Officer.

The veins in his neck and head were standing out, and I thought for a second he'd gone off the deep end. As he caught his breath, I explained what I was doing. "Idiot! Who told you to do such a stupid thing, wasting water like that?" I told him I was acting under the direct orders of the air group commander (who outranked him). I wasn't really sure if I was, but it sounded good at the time, and the words "direct orders" had the desired effect. What I longed to tell him was that I'd like to see him down in the ocean in a raft with no water, and see how he'd like it.

During my four years in the navy, that's the only time I crossed swords with a General Service officer. If nothing else, the incident verified my good judgment in choosing naval aviation.

When operations permitted, many fled the steaming compartments at night for the warm breezes of the flight deck. Hundreds of bodies covered almost every space in and around the parked aircraft. Most evenings, this al fresco slumber posed no problem. On occasion, though, tropical squalls would strike without warning, drenching many a snoring sailor. As aircrewmen, we often converted the rear compartment of our ADs into makeshift bunks. When we opened both hatches for a breeze, a thin mattress could easily fit across the seats in front of the radar.

Our flight deck could be hard even with a mattress, but the heavens offered real compensation. The night sky was a gift not to be wasted. Our night vision wasn't impaired by any residual light, for with the exception of two hidden running beacons, the *Lake Champlain* was totally blacked out. This had nothing to do with military considerations (we wouldn't be under "darken ship" orders until Korea), but was done to save the night vision of those on the bridge. The Southern Cross was just one jewel in a broad canopy of diamonds and never had the stars appeared closer than on those sultry evenings. Those perched on the fantail could gaze at our glowing phosphorescent wake: a brilliant trail of sparkling fireflies.

Mornings in the tropics were not much different. One awakened to the odor of sweating bodies, and rubbing the sleep out of our eyes, we joined the crowd shuffling toward the head. Some were in skivvies, and some were as naked as the day they were born. Regardless, they all wore identical rubber sandals fastened by a single thong between the big toe and its neighbor.

Anderson, a 1st class mech with ten years under his belt, said to a bitching peach-fuzzed kid at the next sink, "Don't complain! It may be tight, but at least you have a clear field of fire. At home, between my wife and three daughters, I need a machete to cut through the drying stockings, panties, and what-have-yous." Some of us thought how marvelous it would be to find those accouterments on our next visit to the head. Boy, would that raise the reenlistment rate!

As we stood in front of those dull steel sinks, rolling with the ship, Radio Central serenaded us with Peggy Lee's "How Much Is That Doggie in the Window." Later, two songs more appropriate to our situation were beamed through those odd-shaped gray speakers: "Side by Side" and Eddie Fisher warbling "Wish You Were Here," both big favorites of the crew. While some of us finished shaving, others exited the showers, snapping towels at those bare asses at the sinks. I'm amazed no one cut their throat. A lot of profanity accompanied this horseplay. Once Walls exclaimed, "Hey Lou, will you look at this body?" pointing to a naked seventeen year old still dripping wet. "He could enter a Mr. America contest." Calley replied, "Miss America, more likely."

In the passageway, the smell of frying bacon and sausage filled the air. It never changed. Regardless of whatever else was on the breakfast menu, "collision mats," oatmeal, or "home fries," it seemed there was always bacon and sausage. Me, I was partial to cornbread and those warm, freshly baked Parker House rolls.

Morning chow was prodigious. Besides the usual civilian fare with which we were familiar (eggs, hot or cold cereal, oatmeal or cream of wheat), we never lacked for heartier fare. A man was frequently asked to perform strenuous manual labor in this terrible heat, and our next nourishment wouldn't be served up for five or six hours. Pork or lamb chops, ham, steak, beans, mashed potatoes, or spaghetti often found their way on to our breakfast trays. While this change of diet was accepted as perfectly natural, the one thing we never got used to was the lumpy powdered milk. The old-timers avoided cereal and drank their "Java" black.

When the air group stood down, one of my favorite places to spend an afternoon was way up forward, just below the flight deck. In the heat and wetness of the tropics, there was always a breeze. There were a couple of spaces up there (not really compartments, since they were open on the side) that were used mostly for storage. I'd bring an apple and Thomas Wolfe along for company, and it was an ideal spot just to watch the sea and sort things out. It appeared to be a place no one used, except when we were entering or leaving port. I was always alone.

On a particularly long afternoon, I became restless and extended myself out beyond the hull opening. Up here, in the "eyes" of the ship, the bow flared, and I discovered my perch was positioned way out to the left of the stem meeting the water sixty feet below. I had to lie uncomfortably on some uneven steel plates, but the sight unfolding below me was worth every aching muscle.

The *Champ*'s clipper bow swept away in a sensuous curve that tapered into a honed blade, cleaving the sea like some giant scalpel. Split into nearly perfect halves, the ocean surged back, opening like the petals of a spring flower. Flaring out, they became hissing white waves that finally met in the spume of the dying wake. I say nearly perfect halves, because those couple of inches on the stem (which formed the point of impact) forced a jet of water straight up, much like a fountain in a park. It was a sight few on board had witnessed, and it was an image I never forgot.

It was easy to come under the spell of the sea, for the vastness of the Indian Ocean covered every quadrant. The sounds, smells, and colors could be mesmerizing, and although he would not have admitted it, this spell could be one of the strongest reasons to make a man ship over for another four or six years. After that, the rest was easy. He was halfway to a "career."

Later, when I shared this space with Roberts, Walls, and Munroe, we often played Monopoly. Sometimes, when aircraft were being catapulted, we'd have to hold the board down because the whole bow shook. You couldn't hear the roar of the engines until they cleared the deck, and then, just for an instant, it would be deafening.

One day, after an hour's play, the four of us were evenly matched on the board. I was doing well with four railroads and some other property, but I worried about coming down on Roberts's hotels on Boardwalk and Park Place. The rent on the Boardwalk was $2,000, and that would put a fatal crimp in my chances. Just as Munroe rolled the dice, the *Champ* turned, and a gust blew both of Roberts's hotels over the side. This in itself was not a major loss because our metalsmiths had long since fashioned steel likenesses to replace the originals, and we had plenty of spares. The real problem was that Munroe had landed on the Boardwalk and then refused to pay for anything more than the unimproved value of the land. His logic was that a hurricane had destroyed the structure, and you couldn't expect a man to pay rent on a building that didn't exist. Roberts looked for our support, but George and I were laughing too hard to be of any help.

Chapter 21

Crossing the Line

No TWO PLACES COULD BE AS DIFFERENT as Greece and our next port of call, Colombo, Ceylon. The tropical isle of Ceylon, about the size of Sicily, had about everything a wide-eyed sailor could ask for in exotic charm, and its oriental atmosphere brought us smack into the Far East.

Lying just south of India, Ceylon had through the centuries developed its own uniquely spiritual culture. Overlaid with Chinese and Indian influence, it was still one of a kind. Here, spread out like a hawker's wares, were gleaming temples, precious sapphires, rubber trees, and working elephants, all competing for our attention.

Not far from the sultry capital where we anchored were some marvelous sandy beaches. Mount Lavinia Hotel had possibly the best and was exclusively populated by the British, who ran the country as a Crown colony. (The hotel was later used in the movie *The Bridge on the River Kwai*.) We would stop, time and again, in places that inspired Kipling and Conrad and Forster. The Union Jack had certainly left its mark.

Ceylon was way off the beaten path for the U.S. Navy, or any navy for that matter, so we attracted more than our share of attention. The natives were a bit laid back at first, probably thinking that we were not much different from their colonial masters. Once they realized we were free-spending Americans (and not too interested in haggling), we were instantly accepted. English was spoken almost everywhere.

A pilot and two other aircrewmen (George Walls and Nault from VC-33) hired a car and asked me to join them for a trip into the interior. From my reading, Kandy, the ancient capital, was high on the list of things to see. We all spread out in the backseat of another ancient sight: a Pierce-Arrow touring car. The driver kept his taxi in top condition, and we were astonished at how well the body had stood up after nearly thirty years in this climate.

As we motored along roads heavy with the scent of tropic vegetation, with a turbaned Sikh at the wheel, Ron remarked what a
great recruiting poster this would make. On this long, dusty highway, we passed strolling natives, all with hordes of children. They
labored under enormous batches of fruit and produce, some perched
on their heads. They all wore skirts, regardless of sex. Only the
British wore trousers.

Our first stop was a rubber plantation, where we walked under
a canopy of Royal palms over a hundred feet high. Later, we bought
some carved wooden figures from vendors who dotted the winding
road up into the mountains.

Kandy was right out of *Jungle Jim*, the lost city in the mountains. Crumbling ruins were laced with thick vines that coiled round
and round over the sandstone columns, and in the deep shadows,
bizarre figures of ancient gods and goddesses stood like silent sentinels. A teeming city once thrived here, but now, like Pompeii, it was
dead. After forty-five minutes, we'd had enough of stones and the
droning of the sing-song guides, who always seemed to tell us more
than we wanted to know.

Lunch in a small village next to a narrow stream was welcome.
Over something described as curry that we washed down with glasses
of cold English beer, we watched children scampering in the shal-
lows as their mothers beat their laundry on the smooth rocks.

As we drove back to Colombo, our driver regaled us with elephant stories. He explained how a young bull was matched to a small
boy, who trained and remained with him for life. No sooner had he
finished, when around a turn in the road, we came upon a group of
elephants being used to uproot trees and clear the land for a new
highway. Our driver stopped, and after a short chat, asked if any of
us would like to ride an elephant. He said it was perfectly safe, so
after a few embarrassing moments of silence, I volunteered.

The trainer tapped the huge animal with his staff, and the creature immediately dropped to a kneeling position. I was helped onto
his back and straddled the beast just behind his leathery ears.
Another tap with the rod, and I was lifted ten feet into the air. George
took my picture, and after a short walk, I was deposited back on the
road. I gave the trainer the last of my cigarettes, and he almost broke
the fingers of my hand with gratitude. Then I fed the elephant some
of his favorite leaves from the wagon. For me, this experience was
the highlight of the trip.

Colombo was a congested metropolis baking under the harsh
equatorial sun, where hundreds of vendors came to feast off the
"rich Americans." On every corner, Buddhist priests in their bright

yellow robes competed for space with jabbering natives who were hawking star sapphires and other "precious" stones. Tiny Morris-Minors and London-style buses inched their way through this mass of humanity. There were scores of vivid images to take back to the ship, but what stuck in most memories was the strong odor hanging over the whole city. It had a quality of decaying vegetation, among other things best left unsaid. The general opinion was that it was just plain rot. George said Colombo should be labeled the "Norfolk of the East." This oppressive smell followed us for over twenty miles out to sea. After three days in Ceylon, we were all glad to be underway.

One amusing footnote to our visit was the VD bulletin put out by Commander Hunley, our chief medical officer. To paraphrase his message, he said he could understand how horny some of us were after a long time at sea, but he couldn't urge us more strongly to remain celibate, at least until we reached Manila, our next port of call. There, he said, the medical books "probably" had names for the diseases. Here, you might be breaking new ground. If you went into the back alleys for pleasure and only came down with some form of VD, he'd consider you very lucky indeed, for you could easily come back with leprosy, elephantiasis, or worse.

Months later, in Tokyo, I ran into Hunley at the bar at the Nigatsu Hotel, and I asked him how successful his admonition had been. He smiled and said it was the most effective medical bulletin he'd ever issued. Sick call produced about twenty cases of dysentery from eating unwashed fruits and vegetables. Nothing else.

A swabbie rarely gets a chance to rub shoulders with a "three striper" (commander), but medical officers were something different. In a way, they were like chaplains, operating a world apart from the navy of gunnery and navigation. Neither group were "line officers" (those who could eventually achieve command), but were tolerated simply because we couldn't get along without them.

Hunley was looking for company and bought me a Scotch. After a couple of drinks, we seemed almost buddies. When he discovered I'd gone to Fordham (where he knew some of the profs), he started to tell me some of the oddities of his seagoing profession. It was remarkably different from the average civilian practice. For a start, almost every patient was in the pink of health. With an average age of twenty, this was to be expected. So his professional day was spent treating sprains, sunburn, and an occasional bad back. As the ship neared some decent liberty ports, a few of the medical inquiries became unusual, to say the least.

The good doctor (now on his fifth Scotch, by my count) recalled a session with an old-timer, a chief about forty (in the navy, anybody over thirty is an "old-timer"). The chief was deeply worried. He wanted the "Doc" to check him out. His problem, it developed, was that he could only achieve two ejaculations on the same erection. Hunley said his patient was lucky he didn't throw him over the side.

The *Champ* sailed east into the waters of the Malay Barrier. This archipelago, which is now almost entirely the country of Indonesia, adorns the equator like an elaborate necklace, its islands dangling north and south from an imaginary chain dividing the world into hemispheres. The *Lake Champlain* moved past Sumatra and into what was once known as the Java Sea. Here, twelve years before, the combined American, British, Dutch, and Australian naval forces were decimated by the Japanese in the early days of the Pacific War. Our first aircraft carrier, the *Langley* (*CV-1*, converted into a seaplane tender), was sunk not far from where we were steaming. We were *CV-39*. The navy and the world had come a long way in those few years.

The shortest route to Manila would have carried us about thirty miles north of the equator, but the *Champ* diverted so we could all partake in what is probably the most treasured of all nautical ceremonies: Crossing the Line.

For three days, verbal and printed warnings were fired off by the "shellbacks," those who'd crossed the equator, to the "polywogs," the uninitiated, or about 95 percent of the crew. They proclaimed the untold terrors awaiting us before we could be deemed worthy enough to enter the realm of King Neptune.

The appointed day opened with a flat gray sea unruffled by the slightest breeze. Our Plan of the Day bulletin called for the wearing of the oldest dungarees and shirts we could find. Selected groups wore half blues and half whites, with the jumpers reversed. This, I surmised, was to show King Neptune just how unnautical we were. It made for great picture taking, anyway.

One of the aircraft barriers was raised in the middle of the flight deck "to separate the men from the boys." All hands had to pass through the gate. Unless you could prove "shellback" status to guards stationed there, you had to run the gauntlet.

Immediately behind the barrier, a large canvas pool was erected. A long wooden table abutted this, at which sat the senior shellbacks in royal splendor. Here, sentences were passed and punishments carried out.

Next to this table, raised high up on a throne, sat King Neptune himself. He was a chief boatswain's mate, the veteran shellback of all 3,500 men on board (he'd crossed in 1932). Earlier that morning,

Equator crossing, USS Lake Champlain, *30 May 1953.*

he'd arrived by chopper on the flight deck. He'd been greeted by the captain and was rendered all the honors befitting a king, not forgetting the twenty-one gun salute. His imperial status was reinforced by a long white robe, a full beard, and, atop his balding head, a gleaming gold crown.

King Neptune's staff made certain no one escaped his wrath. Some were armed with clippers, which they used liberally. Cutting this way and that, they fashioned odd designs where once wavy locks had sat. Those with the most luxuriant growth were singled out for special treatment. Other lieutenants used prodigious amounts of mustard and catsup, which they poured with special delight over the hapless polywogs.

Probably the most dreaded sentence was the order to kiss the "royal baby." This fantastic character was a short fat sailor, sitting stark naked except for an oversized diaper and infant's bonnet. Lubricating grease covered his huge beer belly, and that's exactly where the kiss had to be planted. My buddy Rich Murphy was one of those singled out for this dubious honor.

These preliminaries over, the victims were then seated on wooden stools overhanging the pool. Upon orders from the king, they were unceremoniously dumped into the water, where more tormentors beat them with canvas whips. Emerging at last, all were forced to crawl through a nylon target sleeve, filled with the foulest remnants of the *Champ*'s garbage. These mess tray scrapings had been saved for days in the tropic heat to give it a special odor. Finally seeing daylight once more, these freshly minted shellbacks were hit with a high pressure hose, both cleaning them and ending the ceremony in one fell swoop.

Commander Weisman, our navigator, was the most senior polywog on board. He was just starting to go thin at the top and no doubt feared that what they lopped off wouldn't grow back. As a small consideration, they passed up his scalp, but shaved the thick hair from his chest with a dry razor. He was still laughing through the pain when he was dumped. No one held any grudges, and at the end of the day all agreed the initiation had been carried out in style. May 30, 1953, would be remembered for a long, long time.

Chapter 22

Rained Out

W E STEAMED NORTH NOW, past Bali and the Admiralties, into the South China Sea. "China Seas!" What adventures those two words evoked. We half expected to see Clark Gable and Jean Harlow appear out of the haze, fighting Malay pirates. But alas, nothing so exotic awaited us. Only more long green swells, more sudden, violent rain squalls, more humidity, more sweat. Staying below decks, except for the air-conditioned ready room, was nearly impossible. We exerted our utmost professional skills to make repairs in the planes, rather than hauling the gear into the ovenlike space of the radio shop.

By now, the detachment had really started to shake down. Despite the fact that flight operations were held only once every five days, we'd become familiar enough with the ship's electrical supply to have our planes spotted properly. We owned the only aircraft in the air group using three-phase AC power. We needed this for our radar. The *Lake Champlain* had only three outlets on the hangar deck (no doubt an afterthought). This cable weighed a ton, and if your plane was spotted in a poor location, it could easily mean hauling this monstrous extension two hundred feet. Snaking this cord around tie-downs and parked vehicles and across oil-soaked decks to our aircraft was a not a favorite pastime. To ensure VC-12's Skyraiders were parked exactly where we wanted them entailed some shrewd naval diplomacy.

Ordinarily our detachment, which consisted of three planes and thirty men and was led by a mere lieutenant, would have carried no weight. We had an ace in the hole, however. Our ADs and those of VC-33 were the only aircraft with two seats in the rear. Since we often flew with only one crewman, this left us an empty seat to bargain with.

The one thing almost everyone from messcook to captain wanted to do was take off and land on a flat-top. This became our great equalizer. As a result, we had no difficulty having our planes spotted close to the needed power. Others on our list were "top dogs" in the galley, for obvious reasons.

Sometimes our maintenance on the Skyraider required the dropping of our radome. This odd-shaped bulge, made entirely of a thin sheet of fiberglass, gave our prototype AD its well-known nickname, "Guppy." It also appeared we were carrying an infant Skyraider below our fuselage. In reality, it was merely a covering for our APS-20 radar antenna.

When other aircraft were being serviced on the hangar deck, scarcely anyone from the ship's company noticed. As the chow line wound its serpentine way past both props and jets, there was hardly a sailor who raised his eyes from his Mickey Spillane. But if we dropped that radome, we became the center of attention.

I don't know what they expected to find hidden inside that cocoon. Perhaps a couple of airdales playing poker or a private bar? Sometimes we'd tell a particularly naïve sailor that we had a soft bunk installed inside, so we could "crap out" on long flights. George Walls once told a quartermaster that back in Quonset, we'd occasionally sneak a Wave on board and utilize that bunk to relieve our boredom.

Our electronics boss, Al Talley, was not your average chief petty officer. Soft spoken, immaculate in dress, and finicky about everything that passed his lips, he looked more like an accountant than a sailor. His credentials could not be denied, however. A career man, he'd helped design our radar at the Naval Test Center. He knew the schematic so well he could trouble-shoot the gear from his rack. He'd ask you a few questions, and in no time he'd put his finger on the trouble.

As we were helping load his cruise boxes on board, someone remarked that they felt as though they were filled with rocks. In truth, they were packed with watch parts and repair tools. Talley was a watchmaker with skills as proficient as anyone ashore. Always thinking, Al figured that most officers and men wore expensive timepieces. As grit, vibration, and salt air were in profusion, he had a ready-made market for his avocation.

Early in the cruise, he told "Trigger," our first class, that he had carte blanche when it came to running the team. In essence, he'd stay out of our hair, but would be available if we needed his expertise. We couldn't have asked for a better arrangement.

Meanwhile, the chief did a land-office business that occupied him about eighteen hours a day. His rates were fair, and good businessman that he was, he never charged the top brass. As far as they were concerned, watchmaking was his "hobby." Later, he made his big mark by buying up a slew of Japanese movements and selling them with new cases for gifts. The watches were sound, the price was rock-bottom, and all hands were happy. Al was not someone you could easily get close to, but he always treated his men with courtesy and respect.

Busy with his work, he rarely left the chiefs' quarters. In contrast to his well-tanned shipmates, I'll always remember his pale countenance during captain's inspections or on liberty. "Seventeen Jewel Talley," as we used to call him, was one for the books.

Kinney ran the maintenance crew. It's far more comfortable to deal with a whitehat, even a first class, than a chief. For one thing, chiefs are only a small step from rank, and many were far more experienced both in leadership and technical ability. I guess the primary reason was that the chiefs lived in a separate world: a different uniform, a different compartment, a different mess. You could go on liberty with them (on occasion), but they'd never get "falling down drunk" with you.

Always hovering in the background was the fact that chiefs were career men. All would do a minimum of twenty years, and some would serve the maximum, thirty years. This in more ways than one, separated the men from the boys. Some of the older chiefs would fill a father's role for many a mixed-up seventeen or eighteen year old, and often had better results than the chaplain.

From the first moment I met Kinney, eighteen months before, I never heard him referred to as anything other than "Trigger"; I never discovered how he got that nickname. Standing 5'8", he had a perfect sailor's build. Broad-shouldered and narrow-waisted, he was not only strong, but moved with the agility of a cat.

We never pulled liberty together, but I enjoyed working with and for him. He knew his electronics in spades, and no one on the team worked harder. The son of a barber in Rhode Island, he often trimmed our locks in the compartment.

When Trigger shaved, it was always with a straight razor. One of the indelible memories of my days on the *Champ* was gazing in awe while he stood, legs apart, deftly stroking his neck with that gleaming blade as he rolled with each swell. It never failed to draw a crowd.

George and I made up the balance of the radio-radar crew. The other electronic personnel were primarily engaged in air-controlling. From the top down they were Jacques Dupre, ATC; Calley and Winslow, AT1s; and last, Bill Munroe, recently rated AT3. Bill may have been the least senior in experience, but he was a quick study, and under most circumstances would have been an officer. He could have waited the war out with a college deferment, but he left Columbia and enlisted. This gave him very high marks in my book. Blessed with an engaging smile and a great sense of humor, Bill Munroe was probably the most popular man on the team.

Our whole group took tremendous pride in keeping all our equipment on top of the line. Everything else (sleep, chow, movies, or cards) took second place when it came to having all our aircraft in an "up" status.

Early on June 3, under threatening skies, we passed Corregidor and Bataan and entered Manila Bay. Scores of sunken ships still littered the harbor, tombstones of the Japanese navy and merchant fleet from the carrier raids of late 1944. We dropped our hook off Cavite, a suburb of Manila. The air was so leaden with moisture, the last thing we felt like doing was crawling into whites, but Manila was beckoning just over the horizon, so I shoved off on the first liberty boat, joined by Les Conlon, an AC from a sister squadron, and Mike Groshan, a yeoman I knew from the library. Les was another college dropout, so he fit in well with our circle. The rest of our group had the duty.

We took a train to the capital. The countryside didn't look very different from Ceylon: mountains, lush vegetation, shacks roofed with corrugated metal, and, everywhere, barefoot children. This was the recurring tale of a struggling country trying to feed too many mouths and losing the battle.

But the Philippines were different. This country had once nearly been America, and our trademarks abounded. Fords and Chevys crowded the roads. Signs announcing RCA, General Electric, Singer, Woolworth, and as always, "Coke." Only the beer was homemade. It was San Miguel, and it made Budweiser and Piels taste like water. I was not ordinarily a "brew" man, but this beer was great.

This was also American history. Not Washington or Stonewall Jackson, or even the doughboys, but recent enough for the youngest sailor to remember. Bataan and Corregidor had burned themselves into the national consciousness as indelibly as Valley Forge or the Alamo.

In the first six months of the Pacific War, except for a brief encounter at Wake Island, the Philippines were the only place the Japanese didn't have a walkover. We fought a good battle but lost. Without strong air and naval support, the islands were virtually undefendable. Our air force was caught on the ground a full day after Pearl Harbor, so our army's fate was sealed. It was just a matter of time. In Hawaii the top heads rolled, and they had been surprised.

Here, the top general moved up to the best command and the Medal of Honor.

As the train neared Manila, road signs evoked the past, Santo Tomas, Clark Field, Sangley Point. In the old city, vivid scars still remained of the terrible last-ditch battle the Japanese had put up in January 1945. The rest of the capital, especially the commercial district, looked like Main Street, U.S.A. Rows of stores, hotels, bars, and churches.

After a lunch of grilled seafood and some of that powerful San Miguel, we took a tour of Manila by taxi. The driver was all broken up because we didn't want to patronize his favorite bordello. The girls he showed us didn't stir the least flicker of desire, but even had they been Rita Hayworth or Grace Kelly, we weren't in any shape to do much damage. At this point, we were just looking for a quiet place to sit down and have a few drinks. He suggested a cocktail lounge near the bay, and we all agreed.

The three of us (along with everyone else on board the *Lake Champlain*) were suffering from some sort of dysentery that had plagued the entire crew since we had left Ceylon. One theory laid our problem in the lap of the commissary officer, who, meaning well, had taken on tons of fresh fruit and vegetables at Colombo. Regardless of the cause, it obviously put a crimp in our sightseeing. At the lounge, the bartender's solution to our problem was a couple of stiff shots of blackberry brandy. We figured it couldn't hurt, so we took his advice.

While this was not a "house" in the strict meaning of the word, it wasn't far from it. In Manila, it was hard to go anywhere except church and not be propositioned. At the bar were four B-girls. I guess what set these girls apart from their more direct sisters was that their main object was to get you to buy them drinks. Of course, we all knew that their drinks were watered down, so if you had any idea of getting them drunk, you'd need at least another enlistment to carry it off.

But they were pretty, shapely, and talkative, and it was the first time we'd been close to anyone who resembled an American girl in a long time. We were out of the crushing humidity and near a men's room (no minor consideration, in our condition), so it wasn't too bad a spot to spend a couple of hours. Pretty soon, the girls were sitting on our laps, and they were not exactly shy. Groshan was hot to go, but soon discovered his partner couldn't leave this place until midnight. By then, we'd all be back on board. The girls kept jumping up and down every time Les told a joke, and it wasn't long before the pain in our gut had moved to another part of our body. Conlon's

partner had a fantastic build and hadn't wasted any pesos on underwear. Her breasts were the kind I'd only seen in *Esquire* drawings,
and Les had more than a little trouble controlling himself. All the
girls projected a kind of animal sensuality that left no doubt about
their intentions. While the experience was not unpleasant, we knew
it couldn't lead to a logical conclusion. In fact, the only thing it could
lead to was a bad case of frustration.

The arrival of some destroyer sailors solved our problem, and
the girls moved on to greener pastures. We had some spareribs and
more brandy, and it wasn't long before we started thinking about returning to the fleet landing.

The brandy (on top of all that beer) took our minds off our stomachs, to say the least, and we were easily convinced that a taxi was
a more comfortable means of transport back to the naval base. In
the cab, Les kept raving about his recent companion, whose name
was Maria. He said that in all of his life he'd never met another
woman who had turned him on so (we reminded him of how long
he'd been away from home). He could have had her right on the floor.
He turned to us and gasped, "God, she was a voluptuary if I ever saw
one." Groshan replied, in a surprised tone, "No shit, and all the while
I thought they were Filipinos."

By the time we arrived at Cavite, the sky had opened. In an
instant we were drenched, and we joined a group of forlorn sailors
milling about in sodden whites. Most of them hadn't ventured more
than a few steps from the fleet landing and had been drinking all
day. To most sailors, drinking is a second language. The effects of
the brandy had worn off on the ride back, so I was cold sober (actually a little bit of both). Munroe and Roberts joined a bunch from the
air group who still had a capacity for more booze, but I'd had
enough. I obviously stood out in that crowd.

Everyone who knew me gave me their camera to hold before they
passed out. Soon I looked like I was covering the war for *Life*, *Look*
and *Pic* combined.

When I inquired to a shore patrol chief about the next liberty
launch, he said there wasn't going to be any, at least not until daylight. A typhoon had veered toward us, and the *Champ* had gotten
underway to avoid being blown aground. I took one look at the huge
seas pounding the wharf and realized that no one in his right mind
would run a launch in this weather.

As the endless night slowly wore on, I started to regret coming
ashore. Shivering in my soaked uniform was no fun. To get warm, I
went on board an LCI (landing craft infantry) that was moored near
the landing. A Good Samaritan radioman recognized my electronics

insignia and invited me into his tiny radio shack. At least it was dry, and as always, there was hot coffee.

Around 0200, the bars closed and a surge of whitehats headed for the piers. Most of this lot could barely stand, and some had sold their shoes to buy more booze when their funds ran out. In a short time, many of these swabbies had boarded the LCI and passed out on the open deck in a pile of kapok life jackets.

During the early morning hours, the never-ending rain caused the water level to rise on deck, and there were fears that some of the unconscious sailors might drown. I wouldn't want to be the one who had to compose that telegram. The shore patrol rounded up all the sober people they could find (me) and moved the bodies out of immediate danger. Trying to drag dead weight in a driving rain (while loaded down with six 35mms) was not my idea of seeing the world. To make matters worse, everyone wanted to know what I was doing with all those cameras.

At about six o'clock, the rain slackened, and the word was passed that the *Lake Champlain* had returned. For the one-third of her crew that had gone ashore, it was none too soon. We would return via the LCI because the waves were still too high for a conventional liberty boat. About 300 men finally got on board, and we headed out into Manila Bay. The wild pitching soon finished off those few sailors who were finally getting their insides under control, and loud moans greeted each roll. For a long while we couldn't see anything through the fog and rain, but finally the *Champ*'s outline appeared, a truly welcome sight.

When the LCI hove to alongside the carrier, we rose and fell twenty feet with each swell. Any thought of using the side companionway was out of the question. After a quick conference, it was prudently decided to employ the *Champ*'s huge cargo net to haul us back on board. The OOD wisely sent an able-bodied working party down with the first net. Moving quickly yet gently, they positioned their sodden shipmates into the center, and they were hauled aboard to the deck-edge elevator. Each division had assigned a couple of men to identify and help carry these orphans of the storm below.

Because of the still present danger of typhoons, it was sensibly decided to cancel the rest of our stay and get underway for Japan as soon as the last men came on board.

Once the *Champ* had raised her hook and a muster was taken, one man was still unaccounted for. While a search was underway, word was received from a hospital in Manila that an aviation bos'n, David Marks, had died from injuries sustained in an accident.

As we steamed out of Manila Bay, I'm sure there were some

regrets from those who never made it ashore on that brief (but not uneventful) liberty. I, for one, was happy to be moving again. I'm sure many of my erstwhile companions in that landing craft shared my feelings.

Before reaching Yokosuka, the *Lake Champlain* had one more brush with history. Later that afternoon off Lingayan Gulf, we passed a patch of ocean where the U.S. Navy had been tested as it had never been tested before. It was here the fleet had its baptism of fire with the dreaded kamikaze in late 1944.

All through the campaign for Luzon, the attacks mounted, reaching their culmination at Okinawa four months later. Against these "manned bombs," there was really no defense. You literally had to shoot them out of the sky with your own CAP (combat air patrol) or try to down them with AA. It was fortunate these suicide planes made their debut relatively late in the war. Our losses, great as they were, did not affect the fleet's ability to carry out its mission.

It was obvious that the earlier incoming attacks could be plotted, the greater our chances of destroying them. The longest range radar at the time was mounted on picket destroyers and stationed at the periphery of the task force. Since the sea-level range of their radar was limited by the height of the antenna, the Japanese soon learned to fly in at wave height. What was desperately needed was some way to locate these "bandits" much further distant from their targets. This life-and-death problem led to the development of what later became known as airborne early warning. VC-12, Detachment 44, was the latest embodiment of that idea.

At 1437, 9 June 1953, the *Lake Champlain* moored to buoy #11 in Yokosuka harbor. The long voyage, three quarters of the way round the world, had ended. The recruiting poster part of the cruise was over; now we had to earn our pay.

But first we thought about liberty, especially after what had happened to us at Manila. In spite of stops at Athens and Colombo, the captain hadn't been exactly overgenerous with time ashore. Allowing that only one-third of the crew is permitted off the ship at any time, the maximum amount of liberty that any enlisted man could have enjoyed since leaving Norfolk was three days. Whites were spiffed up, and dress shoes gleamed in anticipation. To put the icing on the cake, we'd just enjoyed a payday.

It only took a few minutes after mooring to dash our hopes. Captain Mundorff, not normally one to bring us into his confidence, wasted no time in telling us he had just received orders to proceed with all haste to the combat zone. Replenishment would commence immediately, and all hands would turn to, no exceptions. We moved alongside Piedmont Pier, and the onloading began. It would last until 1104 the following day, when *CVA-39* was declared ready for sea.

In the past, the air group would usually detail a certain number of lower-rated men from each squadron to help out. Now it was everyone except chiefs, and even they were pressed into service as supervisors. Chief Talley told us we were not going to be involved in this operation, but he suggested that when we listened to what was on our plate, we might want to trade places.

Through a typical communications foul-up, we'd been told the Pacific Fleet air force had already converted to the new UHF radio, ARC-31. Factory personnel had performed the conversions on our Skyraiders before we left Rhode Island. They'd even sent us to school. Now, we learned the people out here were still using the old VHF equipment, ARC-1. Since this job did not lie within our expertise, we would normally have waited for some O & R (overhaul and repair) people to do the changes, a task usually requiring a couple of days. Both radio transceivers (one in the wheelwell and the other behind the crewman's seats) would have to be replaced, along with all the wiring. In addition, the VHF antennas had to be substituted for smaller UHF models and the antenna wire run through the wings. None of us, not even the chief, had ever tackled anything approaching this. The only alternative was to leave the planes behind when the *Champ* sailed.

All the ATs (controllers and technicians) were called together and, after a short discussion, decided to give it a try. For the next forty-eight hours, even as the ship relieved the USS *Valley Forge* and sailed for Korea, we worked around the clock. We drank gallons of coffee, and other than a few cat naps, never stopped. Finally, at about 2100 on 11 June, we finished, and all the newly installed equipment checked out. Our arms were cut up from snaking the antenna wire through the small recesses of the wings, and we were exhausted, but it was worth it.

Along with the controllers, George, Bill, and I had provided the muscle. The planning and execution (the bulk) was the sole achievement of Talley and Kinney, however. They later received medals, which they richly deserved. The rest of us got letters of commendation.

While we were sweating our guts out on the hangar deck, the *Lake Champlain* had some new arrivals that made us the flagship of Task Force 77. Rear Admiral W. D. Johnson embarked as commander of Carrier Division One, and a squadron of F4U Corsairs landed aboard. Fighter Squadron 44 replaced the group of F3D night attack planes of VC-4, which departed CVA-39 on 19 June. The F3D

The four VC teams in descending order: VC-4, VC-62, VC-33, and VC-12. Official U.S. Navy photo.

Skyknights were too heavy and unwieldy for our catapults and crowded flight deck, so they were flown to Korea, where they operated from K-6 airfield.

The Corsairs were of World War II vintage and had made a name for themselves shooting down Zeros and Bettys. Technically obsolete, they were ideally suited for close support of the army and marines, as they could remain over the target far longer than the fuel-guzzling jets. So, as the *Lake Champlain* joined Task Force 77, Air Group Four was composed of the following units: VF-111 (Fighter Squadron 111, 16 F9F Panthers), VF-44 (16 F4U Corsairs), VF-22 (14 F2H Banshees), and VA-45 (Attack Squadron 45, 16 AD4 Skyraiders). Completing the complement of CAG 4 were the four VC teams for special missions: VC-62 (3 F2H Banshee photo planes), VC-33 (4 AD4N's Electronic Countermeasures), and, finally, our detachment, VC-12 (3 AD4Ws Skyraiders, Early Warning and ASW). VC-4, as previously mentioned, had gone to Korea.

While we were steaming across the Tushima Straits (where Japan had become a world naval power fifty years before), drills were held to test every department. In the past three years, the ships of TF-77 had never been attacked. This was no guarantee that it wouldn't happen, and both the Chinese and the North Koreans clearly had the capability, both above and below the surface. It was estimated that the Chinese had over two hundred bombers, and both countries had submarines. A lot of their equipment came from the last war, but so did ours.

The sound of running men reverberated throughout the ship as all hands went to their General Quarters stations. When GQ sounds, everyone runs like hell. Aside from getting to your battle station in a hurry, if you don't move fast enough, you'll be trapped and won't get there at all. Every hatch and manhole is dogged down tight. This insures water-tight integrity and prevents the spread of fire. The carrier is transformed into hundreds of sealed compartments, like some gigantic steel beehive.

The 3" 50s opened up at a target sleeve towed from one of the F4Us. I recalled the day the British jets swooped in at wave height on the *Midway*, and hoped we'd never have to meet jets with AA (antiaircraft guns). In the middle of all this gunfire, damage control parties were directed to frame number so and so, to answer simulated bomb or torpedo hits. We all wished aloud that they would remain simulated.

BOOK THREE

Chapter 23

The Real Thing

AFTER NOON CHOW, IT WAS THE AIR GROUP'S TURN, and we launched 119 sorties. We flew throughout the afternoon and into the evening. VC-12 flew antisubmarine missions, as the rest of the jets and props fired rockets and 20mm at targets towed by our escort, the destroyer *Cushing*.

That night, when the order was passed to darken ship, it was executed with a diligence and thoroughness not seen since we left Norfolk. The *Champ* and her air group were as ready as they would ever be.

A little after midnight on 13 June, we entered the war zone.

On board a carrier, one day is pretty much like the next, with most sailors not knowing what day it is or the date. If anyone was concerned about it being the 13th, they kept it to themselves. As it developed, we would have had good reason to worry.

Our solitude ended at 1300, when we joined the rest of the task force. All around us, the sea and air were filled with increasing power, as more and more ships came into view. The USS *Philippine Sea* (*CVA-47*), *Boxer* (*CVA-21*), and *Princeton* (*CVA-37*) made up the group of carriers, and the heavy cruiser USS *Bremerton* (*CA-130*) and nine destroyers comprised our screen. After days and days of only seeing the occasional DD, the sight of all these ships gave us a heady feeling of confidence for the job ahead.

With four CVs, there were always aircraft to watch that were launching, landing, or massing for a run to Korea. Plane guard escort destroyers (DDs) cut through the waves with a bone in their teeth, using all their power to keep up with the high-stepping carriers. These flat-tops often exceeded 30 knots in the air-still waters of the Sea of Japan. That day our force sent off 283 sorties, and the *Champ* contributed two squadrons. Rail and supply depots were bombed and rocketed at Wonson and Chongjin. Dupre and Munroe flew an ASW op for our team.

All our planes returned safely and were taxied forward of the barriers. When the last plane had been recovered, the plane captains secured the control sticks with the pilot's safety belt to lock the elevators. This prevented wear on the control cables from the strong gusts on the flight deck. On one of the Banshees of VF-22, the arming circuit had not been deactivated, and when the stick was pulled back, several rounds of 20mm were fired into a jet parked forward.

The aircraft caught fire in its main fuel tank, which fortunately didn't explode. As alarms sounded and scores of flight deck personnel raced up with foam and fog hoses, the flames roared like a blowtorch. The burning plane was parked smack in the middle of gassed aircraft, and it was only by the grace of God that everything else nearby didn't explode. About half a dozen men from the flight deck crew crawled right under the flaming jet and directed a stream of foam into the heart of the blaze. If the main tank had blown, they would have all been instantly incinerated. I witnessed this from the O-5 level, and it was about the bravest thing I'd ever seen. I wouldn't have gotten within 100 feet of that fire.

It took an hour, but the fire was brought under control without the loss of any more aircraft. A year before, a similar blaze had started on the hangar deck of the *Boxer*. The giant fire doors were closed, but four planes on the after hangar deck had exploded and burned, killing eleven and injuring forty-three. Over a dozen men had to jump into the sea to escape the flames. We were indeed lucky on this 13th.

A month later, just before departing the ship, Captain Mundorff held a Commendatory Mast on the flight deck. There wasn't a white-hat on board who didn't feel a tremendous sense of pride, not only in the ship, but in his fellow shipmates. It's a rare day in the navy that enlisted men are recognized for anything. The list of citations after a battle is so top-heavy with brass you often wonder if any sailors were actually present. To be fair, this holds true in the army and marines as well. One only has to look at the Medal of Honor recipients from the battleship *Arizona* on December 7, 1941, to see what I mean.

On the *Lake Champlain*, the citations read, "For bravery and complete disregard for personal danger in helping move a burning plane away from possible contact with other aircraft." The following men were decorated: Elton Balch, DDC; Samuel Black, AD1; Madison Compton, AD2; Ralph Pasquale, AO3; John Gercnak, AO3; Gerald Gumpper, AO3; Thomas E. Green, AO3; Roy Bachtell, AD3; John Kruitoff, AD3; Thomas Reeves, AO2; Duane Brickson, AN; Harold Cole, AB1; Robert Smith, AB1; John Adams, AB1; and Andrew Motika, AB2.

Fire on the flight deck of the USS Lake Champlain, *13 June 1953. Official U.S. Navy photo.*

The next day, air operations resumed, and I flew with Calley. He was a terrific air controller, and he never let you forget it. His home was in Tennessee, and if I remember little else about him, it was his comment that, at last, we were fighting on the right side: the side of *South* Korea against the North.

This was my first flight since joining Task Force 77. Looking at all that power steaming below us, I realized that we and a few hundred other airmen were the sole reason for its existence. We were the tip of a lance extending all the way back to Pearl Harbor, San Diego, and (in our case) Norfolk.

We were definitely on the first team. Not only on the team, but calling pitches and positioning players. When we vectored CAP (combat air patrol) out to investigate a target, they relied completely on our experience and judgment, not only to find the "bogie" (unidentified aircraft), but to get them back if their navigation gear went out. We had more responsibility than most people get in a lifetime. Only about fifty enlisted air crewmen in the whole task force had this opportunity and the staggering burden it carried. For some, it was a lure that couldn't be resisted. They made the navy a career. For the rest of us, it was the adventure of a lifetime. Sure, we got flight pay and a chance to wear wings, but if the truth were known, we'd probably have paid to be there.

Later that afternoon, when we were recovered, Calley and I were sent to chow posthaste because lunch was nearly over. Walking into the messdeck, we were stunned. In place of mess tables and benches stood row upon row of bombs. They ranged in size from 250 lb. to 2,000 lb., and all looked suitably menacing. The *Lake Champlain* had taken on a new dimension.

All the sailors were munching away, blithely ignoring these huge cylinders of TNT. The bomb elevators to the flight deck ran directly through the chow hall, and we easily adjusted to this minor inconvenience. Some whitehats broke out their trusty Argus C2s to show the folks back home that we were truly on the cutting edge of this "police action."

There's a rule in naval aviation: if you're going to draw flight pay, you've got to get your time in. Since we often had empty seats and nobody was shooting at us, we became a popular group to fly with. On various occasions, both we and VC-33 carried the flag (admiral) and the air officer, but I never shared this experience. One June morning, my luck ran out, and I drew a "four striper" as a passenger in the right seat. He was chief of staff to the Commander of Carrier Division One. Broken down to simpler terms: he was one big chief.

Actually, he was a real decent guy, and we got along fine. The captain appeared to be in his early forties, with the smooth white skin more associated with a priest or an artist. Every movement revealed a man wound tight as a drum, and I hoped he'd had a recent medical. In as off-handed a way as possible, I pointed out the emergency hatch release in case we had to go swimming. I further cautioned him to be sure and disconnect the headset connection before exiting the aircraft. This drew a weak but knowing smile.

Once airborne, he noticeably relaxed and said, "I'm going to take a nap. Call me a half hour before we land." I gave him a Roger and became immersed in my APS-20 radar. Our ASW op was uneventful, and as we turned to join the returning props, I shook my companion as gently as possible.

After his two-hour nap, he was a different man. I couldn't shut him up. He wanted to know all about our radar. Had we ever picked up any real bandits? (No.) As he spoke, his eyes never left the scope, and he remarked how tough it must be to be locked into this screen for three or four hours. I was tempted to turn his way with crossed eyes (one of my more effective comic gestures), but thought better of it. Those silver eagles cast a spell all their own. I just nodded.

He immediately launched into a lecture about how lucky TF-77 had been over the past three years, never to have been attacked by air or submarine. His boss, the admiral, was concerned we might become too complacent, like the 8th Army in December 1950. The Chinese could be distressingly unpredictable, and he had no doubt they had the power to inflict serious damage on us. He looked me straight in the eye and grabbed my arm for emphasis when he said, "If that happens, you, and a few others like you, could be the most important people in Task Force 77." I screwed on the most serious expression I could manage and busied myself securing the radar. If the Chinese sent two hundred bombers against us, I was confident that even I could plot that on the screen.

On a more serious note, this threat of Chinese bombers (and their accompanying fighters) kept us ever-alert at our radar screens, even after four hours of eyestrain. We lacked guns and speed, but our mission was critical to the security of the fleet. Our sole defense, and only chance of survival, lay in that five-inch screen, for our job was to find them before they found us. Our guppies were the un-armed sentinels of Task Force 77.

Later, I wondered if my VIP companion knew I was an enlisted man. If he had known that, would he have shared these confidences? Captain or airman, we all looked alike in a flight suit, and many high-ranking officers had little knowledge of the nuts and bolts of the lower echelons. I was simply pleased that someone high up thought that what we did was not only useful but might some day make a difference. It was the first time anyone from the top even mentioned the possibility of attack. Three years of immunity could dull even the sharpest resolve. The lessons of Pearl Harbor had not been wasted on this officer, however.

That night after we completed work on our planes, we went up on the flight deck to get some air. At 2030, word was passed that the smoking lamp was out in preparation for fueling. A little while later, a big gray oiler came steaming up our starboard side and proceeded to rig for refilling our tanks. She was the USS *Cimarron* (AO-22). Ever since that first afternoon off the Virginia coast, we awaited every re-fueling with trepidation. This one went off without a hitch.

At 2100 on June 14, in this latitude, it was light enough to view the proceedings. We marveled at the navigational prowess exhibited by both helmsmen. To keep the ships exactly on station required the utmost skill. We were moving at 14 knots, and allowing for currents, wind, and a tremendous difference in size, the slack in the oil lines

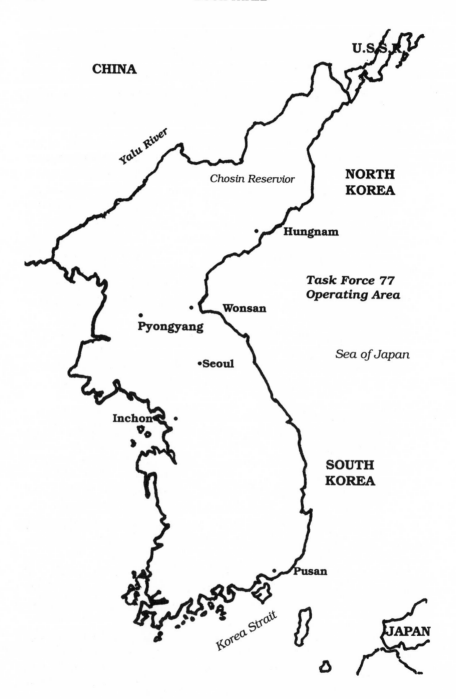

CHINA

U.S.S.R.

Yalu River

Chosin Reservior

NORTH
KOREA

Hungnam

Task Force 77
Operating Area

Wonsan

Pyongyang

Sea of Japan

•Seoul

Inchon

SOUTH
KOREA

Pusan

Korea Strait

JAPAN

was perhaps a hundred feet. This exact distance and speed had to be maintained for nearly two hours. What an outstanding display of seamanship! This was the kind of naval expertise that wins wars, every bit as important as launching the air group or firing a broadside. No matter how often we refueled or replenished, it never failed to provide a good show for all hands. Given the choice, however, I'm sure the quartermasters would have gladly passed up their day in the sun.

The next night, John Williford came up with a welcome surprise: a gallon of grapefruit juice. He, John Robben, and Rich joined me on the fantail after evening chow. Williford, in addition to editing the ship's newspaper, had this knack of always coming up with that extra something to make your day, in this case the grapefruit juice. He always reminded me a lot of Bill Munroe; they both had this laid-back quality that made everyone around them feel at ease. What put Williford in a special class was his fabulous communication skills. I don't think there was ever a man who met him who didn't think he was destined for greater things. I was happy just to be included in his circle.

We drank the juice and reminisced about what we'd be doing if we were home right now. The night was black and there was no moon. Rich said the last place he was in that was this dark was the Tunnel of Love. Williford said, with a smile in his voice, "Don't get any ideas."

Robben told a funny story. It seemed we'd only been at sea a short while when one afternoon he was sitting at Father Kelly's desk, writing letters. The phone rang, and when he answered, it was Commander Best, the executive officer. He was trying to reach Joe Kelly and asked John to have him call him. John said "OK," and Best almost went berserk. "OK? OK? How long have you been in the navy? Don't you know how to address a superior officer?" The next morning, the Plan of the Day had detailed orders to all officers to instruct their personnel in the proper naval courtesy. The correct reply should have been, "Aye Sir."

For the next two days, air operations were conducted with ever increasing intensity. More and bigger bombs filled the mess deck, and soon the novelty wore off. Just before dawn on 16 June, an aviation mech, Delmore Mason of VF-44, fell over the side while climbing the catwalk ladder during a launch. A search was carried out by two plane guard destroyers, but he was never found. The fall from the catwalk to the sea was over seventy feet, so the drop alone was enough to kill a man. He would not be the last man on the *Champ* to die that way.

Those who scanned the horizon on 17 June would notice a new arrival: the battleship *New Jersey*, flagship of the Seventh Fleet. With a raked bow and the sweep of a yacht, she was a sight. Later, "Jocko" Clark, Vice Admiral and a World War II legend, came aboard with another admiral. Watching them alight from a chopper, George exclaimed, "If we get any more brass on board this tub, we'll sink."

CAG 4 flew 97 sorties until bad weather closed us down at 1500. During rosary on the fantail, an ammunition ship, the USS *Mount Baker*, came alongside to fill our magazines with bombs and rockets. Somehow, it seemed the responses to the prayers were a little more emphatic that night.

Chaplain Joe Kelly was an inspiration to all of us. In the hellish heat and humidity below decks, he never dispensed with any of his heavy vestments during morning Mass. Once, he nearly fainted from the heat, but after a short rest he continued. This smiling Irishman was everywhere: organizing tours, comforting those with family problems, and performing his priestly duties. Later in the cruise, he presided over what became the most popular entertainment on board, bingo. During a stay in Japan, he contacted a manufacturer and bought enough cards and equipment to supply 2,000 men. He was one of the few people I ever met who was made for his job.

The 19th was another bad day for the *Champ*. During the launching of our 101 flights, the starboard catapult was rendered inoperative due to a runaway shot. This effectively cut our jet takeoff efficiency by 50 percent. Far worse was the loss of Lt. (j.g.) D. E. Brewer of VA-45. During a bombing run, his AD-4N was fatally struck by flak. Brewer attempted a low altitude bailout, but his chute failed to blossom, and he was killed on impact.

I was flying what started out as another boring ASW mission, but all at once a radar blip appeared on our scope, a surface target not ten miles away. As it wasn't on the screen before, it could be only one thing: a submarine. We called up some CAP (combat air patrol) —two AD4s—and requested permission to make a strike. While awaiting a reply from CIC (combat information center) on the *Champ*, we sighted the submarine, just barely visible. But before we could get a good look, she submerged. Later, the AD pilots said they could have creamed the sub with their rockets, but without permission, we had to hold fire. The rules of engagement were very strict. In international waters, she had just as much right to be there as we did. Back on board, it was determined that it was not an American submarine. In spite of our frustration, we were complimented on our radar skills and reminded that that sub would think twice about surfacing and sending intelligence about our task force.

For the next two days, dense fog caused curtailment of all flight operations. This break allowed the air group to catch up on some much needed maintenance. Closer to home, we all had a chance to recover some sorely missed sleep. Unlike the ship's company, who worked a set routine, we labored until the planes were in an "up" status, even if this entailed working through the night. All the aircrewmen on the team had logged over 20 hours of flight time since leaving Yokosuka, and we were now flying only one man in the backseat to keep our eyes fresh.

Acey-deucy flourished in the compartment, and others played a version of Monopoly, where each dollar was worth a nickel. Players changed as they ran out of money. These stakes were high to people earning an average of $100 a month after deductions.

Each tanker, ammo, or supply ship brought movies and mail along with its nourishment. An hour later, the welcome announcement would be heard throughout the ship, "All divisional mail orderlies lay down to the mail room." We all echoed, "On the double!"

My primary correspondence was, of course, with Marianne, but I also received and answered letters from another dozen relatives and friends. Most of my buddies were in the military, and letters came from Germany, California, Okinawa, and various destroyers and carriers. Because I was not keeping a journal, these letters to Marianne and my parents became my day-to-day record of everything that happened. My envelopes to Marianne and hers to me were numbered. This insured that I wouldn't have to figure out what she was referring to if the letters came out of sequence.

One of her notes contained a set of color photographs. Wow! There was my intended, gorgeously tanned, and standing in front of a Florida palm grove, wearing shorts and a halter. Those legs took my mind off the heat and humidity and just about everything else. That image locked into my brain, and try as I might, I couldn't get it out of my head. Even during an ASW flight the next morning, I still had difficulty concentrating on the radar scope.

Letters were funny. It was a bit like having a long conversation spread out over many days. Sometimes, just when it was getting interesting, the flow stopped. Maybe ten days later, in would come another missive, and you'd pick up just where you left off. One could blot out everything else and treat the time lapse as though it were minutes instead of days.

Much of the mail was from sweethearts and wives, and it would be heavily scented. Some even boasted the bright imprint of two red lips on the back of the envelope and the familiar letters: SWAK. John Robben and I used to laugh about some of the messages from

Marianne and Margie. We'd be burning up the pages with passionate passages (there wasn't much else we could do), and we'd receive
replies telling us how hot it was in New York City. I guess our minds
moved in different orbits.

It was interesting to see who got how much and what kind of
mail. Some would receive mostly newspapers and magazines and an
occasional jotting on lined notepaper. Others literally got bundles of
letters. And, sadly, there were sailors who would never be called.
These people would always disappear before mail call in the compartment.

This influx of news tended to make us feel, if anything, more isolated. Here we were, steaming off Korea, 12,000 miles from home,
floating on a sea no one had heard of, and increasingly living more
and more within ourselves. At home, people were following the coro-
nation of Queen Elizabeth and the conquest of Mount Everest.
Roberts had just received a *Life* magazine, and it was passed around.
It mirrored the good life the U.S. was enjoying: no rationing, no short-
ages. To read the magazine, you'd never know there was a war on.
All the new auto models were being advertised, and to make matters
worse, the full-page ads featured young men behind the wheel. They
were all accompanied by pretty girls and didn't seem to have a care
in the world. Eisenhower was settling into his first term, and the
economy was booming. Back in the States, friends and family were
getting married, having babies, and, in some cases, dying. Often a
letter made one of our shipmates a father, or brought word of a family member's demise, but he could only react by long distance.

In a way, it was like trying to understand what a light year was.
Few of us could grasp the concept that the distant star we were
watching might very well have gone out six months or a year before.
The law of averages being what they were, probably every month on
the *Champ* a member of the crew wrote to someone who was already
dead.

One of the perks of being in a combat zone was postage-free mail
(the other was no income tax). Later, I got some complaints from
stamp collectors, especially the kids, so I'd wait until we hit port,
and then I'd load up on the most exotic stamps I could find.

No one ever read any one else's mail. Some of the incoming stuff
was so unique, however, that it was quickly shared. Bill collectors
hurled dire threats across the trackless oceans, and mothers would
caution sons not to get their feet wet. My mother thoughtfully for-
warded my National Guard discharge. Unbeknownst to me, I'd been
carried on my company's roster for almost three years after I'd gone
on active duty. One of our pilots pointed out that I might hold the

dubious distinction of being the only member of the armed forces entitled to wear two National Defense Service Medals. This decoration was one all servicemen received during the Korean War (just for being in the armed forces), much like the Victory Medal of World War II.

Aside from mail, the other thing that we had incoming and outgoing was our laundry. Each time it was delivered to the compartment, it was a washday adventure. Our shirts and underwear resembled the output of a taffy machine, and our dungarees looked as if they'd been in a tug-of-war.

We learned early in the cruise to tie our socks to the belt loops on our trousers. Socks were stenciled only with our initials, so the ship's laundry never attempted to sort them. More often than not, they simply disappeared. If nothing else, it was good preparation for married life.

Pressing was a luxury only afforded to officers and chiefs, so we placed our whites and blues under our mattresses to keep them wrinkle-free. Yokosuka provided us with decent tailor facilities, and after our first stay in port, we started to resemble real sailors instead of something off the rack at the Goodwill store.

Four days passed, and Task Force 77 marched back and forth across the same patches of ocean while we waited for the fog to lift. From the reports coming in, we knew that heavy fighting was in progress just over the horizon, and many of our people could desperately use our air support.

Finally, during the afternoon of 24 June, the weather cleared enough for the familiar sound of flight quarters to be heard throughout the ship. Eighty dive-bombers and fighters soon roared off the flight deck. CAG 4 geared up for a big operation the next day because the forecast was for clear skies. But again we were denied, and this time fate struck close to home.

At 0245, on a pitch-black flight deck, an AD4N from our sister detachment, VC-33, was catapulted. Immediately, something in the cat machinery failed, and Bill Naster, our buddy, knew they were going in the drink. Lt. Fletcher desperately tried to stop the slewing Skyraider, but it was hopeless. There just wasn't that much deck space. In a cat shot, you either made it or you didn't, and they weren't going to make it.

With full power, they didn't fall over the edge of the flight deck. Instead, they pancaked about 100 yards off the port bow, directly in the path of 40,000 tons of aircraft carrier moving at close to 30 knots.

The landing, Bill thought, wasn't much different than a normal recovery. In fact, there wasn't even the expected jolt, just a deadly sinking feeling as the AD-4N mushed in. Even in the pitch black compartment, the two aircrewmen had no difficulty in disconnecting their headsets and safety harness. It was as if they'd been doing it everyday.

Both hatches fell away as they pulled the emergency toggles, and seawater poured in on them. She was going down fast, much faster than Bill had thought she would, and before he knew it, he was treading water alongside. All this had taken less than ten seconds.

St. Clair and Lt. Fletcher, the pilot, went out on the left side of the sinking AD, leaving Bill alone. He inflated his Mae West and looked around. It was dark, but the massive hull, a few feet away, was darker. Bill could almost touch it. All at once, he realized the pounding, killing screws were only seconds away. Bill saw no way out.

Then a miracle happened. The big, fearsomely moving side suddenly pulled away, leaving him in the turbulent wake, choking on what seemed to be half the ocean. Quick action on the part of the bridge had saved all their lives.

Luckily, Fletcher managed to free his raft before the plane went under. Now, the three of them bobbed about in the warm water, watching the dark ships move smoothly and steadily into the night. The survival lights on their Mae Wests were lighted, and they settled back to be picked up by the plane guard destroyer.

Those in the water rarely understand how nearly impossible it is to sight a man in broad daylight, let alone at night. Observing the force disappearing in the distance, they decided to use their flares to attract attention. Between them, they had six. The first five fizzled. The last one burned brightly, and soon they were safely aboard the USS *Moale* (DD-693), bedded down in warm racks and drinking medicinal brandy.

The next morning, the three survivors returned to the *Lake Champlain* by highline. Most of the crew was on deck, cheering them on. In keeping with an old custom, twenty gallons of ice cream went back the same way and was greeted with equal gusto by the "tin can" sailors.

We pumped Bill with questions about the crash and how he felt watching the fleet move past them into the night. He said that once he got over the shock of nearly being cut into mincemeat, he felt nothing worse could happen to him. At least they were all together. It was only when one flare after the other proved to be duds, that they started to lose their confidence. Apparently, like almost every other piece of equipment in this war, the flares were of World War II vintage. Like fireworks (which essentially they were), they had a limited shelf life. Bill said they were praying aloud when the last one ignited. He'd made a vow out there to say the rosary every night on this trip, and he said, "Believe me, it's a pleasure, not a chore."

George Walls became visibly agitated over the thought that these flares, in which we had so much faith, could fail. George, who knew someone in every department (especially the galley), conned a parachute rigger into giving him six extra flares, more dye marker, and extra shark chaser (the latter being of questionable value). To this inventory, he added a heavy-duty flashlight. He was transformed into a walking survival kit, and we wondered how he managed to squeeze himself through the small hatch on the Skyraider. Winslow told him he wouldn't have to worry about being picked up: once he hit the water, he'd sink like a rock.

With both catapults out, the *Champ* was a declawed tiger. Our jets couldn't be deck-launched, and most of the time in this light wind, neither could the bomb-laden props. Repairs would have to be made at the main fleet facility at Yokosuka. On the morning of 27 June, the USS *Princeton* took our place as carrier flag, and we headed for port, accompanied by our recent good shepherd, the destroyer *Moale.*

Unnoticed by probably everyone on board, 25 June was also the third anniversary of the war's start. The *Lake Champlain* had missed the "Big One" by a scant few months in 1945, and all the way over to Japan there was some conjecture that history might very well repeat itself. Was the *Champ* always to be a bridesmaid? In spite of the dubious honor of becoming the last carrier to join TF-77, she justified her return from mothballs by more than carrying her weight during a period of intense naval air activity. It was another example that the Essex class carriers were probably the best military investment the United States ever made.

In spite of the imminent prospect of liberty, some of us had mixed feelings about leaving the task force. We were the newest kid on the team, and after only two weeks of operations, we were heading into the barn. There was no one to blame, but hundreds of people would be stuck on the line because of our mechanical failure. Our leading chief said, "In the navy you take what comes. Sometimes, you get the breaks, and sometimes you don't. Don't forget, they wouldn't be crying if the situation was reversed."

Chapter 24

Hitting the Beach

FOR THE FIRST TIME SINCE LEAVING NORFOLK, we moored at a pier with a chance to go ashore. Now, with a precious liberty card in our hands, there was no waiting for launches to eat up our valuable time. We just walked down the gangway, and there it was—instant freedom.

Our appetites whetted by only the briefest glimpse of Yokosuka Naval Base, we all looked forward to our first taste of Japan. For almost two months, we had sailed 21,000 miles to reach here, and then with all the wonders of the East practically within our grasp, we'd been whisked away. During all this time, we'd had a total of seven days in port. Allowing for port and starboard watches, the average whitehat had spent only about 24 hours away from the carrier during the past thirteen weeks. We were raring to go.

The Land of the Rising Sun did not disappoint us. The country was exotic, but not too exotic. Eight years of American influence made us feel comfortable, but left just enough mystery to stir our imagination. Make no mistake about it: this was a foreign country.

A few steps from the ship, the naval base itself was a revelation. All those huge cranes brought back images of Norfolk, but that's where the comparison ended. This complex could have been designed by a committee of sailors.

Our first stop was a cafeteria the size of our hangar deck. Hot dogs, burgers, pie, and ice cream were served for next to nothing. Best was the ice-cold milk, all you could drink. Not the lumpy, powdery stuff we'd had since leaving the States, but the real McCoy. Freighters carried the frozen butterfat out from home, and a local mixing plant produced the nearest facsimile to Borden's we'd tasted since leaving the States. On every liberty, this would be our first stop.

A short walk down the road were more formal restaurants, located in the officers, chiefs, and petty officers clubs. One could sit there and be served like the gentleman one really was under those starched whites. Did I say served? Pampered would be a far better word.

The first meal I had at the P.O. Club was at a table for four. George, Bill Munroe, and Roberts joined me. Real china and silver-plate utensils sat on a linen tablecloth, and two waiters hovered just behind us. One never had to ask, a movement or a gesture was enough. The salt and pepper magically appeared, and a flaming Zippo shot from nowhere when your hand moved to your breast pocket.

A steak cooked to order, with fries, onions, and greens—one dollar. This included hot rolls, dessert, and coffee. After satisfying the inner man, we went upstairs, where an orchestra played nightly. The bands all had a remarkable similarity to the styles of Glenn Miller, Harry James, or Benny Goodman. Entirely Japanese and impeccably attired in formal wear, they could produce the sound of any American ensemble, almost on call. Young women sat at some of the tables. There were Waves, a few American civilians, and some Japanese locals. Most were dressed in skirts and bobby-sox and could have been "the girl I left behind."

Our eyeballs must have been rolling on the floor, because a friendly marine sergeant wearing a Silver Star and a Purple Heart came over and explained the drill. Drink tickets were purchased for ten or twenty-five cents. The waiters could not handle money, which in our case was military script. This odd-looking stuff resembled Monopoly money and came in denominations ranging from five cents to ten dollars. We were paid in this currency, and on the base or in the PX, it was the "coin of the realm." Outside the main gate, yen was the rule. The exchange rate was 360 to a dollar.

The waiter took our order, which included Haig and Haig Scotch, Seagrams, and good Japanese beer. We piled all our drink tickets into the center of the table and told him to refill our order every twenty minutes (or as long as we were conscious). Two big bowls of chips and peanuts appeared, and we settled down to a delightful evening watching the young girls and listening to the familiar songs. This established a pattern. Barring the few times we headed for Tokyo or R & R, dinner at the club was our first stop in Yokosuka.

High-class dining was only one feature of the P.O. Club. Without leaving the building, one could bowl on any of ten alleys or swim in a heated pool. The facilities, the shoes, and the towels were all supplied gratis. Rounding out the diversions, and within walking distance, were baseball and softball diamonds. A little further on was a supermarket, a PX, and, adjoining the main gate, an enormous movie theatre showing continuous first-run films. After comparing these unexpected diversions to Norfolk, we all concluded we'd spent our naval careers in the wrong fleet.

The following day we decided to taste the real Japan and made our way into Yokosuka. Situated next to the largest naval base in the Far East, it had the inevitable "strip." Tiny shops, cheek by jowl, catered to the sailor's every need, and some he didn't know he had until he got there. Would you like your blues or whites tailored while you wait? Your portrait painted in oil or pastel? A set of china laid out before you? Or help in choosing a gift for mama-san, papa-san or girlfriend-san?

On one of our first excursions, Bill said we had to visit a bordello. George said real men never have to pay for it, which was another way of saying we were scared to death. Bill assured us this was only a "fishing expedition," so we tagged along. An attendant at the door took our shoes and showed us in. Bill remarked that in every stag film he'd ever seen, the actors wore only socks. Maybe they were all made in Japan.

The atmosphere inside was about as romantic as a barracks. Row upon row of wooden bunks were filled with young girls in silk pajamas. They all looked about 13.

A mama-san soon took us in tow and showed off her prize pupils. Whenever she tried to make a deal, Bill would deflect her with small talk. In the middle of this clever repartee, George was becoming more and more unnerved worrying about his shoes. He was sure someone was going to make off with them. Bill tried to reassure him, but he only became more agitated. Finally Munroe gave this den mother some yen and cigarettes, and out into the fresh air we went.

George looked visibly relieved to be reunited with his size 12s. Bill smiled and said, "Walls, only a Japanese King Kong could have made off with those gondolas." I laughed, but I had to agree with George. I'd have to be either plastered or pretty hard up to avail myself of their services.

Hard liquor was rationed. Enlisted men could purchase one quart every ten days. There was no limit on beer or plum wine, and a drink could be enjoyed in the company of a girl (always Japanese) or with a meal (always Caucasian). No one was pushy.

Young girls, mostly in their teens, were everywhere. These baby-sans were not quite what we expected. The newsreels of postwar Japan hadn't prepared us for these narrow-waisted, doll-like creatures. Forever smiling, they answered every question with, "Never hoppon Joe." All the shore-based sailors, and not a few from the

Champ, had steady girlfriends, and some would marry before their tour was completed.

Behind this facade, built to attract our yen, was another Yokosuka. Here tiny frail women, bent to their tasks, shuffled along the narrow streets. Their little short steps reminded me of someone on ice skates for the first time. The steps of their feet clad in white socks and fitted into wooden clogs echoed throughout the town. Regardless of social level, they carried themselves with a quiet dignity that belied their simple dress. It was evident that they'd all seen hard times. This was the country I'd read about. Not the Nippon of Babysans, chock-a-block bars, or souvenir shops, but a nation of proud people, temporarily down, but certainly not out. They'd lost the war, but had fought a good fight. Nobody ever made disparaging remarks about their combat ability.

Yet these were the same people who had stained their honor, not on the battlefield, but against those much too weak to fight: against women and children and starving prisoners. The terrible war in China, Hong Kong, and Bataan (with its infamous death march) was beyond the grasp of civilized people. This was the enigma. Which was the real Japan? Or were they both only fragments of the national psyche, never to be unraveled?

Back on board, the aircrewmen were notified that R & R (rest and recreation) was available, and all we need do was apply. George and I signed on for a weekend in Tokyo, but before our departure, we were caught up in preparations for the biggest blast of the cruise: our team party.

Upon the recommendation of some hot pilots, we reserved the upstairs room at the Kamatsu Restaurant. It was supposed to be the best place in town. When we tried to book, the owner was hesitant at first, until he found we weren't from a destroyer. "Desroyer sayor no good! They break up my prace." Once assured that we were flyers, he was all smiles. Preparations that rivaled an air strike guaranteed that nothing would be left to chance.

Filet steaks with all the trimmings came from the base commissary. All hands donated their liquor allowance so we'd have a variety of spirits, and we stashed away enough cold beer to satisfy the air group. With the catering room suitably decorated, everything was set for the night of 2 July (the way it came off, some wag said we were two days early).

Shoes were removed, and after a few drinks, so were the officers' jackets and our jumpers. The pilots wore civies.

The cocktail party broke down the last reserve between ranks, but fortunately no one took advantage of the situation. We had a few

*Sailors and air crewmen of VC-12, U.S. Naval Base, P.O. Club, Yokasuka, Japan,
9 June 1953.*

guests from our sister team VC-33, including the skipper, Lt.
Fletcher, and the other two survivors of their crash. All hands
toasted their continued good health (many times).

Our steaks were beautifully prepared (one member of our team,
E. R. Smith, was a first class cook who helped out in the kitchen),
and we were served by pretty local girls dressed in bright kimonos.
With the arrival of the geishas, the party moved into high gear. They
were soon followed by an orchestra. The geishas briefly added a degree of class, but it was a losing battle as the glasses were refilled.

It was close to midnight when the strippers came on the scene,
greeted by loud cheers and whistles. Their performance left little to
the imagination, but the high point of the evening occurred when
Trigger, our crew chief, decided to mimic their act. He started to
slowly remove each piece of his uniform, and so perfectly duplicated
their gestures, that the girls broke down and collapsed on the bamboo carpet. Even the band had to stop playing.

By now, the room was a tableau of limp bodies, passed out in
various positions on chairs, couches, or simply where they had fallen
on the floor. By all accounts, the party was a huge success.

My R & R was due to start the next day, so I had tipped one of the waiters to make sure I got out before 0200 to make my way back to the ship. George had followed my lead. The Kamatsu staff fixed me up with hot coffee, and gathering up my bulky souvenirs, I staggered off toward the main gate, a few hundred yards away.

Weaving along the dark street but feeling simply marvelous, I was halfway to the gate when two sailors knocked me to the ground and started groping for my money (it was in my sock). I was too far gone to offer much resistance, but I worried about losing my ID and liberty cards. Without those, I would have kissed my Tokyo weekend good-bye.

Suddenly out of nowhere a group of young Japanese chased off my assailants, placed me in a pedicab, and directed the owner to the ship. I tried to give them some yen, but they brushed me aside and sent me on my way, eternally grateful. From that moment on, I viewed our former enemies in a much different light.

A few hours later, nursing the biggest head of my naval career, I mustered in preparation for R & R, with a half dozen other ACs in similar straits. Many in our team hadn't made it back to the ship, and for all we knew, the party was still going full blast (there was certainly enough booze). We later discovered that some of the detachment didn't stagger back for three days.

Our train left exactly on time. The built-up area around the city ended abruptly, as if someone had dropped a curtain. A few hundred yards from the station, rows of shops gave way to rice paddies. The whole countryside was criss-crossed with irrigation ditches, and hundreds of farmers toiled in the morning sun.

After forty-five minutes, the green ended as quickly as it started, as we stopped briefly in Yokohama. We were again surrounded by huge factories, steel mills, and railroad yards. We looked for war damage but found none. One explanation was that most of the old city had been built of wood, and, quickly burned, it was just as quickly rebuilt.

Japan's national railway was prewar, but meticulously maintained. Our roadbed was dotted with workers, all clad identically in black cap and black boots. The ride was smooth.

Tokyo announced itself by a slowing train, and a skyline pierced by gas tanks and power stations. We eased to a stop, and a soldier I'd been chatting with said, "Follow me." He was billeted in the same hotel.

The Hanlon Hotel was elegant beyond description. Walking through the lobby of the Plaza in New York was the nearest I'd come to this kind of living. Even the Plaza couldn't match the more luxurious touches in evidence here, however. In the early twenties, when the hotel was built, Japan was going through a love affair with all things British. It took me a while to remember, but it finally dawned on me what this ornate interior reminded me of: the *Queen Mary*. Both had obviously been constructed to impress their guests with all the trappings of royalty, and none too subtly at that.

This parallel was reinforced by the lacquered panels and heavy tapestries of the dining room, which by now was nearly filled with khaki and a sprinkling of white. In the center stood a maitre d', suitably attired in tails. Accompanying him was a legion of waiters hovering over their guests, much as they did at the P.O. Club at Yokosuka. The entire ensemble could have been lifted right out of Central Casting.

Chosen by fate to play an unlikely role, their only clients sat in pressed suntans and whites and tried desperately to look worthy of this unceasing attention. All this for the princely sum of one dollar (another buck was charged for the room). During dinner, the three of us celebrated with a bottle of wine. Just before we'd left the ship, we were notified of the results of the service-wide exam we'd all taken in April. Everyone had passed and could look forward to a healthy increase in pay. I was now officially AT2 (second class petty officer) and would be richer by $50 a month.

The army men outnumbered us ten to one and were billeted two to a room. The soldiers, fresh from Korea, were more than glad to be here, and some had harrowing tales to tell. The tiny contingent of navy aircrewmen was treated royally by the army men, who gave each of us a room of our own.

After dinner, we all headed out into the capital. Tokyo was the largest city in the world, but somehow it didn't give that impression. Few buildings rose over five stories, and the whole town was spread over a tremendous area. As we were riding through the city, we remarked at how nondescript the place was. Maybe "ugly" would be a more accurate word.

After sunset, it was completely different. Could any city change so quickly? As the light began to fade, the capital transformed itself into a panorama of neon. New York and Paris had their Times Square and Pigalle, but nothing close to the variety and excitement of the Ginza. Here, the light had a beauty all its own. Rippling and cascading in hundreds of fantastic designs, it was an incredible kaleidoscope.

We split up. I'd met a corporal in the bar who was stationed here, and he said he'd show me the high spots. When he reeled off all the possibilities, I left the decision in his hands. We ended up at the Ernie Pyle Theatre. It was a good choice. A floor show featuring

Author in Tokyo, July 1953.

a couple of vocalists, a comedian, and a chorus line was just part of the evening's offering. It would have done justice to Broadway. We tried some Japanese food as an accompaniment to our drinks, and it wasn't bad. I'd expected it to taste like Chinese cooking, or at least what we called Chinese cooking at home. It was different, but it wasn't raw fish.

It was at the restaurant that I had my only run-in with army men. Two sergeants, who'd obviously been drinking most of the evening, decided to take out their frustrations on me. "The navy? What the hell use is the navy out here? You guys come over on a pleasure cruise, hang around a few months, and go home covered with ribbons, while we get our ass shot off." The corporal unexpectedly came to my rescue. "With all due respect, sergeant (he pronounced the word "respect" with dripping sarcasm), the navy is indispensable to this war. Every shell, every gallon of gas, and yes, every roll of toilet paper, has to come by ship. And who do you think provides our air cover and close air support? Many times on the line we've hit Chinese strong points on the road, and if it wasn't for the dive-bombers from this guy's ship, I might not be here. You neither."

The sergeant with the loudest mouth seemed transfixed by these comments and suddenly had a change of heart. He came over and started to put his arms around us to show there were no hard feelings. Unfortunately, he forgot to put down the pitcher of beer he was cradling and dumped the whole thing all over us. This struck all of us as absolutely hilarious, and we collapsed laughing, ending what could have developed into an ugly incident.

About midnight, we headed back to the Hanlon. The corporal had been up since 6 A.M., and I was still reeling from the effects of a hot train ride and the "party of the century." The mattress was almost too soft to sleep on, but in a few minutes I was out.

Early the next morning, we were rolling again. Our agenda included the emperor's palace, the Akasaka Shrine, and the Ginza. The latter had lost some of its nocturnal charm, but the shop windows displayed an infinite variety of wares probably seen nowhere else on this planet. Tiny bonsai trees stood side by side with the latest in Canon cameras, and brightly painted paper umbrellas vied for space with bamboo wigs. On the streets, another "stage show" was revealed for all to view. Buddhist monks in elegant colored robes, old men carrying the most bizarre advertising placards, and as always, the women, representing all ages and social strata, from the traditional kimono-clad matron shuffling her way through the crowds, to the young baby-san, indistinguishable from her teenage American counterpart.

On another trip later in the deployment, John Robben and I visited Sophia University, a sister Jesuit school to our alma mater, Fordham. We walked the campus and met a priest who was astounded that two American sailors would take time out from a weekend in Tokyo to pay their respects. He gave us some revealing insights into the Japanese psyche.

Father Schmidt pointed out their strong bonds with nature. It touched every facet of their lives and carried over into their lifelong love of music, painting, and poetry. Then he said, "Look at every product, from the simplest wooden box, to a bamboo hat. You'll see a quality of workmanship found in only the most expensive shops in the West. Their extraordinary manual skills, passed down through centuries, place their artifacts in a class by themselves." Some of the weapons produced in the recent war spoke volumes on this subject. Lastly, he reminded us that the feudal system was only abolished in 1868. This tradition of regimentation led to a national discipline unmatched in the West. I mentioned Germany, and he smiled. "They were allies, were they not?" Except for energy, they could be a world power again, especially since they'd rid themselves of the militarists who had led them down the road to ruin.

Did he have any problems with his students? One problem. They studied so long into the night, they often fell asleep in class.

After our meeting with Father Schmidt, we drastically altered our conception of these strange but fascinating people. The Japanese would bear watching.

Back at the hotel, other aircrewmen had found more than the Ernie Pyle Theatre to admire. Roberts discovered the Tokyo Baths right next to the Ginza. He'd started out with a paratrooper who recommended this stop and was so taken by it that he decided to spend the night. After a milk bath, a lemon bath, and a Turkish bath, he joined a bilingual Japanese family who were fascinated by his tales of the navy. He later breakfasted with them.

George found an entertainment closer to the heart of the nation: pachinko. Like a slot machine, it soon turns its players into addicts. We couldn't understand what he was trying to describe, so he led us to a nearby establishment. The noise was deafening, like hail on a tin roof.

As in the case of a pinball machine, one pressed a lever that shot a steel ball to the top. If the ball found its way into a small opening, you won a prize. Most of the time, of course, you didn't. I couldn't see the fascination, but obviously millions of Japanese did, not to mention George.

Traffic on the streets was light, mostly trucks and pedicabs. Surprisingly, it moved on the left: another vestige of that English love affair. The taxis appeared to be driven by the surviving remnants of the suicide corps, and one had to be careful to look right instead of left before crossing the street.

Most of these drivers were former military officers who had a fair command of English. One theory was that, having lost the war, they could take out their frustrations behind the wheel. On longer trips across the city, many were eager to discuss the Pacific war, although none ever expressed regret for their country's policies.

One former naval pilot explained we were lucky to have had the atomic bomb, or the outcome might have been far different. He said we'd never met the main Japanese army in the field, only bits and pieces of it in the island chain. Their army could have mustered over a million men, with tanks and artillery, backed up by 5 or 6 thousand kamikazes. I didn't doubt his estimates one bit. If anything, he might have erred on the conservative side.

Chief Rogers, our leading P.O., had been aboard one of the first ships to reach Yokosuka after the war ended. Since the surrender had come almost without warning, there were no troops available, the nearest being in the Philippines and Okinawa. So the navy stepped into the breach, with landing parties composed of sailors and marines. Carrying only M1 rifles and pistols, they weren't armed much differently than were the members of Admiral Perry's first entry into Nippon in 1856. Since no resistance was expected, this was a symbolic "show the flag" mission with little muscle.

A senior Japanese officer took the chief's detail into one of the many deep caves cut into the hills surrounding the naval base. Here, stacked row upon row, were thousands of rifles, grenades, and machine guns, to be used by the local populace once the invasion came. Dedicated people by the millions was one thing the Japanese didn't lack, and they were obsessed by the fact that in all recorded history the home islands had never been invaded. The last time it was attempted was in 1286, when Kublai Khan's fleet was destroyed by a "divine wind," or kamikaze. Rogers had no doubt that it would have been a needless bloodbath on both sides, with repercussions lasting well into the next century. It was a sobering thought.

The following morning, our R & R over, we hailed a cab outside the hotel for a trip to the railroad station. We were due back on board by 1200. The driver made a pitch for covering the sixty miles back to Yokosuka by taxi. He promised to get us there in plenty of time and give us a more comfortable ride than the crowded train. We agreed but almost immediately regretted our decision, as he took off in a cloud of dust.

No sooner had we left the hotel when the driver changed into a veritable suicide pilot, intent, it seemed, on killing us all. Careening through the rush hour traffic, he kept his hand on the horn and the accelerator down to the floor. We whipped around street cars, and just as it seemed we would plow into scores of pedestrians, they miraculously melted away.

Down the coast we roared, through Yokohoma and Kamakura,

and finally up to the main gate at Yokosuka. He had averaged better than 50 mph on two-lane roads in one of the most densely populated places in the world. He was all smiles, but we were visibly shaken after this death-defying ride. Given a choice, we'd take carrier landings anytime.

While we'd been in Tokyo, the ship had been undergoing a major overhaul. Not only did the *Champ* sport new catapults, but a new teak flight deck was being laid by an army of local shipyard workers. They wore a uniform seemingly favored by most of the nation: the ubiquitous black cap and matching boots.

The hundreds of landings had left their mark, but I'm sure we could have functioned nicely. The labor rate at Yokosuka, however, was but a fraction of what this resurfacing would cost at home, and we were stuck here until the catapult parts arrived from Philadelphia. It was a good decision.

As a bonus, all the workers were permitted to fill their lunch buckets with the leftovers from the galley. Each man bowed deeply to the messcook as the food was ladled out. This gesture, no doubt, put most of our messcooks in shock, as they were the "lowest of the low" in the ship's hierarchy.

The Korean War and the resultant upsurge in the economy had removed many a Japanese from a life of abject poverty and malnutrition. Locals told us that the winter following the surrender had been particularly bad because there was almost no fuel. The cold, linked with an extremely poor diet, had led to many deaths from pneumonia.

The *Lake Champlain* was a maze of cables snaking down every ladder and passageway. Overhead, the ear-splitting din of air-hammers shattered what remained of peace and quiet. There was no escape. Again, the air group was just in the way, so after muster each day, we headed ashore to play softball, swim, or explore the outer reaches of this sprawling complex.

In the PX, I bought a top-of-the-line Voightlander camera for only $99, and others purchased Leicas and Rollies. Strangely, the best buys were ignored for the most part: the Japanese Canons and Nikons. Although they were strongly endorsed by the *Champ*'s photo department, there was still a long-held distrust of anything made in Japan.

John Robben and I had often talked about running up to Kamakura, only about an hour and a half away. A tiny shore-side village, its claim to fame was the great bronze Buddha built in 1252. It had once stood inside a huge temple, but the structure was destroyed in a tidal wave in 1495. The great Buddha now stood alone, in the middle of a park. Armed with this information, we boarded the train in the company of Hal Holman. We had a marvelous day sight-seeing, swimming, and surfing and topped it off by renting a room for the afternoon at the Seaside Hotel. In slacks and sport shirts, we enjoyed a huge steak dinner on the terrace restaurant overlooking the Pacific.

With liberty everyday from 1600 to 2400, we began to build close ties in town. Soon we had our favorite restaurants, where we could enjoy American food with Oriental overtones. I developed a soft spot for the classical jukeboxes. In a country where the love of serious Western music was only slightly edged by a passion for pachinko, one could listen to Jan Peerce singing a Verdi aria while munching chicken and rice.

In the midst of this life of indolence, we were occasionally called on to earn those paychecks that came on the fifth and twentieth of every month. One day Chief Rogers told me I was going to be the petty officer assigned to the Shore Patrol in Yokosuka the next evening. It was a snap, he assured me. The air group would assign a dozen men, and I'd be the P.O. in charge.

My duties included mustering the men on the ship (making sure they were presentable) and seeing that they had the right equipment. This included a web belt, a night stick, and an arm brassard that said "SP." Once ashore, they'd be absorbed into the main force, which comprised about sixty men. When they were out of sight, I could sit in the base security office and drink coffee until their tour was over. Before the men departed to take up their rounds, the senior officer gave a brief talk outlining their duties. Those few words proved, like nothing else, the vast difference between the state-side navy and Yokosuka. He told them we were not a training command, and he wasn't interested in having men being placed on report for minor violations, like being out of uniform. If they saw a fight, they were to break it up, but should make no arrests unless someone was injured or property had been damaged. He wanted the shore patrol to be a presence, but not to interfere with the boys having a good time. From the looks on the faces of my group, they couldn't have been given better orders.

Later, over coffee, I got to know this lieutenant well. He'd been stationed in Yokosuka for eighteen months, and he said he'd stay for eighteen years if they'd let him. Japan could cast a spell on you without you even knowing it, he said. As part of his job (Public Information Officer), he was studying Japanese, and although he'd only learned a few words, countless doors had opened for him. His salary, modest by civilian standards, enabled him to own a car and rent a small home, complete with servants. For the last year, he'd been living with a beautiful young local girl and was thinking seriously of marrying her. The problem was how she'd fit in with his former life. Right now, he was toying with the idea of living here permanently. He said, "Look behind you." There, much as on the post office walls at home, were photos of wanted persons. The difference here was that these people had committed no crime; they were simply "missing persons." The lieutenant said scores of these people, many of them officers, had just "dropped out of sight." They were probably shacked up somewhere in the small towns in the hills. He smiled and said, "The spell of the Orient." I'd often heard the expression "going Asiatic," but this was the first time I'd seen it in action.

There was another spell, and unfortunately it was affecting the *Champ*. The long stays in port had made too many men disregard the basic precautions regarding VD, and there was a major outbreak of gonorrhea. While most of the cases responded well to penicillin, there were some strains that defied all efforts to find a complete cure. A buddy of ours in the electronics shop was a case in point. He came down with a dose, and although he laughed it off at first, his "drip" persisted. Nothing in the doctor's bag of tricks appeared to have any effect. It wasn't painful, but it was damned embarrassing. To protect his clothing, he was reduced to wearing something very close to a diaper. He became listless and melancholy. The doctor further ordered a total abstinence of drinking. One day, practically in tears, he said, "You know, it's bad enough to try to think of explaining this to my fiancée, but what about my mother?"

Despite the efforts of the two chaplains and the medical officer, the proximity of all those pretty "baby-sans" to our sex-starved crew was just too much to overcome. Finally, our doctor, Commander Hunley, MC USN, responded. He wrote a classic warning that was published in the Plan of the Day.

> If you're not *absolutely sure* that the only thing you are going to do in Japan is take pictures and buy souvenirs, you'd better stop by the ship's store *now* and purchase a few rubbers. You may not think you're going to have a car wreck either, but you still carry automobile insurance. The little Jo-Sans on the beach have been plying this trade for a long time and are out to get your yen. That penicillin tablet alone will not prevent VD. Take along the rubbers for insurance. Assuming that you do succumb to the questionable charms of a local Venus, what can you do about it? First of all don't allow her beauty (they all look pretty good in subdued lighting after a few beers), her sweetness and apparent (more apparent than real) innocence, or her protestations of freedom from disease, lull you into any feeling of security, no matter who she is. If you haven't raped her, she's not any more innocent than you are. While you were at sea, there were plenty of other guys around.

At this point, the good doctor went on to the finer points of post-sexual hygiene. He continued, "The penicillin tablet alone will not prevent syphilis, chancroid, non-gonococcic urethritis, or the other so-called social diseases. If you've kissed your little Jo-San and she has syphilis, nothing will help you. The sweetness of the kiss will have to be its own reward!" Hunley was just hitting his stride, as he soared off into a description of the sterling virtues of chastity:

> The gladiators of Rome were not allowed to have coitus. Athletes are advised to abstain from intercourse while in training. Excessive indulgence in intercourse has a depressive effect on the whole body causing physical weakness and mental dullness. It was Shakespeare's Hamlet who said to his friend:
> Give me that man that is not passion's slave,
> and I will wear him in my heart's core,
> Ay in my heart of heart, As I do thee.

To say that this warning, smack in the middle of the Plan of the Day, attracted the attention of the crew, would be the understatement of the cruise. This bulletin was usually filled with such arcane items as the proper uniform, the time of sunrise and sunset, and how much water the ship had used in the past twenty-four hours. Bill Munroe said the doctor certainly covered all the things that could happen to the unwary sailor, stopping just short of blindness. It was no laughing matter, but given the circumstances, it quickly became one. Sailors can always find humor in anything. For weeks afterward, every time a liberty boat pulled away from the ship, someone on board would yell, "Remember, the sweetness of her kiss will have to be its own reward."

Commander Hunley was tops in my book, and I appreciated his concern for the crew's welfare. Fortunately, I never had to see him on a professional basis during the cruise. I did avail myself of his sidekick's attention, however, when one morning I discovered that I'd lost a filling from one of my molars. In my three years in the navy, I'd never sat in a dentist's chair, so it was with some trepidation that I approached Commander Rice. He gave me a quick look and said that the filling replacement was a short job. He also noticed some wisdom teeth starting to appear, however, which he thought might give me some trouble down the road. He suggested that I come in right after muster the following day, and he'd take care of them.

My previous experience with dentists was anything but good, so I wondered how long I'd be out of action. The next morning I was pleasantly surprised when, with a minimum of novocaine, he not only replaced the filling, but extracted all four wisdom teeth in less than 90 minutes. At noon chow, I ate roast beef and felt no discomfort. A year later, I would I have given anything to have Dr. Rice on hand. At that time, in the clutches of the Veteran's Administration, I was butchered by a dentist who would have made a good auto mechanic.

Yokosuka soon lost the excitement it once held at every turn of the corner, but now we noticed little things that we had overlooked before—shopkeepers hosing the street in front of their stores to keep down the dust; small boys playing soldier, each carrying a small wooden samurai sword; and portrait artists in their tiny stalls, painting under naked lamps long after sundown.

Stacked in front of every shop was a mountain of aluminum suitcases. Someone in Japan had hit upon the idea that the Americans would go wild over these shiny cases, and they were right. As our stay in port lengthened, so did the mound of purchases we just couldn't pass up. Our cruise boxes were packed to overflowing. When we couldn't accommodate another piece, we bought one of those aluminum suitcases. China, kimonos, music boxes, lacquer wear, silk, and even trout flies filled our cases, and the excess found its way into our peacoat-lockers. There was always room, too, for some of those crazy toys that the sailors bought on almost every liberty.

Next to the sound of "China Night" emanating from every shop, the thing I remember most about Yokosuka was the distinctive odor that hung over everything. It defied instant description. More than any familiar scent, it was rather the sum of its parts: a sweet-sour mixture of cooking spices, damp wood, kitchen smoke, and open sewers. It was not unpleasant. Almost forty years later, I could open a lacquered photo album in a dark room and instantly recognize that aroma.

Chapter 25

The Last Act

EARLY ON THE MORNING OF 11 JULY, *CVA-39* made a course for the Sea of Japan to rejoin Task Force 77. Just before we left port, there was a change of living spaces within the air group.

As an offshoot to all this shuffling of personnel, VC-12 was finally moved to a decent compartment. We bid a not-too-fond farewell to Dante's Inferno. Three of the aircrewmen, Munroe, Walls, and I, were transferred to a large, airy space just below the hangar deck that was occupied by the Navigation Division. Within these steel bulkheads were probably the most indispensable twenty-five men on the *Lake Champlain.*

The boys in the Navigation Division were "inside traders" in the true sense of the word. They were privy to all the future movements of the ship, long before even most of the officers knew our destination. Besides laying out all the charts, their job also included the processing of all visual signals to and from our bridge. Not the least of their tasks involved steering this carrier under the direction of the captain or officers of the deck. This obviously wasn't a place for "deck apes." These men were hand-picked.

Entering this inner sanctum of the ship's company, we were more than a little apprehensive. Most general service types didn't exactly welcome airdales in their midst. We needn't have worried. Like the uncorking of a bottle of champagne, all tension disappeared with the first greeting. Perhaps it was our sheer novelty that endeared us to them, the most nautical of the ship's divisions. It would be hard to imagine a greater contrast. Aviation radiomen had been around for perhaps twenty years. Helmsmen, however, had accompanied Leif Ericsson and Columbus. Here was a marvelous opportunity for both sides to find a ready and willing audience for all their sea stories. For the men of navigation, our tales of carrier operations never became dull or tiresome. Whether deck launch or catapult shot, they wanted to know every detail.

Our only problem arose because of our difference in working hours. The navigators toiled the normal ship's routine, 0800 to 1600. They were free the balance of the time, save the occasional watch. Our routine, in contrast, was strongly influenced by the weather. If it was good, the air group would be launched, and that could mean flight quarters at 0400, flying through the day, and working into the night. When the fog closed in, we'd do almost nothing.

Our good relations were strained the very first time the three of us sat up most of the night with a radar problem. Simply put, the weather the next day was terrible, and we wanted to sleep in. The compartment cleaners had to trice up the racks (fold up the bunks onto steel stanchions) and didn't know what to do with three sleeping airdales. These poor creatures held us in some awe, for besides wings, we all wore crows (designating petty officers). In the air group, especially electronics, we were a dime a dozen, but in general service, rated men were next to God. Before setting off World War III, we reached a compromise. The sweepers had no objection to our remaining in the bunks, providing they could do their job. To insure that we wouldn't be dropped six feet onto a steel deck, we were strapped in. To get some idea of what it was like, imagine yourself in an upper Pullman when the porter folds it into the wall.

It was a perfect arrangement until one morning when a chief decided to pull a surprise inspection. The first thing he saw was Bill Munroe's leather flight jacket hanging from a rack. Before he reached it, he ran into George's size-12 foot. As I was in the back row, I could observe him without being seen. He stopped in his tracks, and with the flush rising in his face, I sensed we'd soon be the object of his celebrated temper. Before he could utter a word, the cleaner hissed, "airdales." He closed his mouth, let out a sigh, and walked off, shaking his head. We slept on.

In a few days, we were fully absorbed into their midst. Bill regaled them with his Columbia football exploits, and George kept them plied with night rations. I told them what it was like growing up in New York City; to all of them, a place of great mystery.

Hal Holman had the bunk below mine. A little shy at first, he loosened up when I offered to let him read any of the books I stored below my mattress. He was about eighteen, and looked as though he and his razor rarely met. When we became close enough to share confidences, he let slip that something was really eating him. It took me a while to uncover his secret fear.

As he met his buddies returning from liberty, they were overflowing with lurid stories of their sexual exploits, while he stood there, wondering if it was even worthwhile to relate his afternoon's sightseeing. His real test occurred when they all stopped at the pharmacist's mate table for an anti-VD pill. He felt that he was the only one on the *Lake Champlain* who wasn't sampling the local women. Was there something lacking in his genes?

Bill, George, and I reassured him by explaining that the three of us passed the table regularly without stopping, and we suggested he watch the pill-takers closely next time. Nine out of ten tossed the pill over the side before going below. He might try this on his next liberty. Hal was a changed man after that.

Walls soon became a big favorite, and I strongly suspect the division would have adopted him if they could. They were astonished at his prodigious appetite, his never-ending patter of humorous stories, and his skill at cards. Other sailors might gripe about the food, but to George, this was sheer heresy. As far as he was concerned, Escoffier himself couldn't hold a candle to our galley. It was great fun to position George on the chow line behind John Robben, a particularly finicky eater. John would go through the long steam table barely able to suppress his revulsion at what lay before him. Choosing carefully, he'd balance his tray with a green vegetable, a slice of tomato, two slices of bread, and a mug of lemonade. George, in contrast, almost needed help to carry off his largess.

Sitting next to John, he'd plunk down a tray overflowing with greasy pork chops, lumpy mashed potatoes, corn bread floating in butter, and a giant slab of pie. A great friend of the cooks, he was never shortchanged. John took one look at that tray, and, almost visibly ill, moved as far away as possible.

On quiet days in port, Depron or Bill George would show me the bridge. It was a fascinating spot, with the helm, plotting board, alidade, and loran; the latter was the only piece of equipment of which I had a little knowledge. There was the captain's special chair, and when he wasn't on the bridge, no one, but no one, ever sat in it. Outside, row upon row of signal flags stood ready to be sent aloft at a moment's notice. Adjoining these flag bags was a powerful telescope to read the blinker signals from other ships and our lamp for transmitting. On the one hand, it was a world of technical marvels; on the other, it held artifacts that would have been familiar to Prince Henry.

Closer to home, these were the people who would swing the stern and pounding screws away from me, if I was unlucky enough to follow my buddies from VC-33 into the drink.

Our two-week layoff had made all hands a little rusty, so general drills, including target practice, were held. In the afternoon, CAG 4 launched 92 training sorties. All those lazy afternoons (and not so lazy nights) had noticeably dulled that sharp edge so necessary for carrier operations. Some of those early landings were pretty hairy.

The following morning we were at it again. Now, although the deteriorating weather limited our flight time, there was a significant difference in performance. CAG was happy, and so were the ACs.

Our second "thirteenth" in the war zone was just a day like any other. Our rendezvous with Task Force 77 forced us to maintain course and speed, so the air group stood down. We fired our AA guns and refueled our escorting tin can. Long after "darken ship" and "keep silence about the decks," the *Champ* joined the main body. This time, only the *Princeton* and the *Boxer* were on station with seven destroyers. The other units were enjoying their well-earned rest in port.

Despite our eagerness, the fog continued to plague us. Our aerographer's report showed us sitting under a stationary front. There was scarcely a breeze to ripple the waves. The hours dragged.

The month was nearly half over, and none of us had much flight time to show for it. VC-12 flew one of the hundred twenty-eight sorties late in the afternoon, Kinney and Dupre flying with the team leader. Visibility was so bad that all attacks were radar controlled. Our troops urgently needed ground support.

On the 15th, the fog persisted, blanketing us for the umpteenth time. Was this weather ever going to change? Maybe the chaplain had a sun prayer. With his typical Irish grin, Father Kelly said that rain was the only thing he'd ever been asked to request, but he saw no reason why we couldn't try to coax some clear skies from on high. It would be great to report that our prayers were answered and that CAG sent off everything that would fly. It was not that simple. Another week would pass before the fog blew away for good.

During the entire stretch, only on the 17th did we send up over one hundred planes. As a footnote to operations on this date, another record was set, one that literally could have made it into Ripley's "Believe It or Not." Lt. T. A. Francis of VF-22 made the 5,000th landing on the *Champ* since she was commissioned. One might say, "So what?" Well, he also made the 4,000th on 14 June and the 3,000th on 29 April.

On the rest of the long days, we sweated it out, literally and figuratively. Limited ops were flown on the 22d, but during the recovery, an arresting gear cable parted, seriously injuring R. Kilgrove. During one of the 60 sorties, a Banshee was disabled by flak over Korea, but the pilot managed to reach the coast, where he bailed out. He was recovered by a chopper from the USS *Bremerton*.

One day, returning from a four-hour ASW flight, I met Hal

Holman as I stepped into the island. When he looked at me with the wide eyes and open jaw of someone thunder-struck, I realized it was the first time he had seen me in my "work clothes." His surprise turned to awe, and he surveyed me with something akin to hero worship: the romance of flying and all that crap. It couldn't have been further from the truth. If I had to choose a moment in my four-year hitch that was the absolute bottom, this was probably it. Standing in my sweat-soaked flight suit, I had enough "ornaments" hanging from me to trim a fairly good size Christmas tree. The life jacket alone was draped with a flashlight, dye-marker, shark-chaser, whistle, survival knife, and all the flares I could carry. I'd opened my Mae West and removed my crash helmet, but I was still weighed down with the tools of my trade. I saw Hal fix his stare on my .38 peeking out from its shoulder holster under my left breast. If he only knew how useless it was.

Like almost everyone on board, I was suffering from an irritating skin rash. Other than those short times in the Ready Room, it was impossible to stay dry. The temperature on board averaged better than 90 degrees. The steel hull soaked up the heat of the sun all day and radiated it all night. The humidity was even worse, and the *Champ* sweated along with her crew. My heart used to go out to those poor souls working in the boiler room. They were truly the unsung heros of the *Champ*.

My heat rash was worst under my arms and in my crotch, and there wasn't enough talcum powder to make a difference. When I flew, the sores were aggravated by the tight straps of the parachute. In the air, you wore the chute as snug as you could stand it. If you had to exit the plane, it would be a split-second decision, and there'd be no time for fumbling with a harness.

After the long flight that day, my ass was numb. I'd sat in one position for four hours, staring at a five-inch scope, watching the sweep go round and round. This constant attention had made my eyes look and feel as though I'd been out on a three-day binge. I had a dull ache above the bridge of my nose that gradually moved into my skull. It was barely noticeable among the other irritations of flying.

The roar of the engine, almost 3,000 horses, and the constant vibration had taken their toll. The weight of the helmet, the Mae West, and the revolver pulled on my neck and shoulders like some yoke on a beast of burden. I was wiped out.

When I walked into the Ready Room, the frigid air hit me. Somehow it smelled sweeter, reminding me of those days when movies were first air-conditioned. I never wanted to go home. I watched the pilots slowly saunter into the room and collapse into the softness of those high-backed leather chairs. Did I look that bad? They all seemed ten years older than they were this morning. Years later, in Madrid, a matador got into my elevator as he was returning from the arena. He had that same look and sweat-soaked body as the pilots. Both had had their "moment of truth."

I went out into the passageway. The enlisted men flattened themselves out against the bulkhead, and I wanted to yell, "Relax guys, I'm one of you!" Of course I didn't. I found a head and took a long satisfying leak. I'd almost forgotten I needed to take one. There was a mirror over the sink, but I was almost afraid to look in it. It was me all right, a little frayed around the edges, but still recognizable. The pilots were in far worse shape. I only had to watch the radar. They had to get us back in one piece, going through that intricate and deadly approach and trying to remember all the things they hoped were second nature by now.

Another night, waiting for our planes to return, I met Hal again. We decided to have a couple of Cokes by the familiar red machine on the hangar deck. The ocean just below the deck was pitch black. Every few seconds a fan of white foam from the bow wave broke as it raced by into the night. The *Champ* was making many knots, probably close to thirty, as the planes came round to land. We could hear and feel the thump every time one touched down. Hal finally asked the question everyone wanted to ask the aircrewmen. "Where do you find the guts to take off and land on this thing, day after day?" I mumbled something stupid like, "You get used to it." A truer reply would have been, "I don't have the guts not to." The fear of looking bad in the eyes of your fellow crewmen is far worse than the fear of flying.

Sure, I was afraid, especially the night work. One never got used to those predawn launches or the scary landings in the inky darkness. Each of us had our own set of personal terrors. For me, the worst thing I could imagine was being trapped inside a sinking plane. In my nightmare, I was suspended upside down. I'd seen a number of aircraft go in the drink, belly-up. If you blew a tire while landing or came in at too steep an angle, that's the way you'd go into the sea.

None of us ever talked about death, our own or anyone else's. We knew there were risks every time we crawled into the backseat, and we'd all seen enough planes go down to know it occurred on a pretty regular basis. But there was a stronger feeling, that we were all immortal. I don't think any of us ever thought we were going to die, even years and years from now. Before we got too old, somebody would surely invent something, and we'd all live forever.

Flight quarters sounded at 0430 on 23 July. From seemingly every sector came the call for air support. The Chinese had mounted a strong offensive, apparently under the impression that the cease-fire line would be frozen by the truce. Task Force 77 responded in spades.

At 0908, Ensign H. K. Wallace of VF-22 lost his port tip tank as he was being catapulted. This caused his Banshee to flip over as it reached the end of the deck, crashing upside down into the sea. The aircraft sank in seven seconds. The pilot stayed with her.

I flew an ASW op with Bill Munroe and picked up nearly all the flight time I needed in one mission. It was my first catapult shot. Sometimes people ask me what it was like, and I start to explain. After a few sentences, I realize there's no way I can even remotely do the feeling any justice. It's nothing like a roller coaster. I guess being shot out a cannon would come closest, but then not too many people can relate to that.

Our first task was to make absolutely certain there were no loose tools in the "tunnel," that open space in front of the right-hand seat that was used for radar access. Even a ball point pen or grease pencil could turn into a murderous missile when we accelerated from 0 to 100 knots in less than two seconds. Even with your body forced back into your seat and your crash helmet snug against the head rest, it was a shock, albeit an extremely brief one. Once clear of the ship, the plane slowed as if someone had applied brakes. The power that flung you out over the sea produced a far greater wallop than anything an AD could generate, and it lasted only a second. The ship was the bow. You were the arrow.

Later in the deployment, George rigged up a camera to the metal racks holding the radar. He wanted to capture on film the Halloween mask effect the "G" (gravity) forces exerted on our face. For that one instant, all the flesh on our cheeks was forced back into our skull cavity. It wasn't very pleasant to look at, but it gave you some idea of the stress being exerted on the body. Alas, the shock was so sudden that even with a shutter speed of 1/500th of a second, the picture came out blurred. Strangely, its very blurring probably recorded the event far more dramatically than a perfect photo.

At any rate, this "cat shot" was only the first of eight I experienced off Korea. That mountainous coast was notorious for its almost complete lack of wind. In the Atlantic and Mediterranean, for example, the props were deck launched 90 percent of the time.

Task Force 77 broke its record, and the *Champ* chimed in with 157 launches to hold up her end. The flight and hangar decks were teeming with activity all day and into the early evening. There were troubles for all departments, and very few in the air group slept much that night. Kinney, Walls, and I were kept busy with a problem in the radar (and the usual altimeter gripe) until past midnight. Water hours were lifted so we could remove the sweat and the grime. The compartment was well above 90 degrees, but we were asleep in seconds.

Our bugler blew the familiar call for the air group at 0415, and into the Ready Room we shuffled. Talley was out with the flu, and Winslow was down with a head cold. George and I took their places and logged over seven hours that day. The circuits were alive with combat reports: planes making runs on pill boxes, road blocks, supply columns, and artillery positions. The Skyraiders and Corsairs were having a field day.

On one leg of our ASW mission, we passed close to the battleship *New Jersey* (BB63). I prayed our IFF was putting out, because in this atmosphere, people shoot first and ask questions later (IFF, identification friend or foe, was an electronic device that sent out a coded signal identifying us as an American plane). The *New Jersey* looked formidable from 3,000 feet, bristling with five-inch and smaller antiaircraft guns. Flying straight and level at 150 knots, we would have been like that proverbial fish in the barrel.

The battleship was shelling positions about ten miles away on the North Korean coast. Each time a salvo was fired, the shock wave was clearly visibly on the water. We'd been told the 16-inch projectiles could be seen when they reached the top of their trajectory, so we strained our eyes. I saw them once, or at least I think I did. Sometimes when you're really trying to spot an object, like the green flash at sunset, your imagination can play tricks with you.

As we orbited *CVA-39*, waiting for our turn to land, many planes were requesting priority due to flak damage or low fuel states. Our AD4W could throttle back and wait until the very end to come aboard. We had a ringside seat at 1,500 feet, watching jet after jet come in to roost, followed by the slower but more substantial looking Skyraiders. These pros made it look easy, which it never was.

After a bone-jarring cat shot, these pilots had been flying over enemy territory and providing close ground support for the marines and army. For two to three hours, they'd been dodging heavy flak. Now physically and emotionally drained, they had to find their way back to the carrier and land on her pitching deck. During the most demanding days of combat, we had no barrier crashes. All the planes landed safely, except one AD that ran out of fuel and ditched alongside the ship. The pilot was recovered by our helicopter. This was a testament not only to their high level of training, but also to the fortitude and unfailing dedication of each and every airman.

Shortly after we touched down, effectively ending the day's flight ops, the *Champ*'s chopper crashed into the sea. She had been involved in a routine mail drop over the USS *Blue*, a destroyer in our screen, when she lost power. The pilot and aircrewman were rescued by another chopper from the *Boxer*.

When the final tally of TF 77 was made late that night, it was revealed that we had set a new war record for sorties, with an even 600 flown that day. The *Lake Champlain* was the top carrier with 156. Not bad for the new kid on the block. That night we rearmed from an ammo ship, USS *Vesuvius* (AE-15).

The air group had been flying so many missions and delivering such a prodigious amount of ordnance that we were refueling and rearming almost nightly. This, in turn, put a terrific strain on the ship's company. On top of their normal day's work and watches, they were up well into the early hours of the morning, manhandling supplies and ammunition. This was backbreaking labor, and after two or three consecutive nights, it started to take its toll.

For a time, the four CAGs were using over 9,000 barrels of aviation gas a day. Tankers, it seemed, were constantly alongside. These replenishments often took place under the most adverse weather conditions, with visibility down to one hundred feet in fog and mist. Searchlights were used, and "darken ship" went by the boards. The need outweighed the risk.

Witnessing a replenishment, I began to take note of the tremendous organizational genius it took to run this ship. Although the *Lake Champlain* excelled in the performance of her primary function, delivering ordnance to the enemy, she was also home to over three thousand men. This role (which we took for granted), caused us to gripe from morning 'til night: it was too hot, the food was dull, and we never got enough sleep. But if one took the time to think about it, our carrier was a paragon of efficiency. Maybe not that elusive dream of perpetual motion, but pretty damn close.

At times we'd be at sea for close to six weeks, but nothing changed. The showers were always hot, our clothes came back clean from the laundry, and we got three "squares" a day. In short, everything worked.

In the civilian world, anyone with an audience criticized the army and navy. What the services really needed were some good hardheaded businessmen with a profit motive to run things. Oh yeah? Surely, nobody on the *Champ* was in it for the money, but dedication was something you couldn't put a price on.

Before enlisting in the navy, I had worked in a supermarket, a cemetery, and an insurance company. In each job, with few exceptions, people just put in their time. The paycheck was the thing, the only thing. There was little loyalty. We all thought the company was trying to get the most out of us for the least pay.

Out here, I never ran into a man who wasn't giving 110 percent.

In the course of an average day, we had hot muffins for breakfast, and we never ran out of catsup. The latter was amazing because it seemed as if sailors put catsup on everything except their cereal. Soap, paint, and bleach were always in use, and our geedunk stand produced an endless supply of ice cream sundaes. Whether it was razor blades, toilet paper, electronic parts, or 105-octane gas, no one ever said, "Sorry, we're fresh out."

The people in supply did a herculean job. They were truly the unsung heros of Task Force 77. How they kept track of the thousand and one items, from paper clips to light bulbs, from 1,000-pound bombs to spare American flags, was a mystery. When the captain said, "I want sixty planes for tomorrow's strike" or ordered, "All ahead full," he got it, no excuses.

In a larger sense, one could appreciate the latent power of America neatly expressed in this task force. Sent halfway around the world, thousands of men toiled in scores of ships and hundreds of planes. And this great fleet was backed up by huge naval bases like Yokosuka and Sasebo. In spite of our size and tremendous fire power, we were still small potatoes compared to the Eighth Army and the marines fighting just over the horizon.

Two oceans away, another fleet with even larger aircraft carriers supported over 200,000 troops in Europe. And yet, for all this prodigious effort, one could spend a week at home and never know there was a war on. New automobiles and appliances rolled off the assembly lines, new homes and offices were being built, and gasoline was cheap and plentiful. Nothing was rationed. It was business as usual. What a country.

While our asses were dragging from all this flying and replenishing, those with a little historical perspective also got some appreciation of what our predecessors had gone through in World War II. Their flight operations were far more sustained, and they put up a "maximum effort" for weeks on end. When they were finally relieved, they enjoyed no great liberty ports with baby-sans and tender steaks. They usually retired to some God-forsaken place, like Mog Mog atoll in Ulithi, with a couple of beers and a softball game for diversion.

The major difference was that all our ordnance was outgoing. In other words, nobody was shooting at us (at least at sea). We operated in a protective cocoon brought about by political and military considerations which the fleet of the forties never enjoyed. For them,

A VC-12 Skyraider taxiing on flight deck of the USS Lake Champlain, *July 1953.*

anytime, day or night, at sea or at anchorage, death and destruction could come by torpedo, bomb, or kamikaze. Just experiencing a brief taste of the "real thing" gave us an undying respect for those who fought in the "Big One."

On the front, the Chinese had launched another offensive, and General Maxwell Taylor had thrown two American divisions into the gap. Close support was the order of the day. Our entire prop force worked with the Eighth Army, providing reconnaissance and leaving the jets to attack communications. Even the battleship *New Jersey* came up to use her 16-inch guns on the battleline. She was joined by the cruisers *Manchester, Bremerton,* and *St. Paul* and a division of DDs. The navy's role had gone full circle, returning to the missions it had performed so well in those dark days of 1950.

During the previous afternoon's recovery, George and I were up forward inside an AD, checking out a receiver. The last flight had nearly been recovered when the bullhorn announced, "Plane in final approach has hung rocket." This had occurred before, and the missile had remained firmly in its rack. We also knew it couldn't explode because it had been disarmed. As a result, few, if any, moved. The Skyraider landed, caught a wire, and came to an abrupt stop. Its rocket, unfortunately, didn't, and it continued down the flight deck at something close to 80 knots. In the middle of its erratic course, it struck a plane captain and left him with a compound fracture of his right leg; he was lucky at that. The next afternoon, history repeated itself, only this time it was a Banshee instead of a Skyraider. The Air Boss got out the words "Plane in final approach," and I was carried into the catwalk and inside a hatch before I knew what hit me. True to form, this time the rocket stayed with the aircraft. I hadn't seen anybody move that fast on the *Champ* since the first liberty party at Yokosuka.

July 25 was a rare clear day for this time of the year, and again the task force broke its record with 746 flights. Our team flew four ASW sorties, and all the crewmen got air time. Calley and I were up with Lt. Williams, as the four carriers pounded out close to 30 knots to bring their squadrons back on board. We still had another two hours left in our mission, so we were treated to a rare view of the whole force steaming below us.

The carriers were headed into the wind on a course taking them directly into the coast of North Korea. We asked the pilot why the ships hadn't turned. He surmised that some of the jets probably didn't have enough fuel to wait for the carriers to come around again. When only five planes remained, Williams said, "Watch closely and you'll see some fancy maneuvering." Admiral Johnson was quickly running out of sea room, and he'd shortly be in range of the North Korean shore batteries.

Finally, the last aircraft touched down, and before the wire was released from the hook, the entire task force made a 180-degree turn. A dozen ships turned as if guided by one hand, their long wakes cutting white circles in the blue sea. *Life* magazine later ran a spread on the *Champ*, and what we saw that day was captured on film.

Those on board had a different viewpoint, but an equally interesting story to tell. The coastline was clearly visible and getting closer by the minute. As the last plane was in her final approach, the bullhorn blared, "Stand by for an emergency turn to port." All hands hung on. When the order "execute" was given, the ship heeled over and everything not secured rolled across the deck. More than one tool box and some loose pieces of cowling went over the side.

During a later launch, a plane handler was sucked into a jet engine and critically injured. This increased tempo of operations was taking its toll.

That night after chow, all the technicians went to work. Every one of our planes had electronic troubles and had to be ready by the following morning. Three of us manhandled a heavy radar unit down three ladders and into the shop, where we spent five hours locating

and repairing the problem. On top of this, the APN-1 electronic altimeters were out of alignment. Their sensitive circuits just weren't
suited for the rough and tumble of carrier operations. It was akin to
repairing a sensitive timepiece next to a railroad trestle. Later, the
APN-1 became my ticket to a brief moment in the spotlight, but that
was still in the future.

Well after midnight, the radar in 703 checked out and we all went
below to the mess deck for some cool drinks. Tired as we were, we
still needed a drink before sacking out. The cooks recognized us and
wanted to make something special, but we didn't even have the
energy to eat. In spite of the heat and humidity, we collapsed in our
bunks with everything but our shoes on.

It was two hours, but it felt more like two minutes, when we
awakened to the bong, bong, bong of General Quarters and the urgent
voice on the P.A. system shouting: "General Quarters! General Quarters! All hands man your battle stations!"

Previously, all G.Q. drills had been announced beforehand. Our
compartment lights were turned on, and everyone started running. I
heard someone shout, "This is no drill!" (Where had I heard that before?)
Needing no further motivation, all hands on the *Champ* responded with
something bordering on pandemonium. We just made it to the Ready
Room before all the hatches were dogged down behind us.

To save our night vision, the Ready Room was bathed in an eerie
blue light as we changed into our flight suits and Mae Wests. The
teletype revealed many bogies closing the task force. The usual ban-
ter and horseplay were missing as we received our assignments. All
three of VC-12's planes would be launched.

I could hear the jets being "catted" above me as I climbed into
the backseat of 703 on the deck-edge elevator. With Lt. Williams as
our pilot, we would operate as the backup AEW plane. Oddly, it was
703 that had kept us up half the night. The *Lake Champlain* was
pounding out many knots as I propped open the hatch to get some
air. From our perch out over the hull, I could watch the boiling sea
race by. A few yards from the foaming bow wave, the ocean was
black beyond description. I wouldn't want to be down tonight.

On previous flight ops, when a launch was delayed, we usually
passed the time telling jokes or exchanging the latest scuttlebutt.
Tonight was different. Each of us sat silently with our own thoughts.
All of us, I'm sure, made impossible promises to God, and I was one
of them. My gut was wound so tight, it was hard to breathe, no less
talk. For the umpteenth time, I tightened the harness of my chute.
I remember praying, "Whatever else happens, don't make me bail
out of this thing!"

In spite of the tremendous anxiety, between the heat, the darkness, and our overall fatigue, we both dozed off. The next thing I remember was Williams shaking me. We'd been told to stand down and secure from General Quarters, he said. Whatever it was out there had disappeared as our jets closed for interception. We should all get some shut-eye, as there was a full card on for tomorrow, and all of us were scheduled for a 0930 launch in the same aircraft. It was now 0455.

It was a dog-tired crew that shuffled back to their living spaces, carrying steel helmets and fire-fighting equipment. George and I fell asleep immediately in the big leather chairs in our Ready Room, still wearing our useless .38s. It was easier, and far more practical, than dragging ourselves back to our compartment. Besides, the Ready Room was gloriously air-conditioned.

That day, CAG-4 flew 166 sorties, a *Champ* and TF-77 record. Our jets flew deep into North Korea, cratering airfields and attacking communications centers. The props operated around Wonsan. Flak was intense, and many planes returned with holes in their wings and fuselages.

During a deck launch, an AD4B from Attack Squadron 45 went into the sea after an engine failure. The pilot, Lt. Brumbach, was recovered by our helicopter uninjured. While recovering aircraft from our early afternoon attack, Airman L. Woods, a plane handler, was seriously injured when he was blown into a tractor by a jet blast. More serious was the news that Ensign Broyles of VF-22 failed to rendezvous after a bombing run over the North. An extensive search came up empty. He was last seen in a 40-degree dive at 6,000 feet. No ejection was observed, and he was listed as missing in action.

When flight operations ceased that day, crewmen were sprawled everywhere. They were in passageways, on mess tables, in catwalks, and on wings. It was as if the *Champ* had been struck by a gas attack. Some poor bastards were later detailed to take part in a rearming from USS *Vesuvius* (AE-15), and I saw about a hundred of them straining under the flood lights as I headed below decks about 2130. Except for the activity on the hangar deck (which ended at 2300), the ship was a tomb.

On 27 July, another hot, humid day, I flew my twenty-first mission with TF-77. (George and I ended up tied for the most flights in the war zone.) In the final approach, while I was taking a photo of the *Champ*, word was received that truce terms had been accepted by both sides. We became the last plane of the final combat strike to touch down. All offensive operations ceased. After 37 months and 53,629 combat deaths, the Korean War had ended.

Chapter 26

Peace and a New Skipper

THE COMMANDER OF THE SEVENTH FLEET, Vice-Admiral Clark, sent this dispatch to Task Force 77:

> Upon the occasion of an armistice in Korea this date Commander Seventh Fleet expresses his heartiest congratulations to all ships and units under his command on their individual and collective perfor- mance in the fight against communist aggression. During the critical period when the fate of the truce was hanging in the balance you re- sponded in a manner that is in keeping with the best tradition of the Navy and you have materially aided the cause of freedom by persuad- ing the enemy that war is not in his best interest. We pray that we have achieved a lasting peace but we must remain ready and alert to meet any future threat to the security of the free world. I am proud of you. Well done to all hands.

As a bonus for the "well done" received from fleet commander "Jocko" Clark, holiday routine was declared. Some of the crew went to church services, and some played basketball (I don't know where they found the energy), but most people slept. I returned to that big soft chair in the air-conditioned Ready Room and slept through lunch and dinner. After a sandwich at 2100, I wrote a couple of let- ters and sacked out again, this time for eight hours.

Now fully awake, the ship's complement learned some startling news. The *Lake Champlain* had a new captain and executive officer. The skipper was Captain L. D. Schaeffer, and the "exec" was our for- mer operations officer, Commander Lynch.

Under normal circumstances, this would have been "the story of the week" (if not the year). But after the round-the-clock operations of the past five days, it seemed merely a footnote. Soon, however, we were ready to absorb the full impact of this momentous change, and before looking over our new leaders, it was time to evaluate those who were departing.

Rarely does an enlisted man see the skipper or his "hatchet

man." Except for a full-dress Captain's Inspection or (for the unfortunate few) a Captain's Mast disciplinary action, these people were almost invisible. Compared to top corporate leaders ashore, they were nearly omnipotent.

Captain Mundorff was a short, dapper man, always looking as if he'd just stepped out of cellophane. Because he spent most of his time in air-conditioned spaces, that wasn't too difficult to accomplish. Where he lost points with the crew was his lack of communication. Seldom did he tell us where or when we were going, or how long we'd stay there. Sailors expect and depend on regular announcements. This makes a routine, and that very certainty is what the navy is all about. Mundorff looked and acted aloof, rarely rubbing shoulders with the "dungaree set."

Commander Best (not his real name), the X.O., had the demeanor of a miserable S.O.B. If he was only assuming that role, he could have won an Academy Award. He never smiled and wore a perpetual scowl. He was someone you never wanted to cross. It was his job to carry out the captain's orders, and he excelled at it.

No one knew whether it was he or the captain who initiated the policy of "cleanliness or death." The effects of this official decree permeated the *Champ* from stem to stern and affected every waking moment of our lives. One of the standard jokes at the time was, "The *Lake Champlain* may not win a Presidential Citation, but she'll surely garner the Good Housekeeping Seal of Approval." Regardless of whose order it was, it wreaked havoc on the crew's morale. At any time of the day, it always appeared that two-thirds of the ship's heads were "secured" for painting or cleaning. The junior officers said they suffered the same fate. Half the people you passed in the passageways had a pained expression on their faces.

On the credit side, the navy doesn't choose senior officers on the basis of popularity. As important as morale may be in the overall performance of the complement, it's not the captain's highest priority. Mundorff and Best recommissioned the *Lake Champlain* out of mothballs and turned her into an effective combat unit. Other than a brief flirtation with disaster just outside of Norfolk, the *Champ* had done everything expected of her. *CVA-39* may not have been an overly happy ship, but it was a place where things worked and orders were carried out. In the final accounting, that's what gets you promoted.

Captain Mundorff was passed over for promotion for medical reasons (a back injury from a catapult shot), and he retired. Best on the other hand, not only got his own command, but eventually achieved flag rank, Vice-Admiral. As task commander, he presided over the search for an errant H-bomb off Spain in the late 60s.

The new team couldn't have been more different. Leonard B. Schaeffer was a tall, lanky "Lincoln in sun tans." His uniform hung, rather than fitted his frame. A lock of undisciplined hair fell over one eye, and his right hand was constantly sweeping this back.

In 1944, as Air Officer of the *Lexington*, he'd been badly burned in a kamikaze attack and had spent six months in the hospital. He came to us with a great combat record that included a Navy Cross, D.F.C. Purple Heart, and a fistful of Air Medals. His record as "Air Boss" and Operations Officer on the *Blue Ghost* made him a perfect choice for command.

In contrast to Mundorff, who had lived a monastic life on the bridge or with his staff, Schaeffer was everywhere. His style was simple: "This is my ship, and I want to know every nook and cranny in it." In the first few days, his approval rating soared.

For starters, his timing couldn't have been better, coming in just as the war ended. His slow drawl dovetailed perfectly with our new scenario, calling not for urgency, but rather, "steady as she goes." The ship's company was as tautly efficient as before, but now it appeared to be fueled by a desire to please, rather than any fear of punishment. Some thought it was just a brief honeymoon, but the relationship matured into a good marriage all the way back to Mayport. To me, this was the ideal way to lead, but I'd only seen a handful of men who could pull it off.

Our new "exec," Commander Lynch, was a known quantity. He had served us well as our Operations Officer. A big smiling Irishman with a fine combat record, he set the tone for a happy ship. Although he was no pushover and discipline stood firm, he made small changes that endeared him to the crew.

Side cleaners no longer had to work in undress whites. Scraping and painting the side of the ship in port was one of the dirtiest jobs on board. Our former exec. thought it would look better to have the cleaners in whites rather than in work clothes. This was as about as logical as cleaning out an outhouse in a tuxedo.

In retrospect, it was these degrading and senseless orders, rather than the low pay and long family separations, that were the major factors in the low reenlistment rate. It's one thing to be tough; it's another to be needlessly demeaning. These were the things sailors remembered. I think most of us felt, "I'll work like a dog, just don't treat me like one."

The word was passed to the 1st lieutenant, and then to the Chief Master-at-Arms (our police chief), that minor uniform infractions during work hours were to be overlooked. Sometimes the wearing of a white hat just wasn't practical. More liberal shower times were set, with the condition that if they were abused, the old restrictions would be reinstated. The crew had been living with the old water hours for nearly four months, and since no one took advantage, consumption remained the same.

In what was the biggest boost to morale, the heads were open for business when and where you needed them. According to one theory, it wasn't the change of command at all. The ship had simply run out of paint. Whatever the reason, the new team was given credit.

So gradually, over the next few weeks, the atmosphere on the *Champ* took on a more relaxed tone. There were more smiling faces and fewer fights in the chow line. It was a time we all started to enjoy being in the navy.

The pace slackened. Our cruising speed diminished, and those exhausting rearming and replenishments at sea became a thing of the past. No more bombs in the mess deck. No more bombs, period.

The air group was not immune to these changes. Flight operations were reduced to a bare minimum, with just enough air time to keep the pilots from becoming dangerously rusty. There were still AEW and ASW missions, but now they were primarily training in nature. Although they no longer toted bombs and rockets, the fighters and dive-bombers continued to carry .50 caliber and twenty millimeter ammo. One had to remember that this was not really peace we were living under, but an armed truce.

Having the twin advantages of long endurance and advanced radar, our planes were used to provide the ship with reconnaissance over a wide sector of the ocean. One of these routine flights became anything but that on one memorable afternoon.

After being aloft for an hour, the pilot asked me to take a look at the starboard wing. Did it appear any different from my angle in the rear compartment? After examining both wings closely several times, I had no doubt that the starboard wing had not locked.

On carrier aircraft, the wings fold to save space. Just before launching, as the planes taxi forward, the wings are extended. When the wing is fully lowered, a steel bolt moves back into place to lock it in the down position. On our aircraft, the bolt had not seated. We were literally flying on hydraulics.

When the pilot called the ship, he was instructed to keep it straight and level and not to attempt any violent maneuvers. Violent maneuvers! Whoever was on the other end of that radio had obviously never flown a "guppy."

After a few more transmissions, it was clear this type of problem had never occurred before, at least to those on board. The general opinion was that if the AD had remained airborne well over an hour

Two F9F-Panthers over USS Lake Champlain, *August 1953. Official U.S. Navy photo.*

with an unlocked wing, it could make it back to the ship. We landed without incident after a long shallow approach, but my adrenaline generator was working overtime. We all told jokes to break the tension, but we weren't fooling anyone, least of all ourselves. Mr. Madison was normally not the joke-telling type, but that day it didn't seem to make any difference. He told us that he'd hit the "bailout bell" once if he started to lose control. Bill and I kept our harness tight and one hand on the hatch release all the way back to the ship.

After we landed, my hands were shaking so badly, I needed help getting out of my gear. I'd never been so terrified in all my life. I was numb. If that wing had collapsed, the chances would have been almost zero that we would have been able to exit the plane. God, I'm sure, received a few more heartfelt promises that day. Madison added, more in truth than jest, "We all earned our flight pay this afternoon." In the end, it was determined that the wing lock was inoperative.

What made the whole incident so unique and all the more terrifying was the prolonged tension that had built with every minute.

Most airborne incidents occurred too fast for us to feel fear, and it would be only much later that the touch of the angel's wing returned to haunt us.

In the rest of the navy, death was the rare visitor. On our beat, it was always present, hovering over your shoulder. Considering the infinite number of things that could go wrong, it was a miracle we didn't lose more planes. The fact that carrier pilots are the best of the best made all the difference.

At this time, two oceans away in the Mediterranean, an event took place that brought home our relationship to "Lady Luck" with startling clarity. Two of the casualties were from our own squadron and well known to us. They were part of one of our teams on the USS *F.D. Roosevelt,* operating off Crete. Most of the air group's morning recovery had been completed, and one of our guppies was perched at the extreme end of the flight deck. A plane captain was standing on the wing, leaning into the cockpit. A radio technician had just emerged from the port wheel well, where he'd checked the connection on a receiver. A Banshee came in too fast and at too steep an angle. Hitting the flight deck with tremendous force and speed, the aircraft bounced back into the air before engaging a wire. Soaring forward, it leap-frogged the barriers and came down into a group of parked planes on the port side. All this happened in the time frame of perhaps five seconds, so first impulses spelled the difference between life or death. I later saw a film of this incredible accident, and while watching it, I found it nearly impossible to believe that this was real life, and not just a movie. Sadly, though, it was all too true.

As the jet returned to the deck, its port wheel just grazed the head of the driver of a mule (one of the small tractors used to tow aircraft). Had he not instinctively ducked, he would have been decapitated.

Up forward, the two airmen from VC-12 had perhaps two extra seconds to make a decision. The radioman catapulted himself into the port catwalk, breaking an arm and a shoulder. The plane captain was on the wrong side of the cockpit to follow him, so he took the only remaining path.

Just as the errant Banshee started to sweep the parked planes into the sea, he leaped over the forward edge of the flight deck and fell twenty-five feet into a gun tub. He broke his back, but lived to tell the tale. A moment later, his Skyraider was enmeshed in the wreckage of the other four planes, and they fell into the sea. Two pilots died.

A week after our incident with the wing lock, "Preacher" Williams gave me an envelope in the Ready Room. Inside was one typewritten page containing the lyrics to a famous World War II song, "Coming in on a Wing and a Prayer." It couldn't have been more appropriate.

Williams, incidentally, was tops as a pilot as far as I was concerned. On one takeoff, his engine started cutting out halfway into his flight deck run. He had already reached the point of no return. With only a few seconds to act, he switched gas tanks, assuming condensation was the cause of his erratic engine. Most of the other pilots I knew said it was a fabulous decision, especially when you only had one shot. I wasn't in the backseat that day (I'm glad I wasn't), but I can imagine the feelings of the crewman watching the air speed indicator. He was so sure he was going for a swim, his hand was still locked on the emergency door release five minutes after they were airborne.

Ten days after the truce, the task force cut its carrier strength to two. We were further advised that each ship's time at sea would be reduced, and, conversely, our port stays would be lengthened. "Darken ship" routine was scrapped, and movies on the hangar deck were resumed.

For the first time, the fighter and attack squadron pilots started to feel that they had a reasonable chance for a normal life. If the furious pace of the past week's action had continued, there would have been more empty seats in the Ready Room and a lot more space in the hangar deck.

Chapter 27

A Summing Up

THE WAR'S ENDING BROUGHT WITH IT feelings of both relief and bitterness. It was difficult for us to accept the restrictions, both military and political, of our first "limited war." The absence of a clearly defined victory left many with a sour taste in their mouths.

Everyone on board had fought in or lived through World War II, a very black and white conflict. Our goals had been clear: the absolute destruction of the Axis powers and their unconditional surrender.

Korea was a different story. The U.S. didn't have two years to weigh its options. We plunged right in, clearly out of necessity. Any protracted debate would have resulted in a North Korean fait accompli.

The initial six months were almost a microcosm of the "good war" that had ended five years before. After nearly being pushed into the sea, we rallied and went on the offensive, and by November we appeared to have things neatly wrapped up. Entering the war under a UN sanction to preserve the integrity of South Korea, we expanded our role after Inchon to the occupation and reuniting of the whole peninsula. The speed of our military success ran far ahead of our long-range political planning, however, and no one in the corridors of power reflected on the implications of crossing the 38th parallel and its impact on China. Washington was reacting to, rather than planning, our ground movements. So rapid was the disintegration of the enemy's front in October and November that MacArthur was given his head. It looked like 1940 France all over again.

There was one major difference. In 1940, France had no powerful ally on her border. China was a huge military and political question mark. Would she stand by while her smaller neighbor was defeated and strong unfriendly forces marched up to her northeastern border? The U.S. still recognized Chiang as the legitimate leader of China, and leading factions in our government hoped to put him

239

back on the mainland. It wouldn't be stretching the imagination to think that Mao might consider the massing of U.S. forces on the Yalu as the first step in a two-pronged invasion, the other coming from Formosa.

Since 1949, Red China had been isolated from the United States, economically and diplomatically. We never recognized the Communists as the true government and effectively barred them from UN membership. This isolation only fueled their paranoia about Western encirclement. With the bulk of our forces in Europe, we, of course, had no such plans for supporting an invasion. Wars, unfortunately, have started on lesser misunderstandings.

China's sudden entry into the conflict in December 1950 threw a wrench into our Asian strategy. What had started as a "police action" against a third-rate country turned into a land war on the Asian continent, which none of us wanted. China had the largest army in the Far East, an army battle-hardened from World War II and a recent civil struggle. Clearly, this was not our plan for a showdown with the Reds. This would be the classic wrong war at the wrong place at the wrong time. Our postwar commitment was to Western Europe, and we couldn't maintain that commitment while fighting a full-scale ground war in Asia. An agonizing reappraisal took place, and our objectives were scaled back to our original goal, the preservation of South Korea.

At the time, this led to a great wringing of hands in Washington. The major adjustment required to accommodate this new geopolitical and military reality caused many heads to roll, MacArthur's being only the first. Was the uniting of the two Koreas worth an atomic war with China and the strong possibility of Russian involvement? Most people on both sides of the Atlantic didn't think so. The action would be fought to a conclusion on the ground and in the air with conventional weapons: American technology versus Chinese manpower.

Eventually, we forced the North Koreans and Chinese to the truce table because we made it too costly for the Red Army. They may have had an almost bottomless supply of manpower, but they only possessed so many trained divisions, and Ridgeway and Van Fleet were putting them through a meat grinder. Korea, with its rugged mountainous terrain, was an ideal defensive platform, especially for forces with superior firepower and complete control of the sea and air. Mao's generals soon realized that we could never be dislodged by force and that our commitment was firm. It was they who asked for the initiation of the truce talks in 1951, and, although the war dragged on for another two years, the outcome was never in doubt.

In the years following, it became popular to think we lost the war, no doubt because we didn't reunite Korea and because we were pushed out of the North. Well, the North Koreans, and later the Chinese, were pushed out of the South, not once but several times. In all the arguments over the past forty years, one fact has been ignored. Were the goals of North Korea's aggression in June 1950 realized at the end of the war? The answer has to be a resounding no. The borders were essentially the same. Behind our military shield, South Korea has become the industrial miracle of the Asian mainland, second only to Japan. On the other hand, the North retreated deeper and deeper from the family of nations, falling into the backwater of a fourth world status, the Albania of the East.

In the end, the war proved a disaster for any far-ranging Communist goals. America, the sleeping giant, was now fully awake. Never in our lifetimes would our armed forces again fall to such a sorry state.

Our military leaders learned some important lessons, too. Nuclear weapons had little effect in limited wars, and air power alone would not stop a determined aggressor on the ground. In meeting our obligations all over the world, the navy was finally restored to its rightful position as an equal partner, and not merely a stepchild, of the air force. Lastly, the marines, who had nearly been disbanded in the unification process, took on a new luster after Inchon and Chosin.

The Korean War, then, brought us into the years ahead, ready to face the new realities. Regional conflicts would be the order of the day. Rarely would the superpowers go toe-to-toe, as they did in Cuba. More often, the battles would be fought in (and by) third-world nations, with the U.S. and Russia providing aid and advisors. Twice, both sides got in over their heads and came out losing far more than they gained: the U.S. in Vietnam and Russia in Afghanistan.

The Korean War left a bad taste. There are many reasons for this, and few have been explored thoroughly. Coming on the heels of World War II (less than five years separated them), it always suffered by an unfair comparison. Our memories of the "Big One" were dominated by smashing victories on all fronts. These recollections were further enhanced by countless war movies that focused on our invincibility. The early days of our rearmament, when the army practiced with wooden cannons and motor cars marked "tank," were conveniently forgotten. The terrible defeats of those first six months were ignored or glossed over.

In the mind of 1950 America, our forces were still the well-equipped victors of World War II. Nothing could have been further from the truth. Through a combination of overconfidence in the big bomber and severe budget cuts, our armed forces had fallen to a precarious position by the spring of 1950. The Eighth Army in Japan was composed primarily of draftees, and those who had enlisted had been wooed on a recruiting theme of a soft life in the new army. Trucks and tanks lacked regular maintenance and suffered from a shortage of spare parts. Our antitank weapons were out of date and pitifully inadequate against the Russian T-37s manned by the North Koreans.

Our navy, after the terrible unification fight which resulted in the infamous "revolt of the admirals," was in even worse condition. When the North Koreans invaded their neighbor, we had exactly one aircraft carrier in the western Pacific, the USS *Valley Forge*. The second CV to arrive on the scene was British.

We literally had to scrape the bottom of the barrel to keep our forces from being pushed into the sea. Active and inactive reservists were called up and hastily thrown into the breach. Unfortunately, little of this information reached the general public. They always thought it was a political decision not to commit more forces. As a result, Korea suffered from an unfair comparison. In later years, historians have put the war into a more favorable context, but that viewpoint has never been shared by the general public. If nothing else, the war should not be forgotten.

To me, it always seemed that this "police action" was conducted in the long shadow of its big brother, the "good war." Every ship and base I saw was built for World War II. Practically all the weapons, except for jet aircraft, were the instruments of the 40s, and even the uniforms hadn't changed. Only the air force, which hadn't existed as a separate service back then, sported new distinctive togs. Unfortunately, they had an uncanny resemblance to the U.S. Postal Service uniforms.

I've often thought the Korean War shouldn't be termed "the forgotten war," but rather the "second-hand war." Our air group fielded Corsairs, and from Japanese bases came Superforts and Mustangs. Now, though, pilots worried about MIGs, instead of ME109s and Zeros. Sometimes it seemed as if the old conflict had just taken a brief pause, and most of the same characters had come back on stage after intermission. MacArthur, Radford, Mark Clark, Bradley, and Ridgeway were just some of the leaders who were giving the same orders they had given in Luzon and Normandy. The script was unchanged; only the face of the enemy was different. If you were a World War II buff, you often felt as if you were in a time warp.

But in spite of all the statistics, the resurgence of South Korea, and our dominating military position, I still had some recurring personal doubts. Was it really worth four years of my life and the lives of countless others? Did our accomplishment outweigh the cost in treasure and human life? In this situation, one emotional experience was far more telling than all the figures in the world.

One afternoon in 1985, I was sitting in my insurance office in Flushing, New York (Flushing has one of the largest Korean communities in America). I was just completing an application for an Oriental woman in her midforties, when she glanced over my shoulder to the photos on the wall. There was a picture of my Skyraider, flying over Task Force 77. She said, "Were you in World War II?" I laughed and replied, "No, I'm not that old. I was in Korea." She stared at the picture for a moment, and then at me, with a look that spoke volumes.

With tears welling up in her eyes, she said, "I was very young when the war started. We lived on the Han River just south of Seoul. My family *walked* to Pusan." It was well over a hundred miles. She reached over and ever so gently touched my arm, saying, "Thank you for saving my country." That last doubt had finally been put to rest.

Chapter 28

"We All Hear You, Dick"

My NEXT R & R TOOK ME TO the mountain resort of Karuiazawa. Located about 70 miles northwest of Tokyo, this Swiss-like village had been a favorite of the expatriate German community since the early twenties. Once again, the vacationers were primarily army personnel, and the food and facilities were outstanding. Street signs in both Japanese and German were a real oddity, however.

The mountain air was bracing, and our long walks into the hills gave us just the appetite needed to do justice to the enormous portions. Saturday evening the hotel featured a young Japanese soprano who sang arias from *Madama Butterfly*. The program included a brief synopsis of the opera, and Roberts quipped, "Only a crummy officer would treat a baby-san like that. He shudda' croaked in the end, not her."

On the train back to Yokosuka, I met Cal, an aviation storekeeper from New York City, who was stationed at the fleet supply depot on the base. We became fast friends and shared many meals at the Petty Officer's Club. This friendship indirectly gilded my reputation as a technician, one that was not completely deserved. Before my moment in the sun, however, I had to endure what was probably the low point of my electronics career.

Shortly after our return to sea, a pilot reported a noisy radio switch. This switch, located on the "joy stick," is thumb-actuated and controls both the intercom and the radio. For all the maintenance I'd performed on Skyraiders in the past two years, I'd never ventured into the cockpit. It looked like a five-minute job. Remove the plastic cover and clean the contacts.

When I took off the cover, however, six tiny wires jumped out, as if from a Jack-in-the-box. I cleaned all the exposed metal and refitted this maze, following the color code from the manual. It was an extremely tight fit, and only after a few attempts was I able to close the cover and tighten the set screws. To test my work, I called the

Champ's communications for a radio check. They heard me, noise free, "loud and clear."

The next day, as fate would have it, I was flying in the backseat of this very aircraft, with Lt. Gilmore as pilot. An "Academy man," he was a rather finicky individual: all business. After reaching altitude, I asked for permission to fire up the APS-20 radar. No reply. I asked again, thinking he might have been distracted by something in the cockpit. Still no reply. All I could hear was a clicking sound.

On the radio a few minutes later, I heard someone shouting over and over, "Can you hear me, Jack?" Finally, from another plane, came the booming voice of our team leader Commander Herman, "We all hear you, Dick." Silence.

We no sooner climbed out of the plane than Gilmore said, "Wait till I find the numbskull who screwed up my radio." I said, "Lieutenant, you just flew with him." He glared at me and stalked away.

I was puzzled. I couldn't figure out how the switch checked out perfectly the day before, but failed during the flight. After listening to my story, Kinney and Talley figured the leads were probably touching when I pushed them back into the receptacle. Being so close to the ship's antenna, the intercom registered the same as the radio. For weeks the cry "We can all hear you, Jack" followed me around the shop and Ready Room.

As long as I'd been flying from carriers, the APN-1 electronic altimeter had been plaguing the pilots and technicians. It was just too damn erratic for this type of work. The output circuit was composed of four vacuum tubes so sensitive that the manufacturer had them zoned A, B, and C. If you couldn't locate matching tubes (and, for some reason, there was always a shortage), a painstaking alignment had to be completed in the shop. This alignment held only until the next cat shot or landing. Since knowing his height is critical to a carrier pilot, there was no end to the complaints. Altimeter maintenance was always relegated to the lowest man on the totem pole, in this case, me.

During the *Champ*'s next stay in Yokosuka, I told Cal about my gaffe with the switch and happened to mention in passing my continuing frustration with the APN-1. He said he didn't know if he could help, but why not stop by with a list of what I needed, and he'd see what he could do. As a ranking AK (Aviation Storekeeper), it turned out he could do a lot. I picked up three large cartons of these ornery tubes, probably more than the whole squadron's allotment at Quonset Point.

Later on board, as I realigned the altimeters, each output circuit now had matched tubes (I kept a record in my flight suit of where each zoned pentode was). The immediate result was a marked improvement in the accuracy and stability of the equipment, but my real achievement came when I was airborne.

It wasn't long after takeoff that the pilots started to sing the same old song about erratic behavior. I'd tell him I couldn't guarantee anything, but if he'd hold it straight and level for a few minutes, I'd see what I could do. As the APN-1 sat directly behind the left rear seat, I had easy access. I'd switch tubes (I carried spares in my flight suit) until the gear was steady as a rock. In one stroke, my reputation was reversed.

Unfortunately, I never had the chance to exercise my genius in front of Lt. Gilmore. Maybe he requested I not be assigned to him, or perhaps it was just the law of averages. After we left Japan, air operations were limited to once a week.

This incident broke up what (for most of us) was an intolerably boring period. Bill Munroe also helped with his "flight commander" routine. Whenever flight ops were on, Bill (a third class AT), whether flying or not, would stroll around the passageways, clad in his flight suit, Mae West, and the biggest pair of sunglasses on the *Lake Champlain*. Standing orders for ship's company when they saw a pilot was to yell, "Attention," and flatten themselves against the bulkhead. Bill would put on his best MacArthur pose and say, "As you were, men," never breaking stride. The rest of us would stand some distance away, barely able to control ourselves. Occasionally, he'd get some odd looks in the chow line, but no one ever broached the subject.

Another time, a driver towing planes on the flight deck had a freak accident. He misjudged the distance below the elevator of a parked Banshee and neatly sliced open his forehead. He wasn't badly hurt, but he was knocked cold. Everybody was sympathetic but Munroe, who in his usual manner had the last word. "Don't feel sorry for him. He's the only guy on this tub who's had a piece of tail in the last two weeks."

At other times, it was no joking matter. When the weight of round-the-clock operations was lifted from our shoulders, it created another problem, one we thought we'd put behind us. In its place, the terrible loneliness returned and cloaked the ship, seeping into every space and compartment. We could see it in the glazed eyes on the chow line, and in the vacant looks of working men whose minds were miles away. We could see it in the faraway gaze of sailors standing for hours on the flight deck or in catwalks, trying to project their hearts and minds back across the sea. In World War II, they used to talk about the "thousand-yard stare"; here it was the ten-thousand mile longing.

While this loneliness was deeply personal, the hurt was too great to keep inside. Some of the guys could no longer remember what their sweethearts and mothers looked like, and for others, the fact that we still had more than half the time left in this deployment was nearly impossible to imagine. So we talked it over, night after night, in the gun tubs at sunset and over the fantail in the glow of the moon. It turned out to be the best therapy.

On those nights when talking didn't help, I'd write a long letter to Marianne. After an hour, I'd almost recapture that intimate feeling of being near her, for that long-range sharing of thoughts did the trick.

One night after finishing my letter, I reread a few of hers, and I could almost feel her presence. After tossing and turning for an hour in the oppressive heat, I awoke, exhausted and drenched in sweat, certain that I could smell her perfume. It was uncanny. I thought it was a dream, but it persisted. At last, I got up and made my way to the fantail. Here, I sat on a bollard and watched the wake boiling up under the stern. The turbulence was clearly visible in the full moonlight. It proved to be a poor choice to get rid of the depression.

If there was one spot on board that was guaranteed to stir your memories, it was the fantail. Unless you were a navigator, it was the only place one could record the tedious passage of distance. Underway, one patch of ocean looked exactly like the other. Watching the long wake stretch out into the night, I thought of how similar this phenomena was to the physical act of writing. A letter, once written and read, disappeared into nothingness. In a sense, the *Champ* was using this placid sea as a slate, stroking her "lines" with the action of the screws. Her message was powerful, but soon faded into the gloom. The long white road stretched into an ever fainter path until it only existed in our imagination. When I told John and Hal about my experience, they confessed to having similar sensations, but they never got out of their racks. Of all the hardships we endured, this was the worst: the cruel, bitter, grinding, unceasing loneliness.

While the fighting ensued, the crew felt their presence had a purpose, and an important one at that. In spite of the pronouncements about our preserving the peace, it was hard to generate any enthusiasm when the missions changed from close-air-support to training. Now that the war was over, the universal feeling was, "We did our part, now let's get the hell home." We resembled a group of actors who, having played a leading role "on the line," were now relegated into the endless rehearsals of training exercises. As the days wore on and the *Champ* sailed up and down the coast with her consort, it appeared as if we were just going through the motions. We had, in effect, become a task force without a task.

Chapter 29

A Mountain
in the Clouds

ONE NIGHT IN THE LATTER PART OF AUGUST, a few of us were sitting around the library when the topic turned to mountain climbing. Hillary and Tenzing had just conquered Everest, and this formerly impossible feat probably inspired even the most timid of us to think about scaling something. Murphy said with a straight face, "For openers guys, let's cross Everest off the list." Fuji seemed the right size and had the added advantage of being within a few hours train ride of Yokosuka. After talking with some of our shipmates who'd climbed it on an earlier R & R, we determined we'd need a minimum of three days. The immediate problem was choosing a time.

Initially, our band numbered three: John Robben, Rich Murphy, and myself. Later, more whitehats joined. We finally had to call a halt because each additional participant complicated our scheduling. Every man had to be in the same liberty section and be chosen for R & R at the same time (only one-third of the ship's complement is away at any given time). Luckily, Commander Lynch came to the rescue and changed some R & R assignments.

These logistical hurdles behind us, we set off for Fujiyama on the morning of 26 August. On the train we discussed what might lie ahead of us. It only took a moment to realize that most of us thought this would be a lark. Hadn't thousands of people, many of them very old, already reached the summit this year, and countless others in times past? We'd heard most Japanese considered it a religious duty to scale it at least once.

One salient fact tempered our optimism, however. Regardless of how one minimized the difficulties, Fuji still stood 12,305 feet, and none of us had ever climbed anything higher than a bar stool.

At the right time of the year, middle June until early August, the climb is relatively easy. After that, because of high winds and sudden storms, it's not recommended. Due to our diversity on board, late August was the only time slot available. No one showed any concern as the train wound its way through the mountains on the way to Hakone National Park.

That afternoon we checked in at the Fuji New Grand Hotel. With its peaked roofs and timbered ceilings, it could have been a chalet in the Swiss Tyrol. It was not out of place. Walking among the towering pines and inhaling that sweet cool mountain air, we wouldn't have thought it unusual to hear yodeling echoing through the hills.

At supper, the talk centered on the next day's journey. We had almost no idea what type of terrain lay before us or how long it would take to cover it. We were the only prospective climbers among the registered guests. One older army sergeant said it was obvious the navy didn't do a lot of walking. The infantry would have more sense than to engage in what was essentially a forced march on a weekend pass.

Not the least of our concerns was food. The manager said there were no eating facilities once we left the hotel. This was another disadvantage of making the ascent out of season. He advised taking boxed lunches, and it turned out to be good counsel.

A little before dawn, the six of us downed a quick breakfast and headed out onto the trail. Under a light drizzle, we completed the first twenty-five hundred feet on horseback. It was painfully slow. Leaving our animals at the timber line, we started climbing in earnest at the 6,000-foot level. Shortly before, we had purchased climbing sticks. These not only helped us keep our footing, but enabled us to record each thousand-foot stage with a marker burned into the wood. Tiny wayside lodges dotted the mountainside where, besides marking our progress, we could stop for a hot cup of tea.

Our earlier feelings of optimism quickly faded once we took a few steps in that loose black volcanic ash. After about ten minutes, I started to sense some real doubts about our ability to make it all the way. Sharp pieces of this mixture found their way into our shoes, and we seemed to be stopping as much as we were climbing.

We'd expected gorgeous vistas once we cleared the trees, as all the postcards in the hotel lobby proclaimed views that rivaled Everest. Instead, we were enveloped in fog and low clouds. No matter how much we struggled, we always seemed to be stuck in the same place. It was as if we were on a treadmill.

The first couple of hours of starts and stops behind us, we began to get our second wind and established a rhythm. Moving steadily, we reached the seventh station at 2:30 P.M., and we were now at 8,000 feet. It started to rain. We agreed on a twenty-minute break and drank some cold tea. I'd brought a small bottle of saki, which I'd saved for a time like this. I needed warming up. For all the effect it had, it might as well have been Coke.

Fuji, which looked so symmetrical in photos, was now shapeless. Our progress was difficult to record because one rock looked like the other and there were no landmarks. This was a mountain with seemingly a beginning and an end, but no middle.

At 9,000 feet, we were reaching the limits of our endurance. Each step was an effort. The wind came on with a vengeance, the rain pelted, and the sky grew dark with angry menace. Murphy and I became separated from the others. As we climbed higher, violent gusts of wind caused us to flatten ourselves against the rocks to keep from being blown over the side. In the thin air, our lungs ached, and it seemed we could never get enough oxygen. I reached a point where I was certain I could go no further, but I was equally certain I must.

Looking down, we could make out John, Al, Don, and Ken making their way tenaciously along the trail. The mist had already blanketed the last way station from view. Every few minutes, a sweeping gust would punch a hole in the gloom, revealing patches of blue and even fleeting glimpses of the valley and lakes below.

We had little time to enjoy the views, however brief, because our daylight would not last much longer. This was another reason the climbing season centered around early summer. Murph and I decided to pull away and see if we could find an occupied hut up ahead. The one at 10,000 feet had been locked.

The cold rain started to fall in sheets, and we lost the trail. It took us nearly forty minutes to locate the familiar stakes imbedded in the rocks. By now, what had previously been an annoying rain was turning into sleet. My lungs burned, and to add to my misery, rainwater kept running down my back. In the sleet, I had trouble watching the trail and often fell into sharp outcroppings, cutting my knees and shins. Rich shared my pain, but never complained.

The hut at the 11,000-foot level was open. It was 6 P.M., and the temperature outside was 34 degrees. Here we met other climbers for the first time since we'd left the horses. Horses? Had that been the same day? It seemed like a week ago.

Our new companions were an air force sergeant and his two Japanese guides. Murph and I asked them if we could accompany them to the summit, only a little more than 1,300 feet up. They didn't think that it was a good idea; they, in fact, were on their way down. In less than half an hour, it would be totally dark, and it would be too hazardous to continue in this high wind. They estimated the gusts near the top to be close to sixty knots. When they'd met a descending climber 500 feet above us, he told them that the summit lodge was closed for the season. They continued climbing for a while, hoping the light would last long enough for a round trip, but finally conceded it was foolhardy. They suggested we all bed down here for the night. Tomorrow we could continue.

Sadly, we knew there'd be no tomorrow for our group. We had to be back at the Fuji New Grand by afternoon and on a train by early evening. For a moment we half wanted to push on. That damn summit was so tantalizingly close. But deep down, we knew we were just kidding ourselves.

Twenty minutes later, the remnants of our party appeared, frozen and exhausted, and we all collapsed on the bamboo floor of the station. Our hosts could offer us only a few rice balls, but it was warm, and there was no lack of hot tea. It was fascinating to watch the young Japanese couple eat their rice and feed their baby-san around the glowing embers of a coal fire. It wasn't long before we all fell into a coma. Luckily, we were too exhausted to realize how hungry we were. While we were asleep, the young woman hung up our wet clothes to dry over the fire.

Bright sunlight streaming through the window had us up at dawn (this was getting to be a habit). Outside, it was almost dead calm, and though it was only 38 degrees, we felt 100 percent better in dry clothes. After some hot tea laced with the remainder of my saki, we started down. Our "hosts" charged us the magnificent sum of 35 yen for food, tea, and lodging—about ten cents American.

Now we had long stretches where the green valleys and distant mountains were revealed in picture-postcard glory. It was as if the mountain, having beaten us, was finally giving out with a small reward. We even forgot our aching muscles and sore feet. By 9 A.M., the clouds returned, teaching us a lifelong lesson: mountain viewing is for the early riser. On a straight and level road about a half mile from the hotel, I severely twisted my ankle and had to limp the rest of the way with my weight on my climbing stick. After hot showers and steak and eggs, someone at the hotel taped my swollen ankle so I could walk without too much pain. My climbing stick was now a cane. We all breathed a silent prayer of thanksgiving that no one had been hurt on the upper reaches of Mount Fuji. None of us wanted to speculate on what might have happened.

As we departed, the manager was kind enough to ask about our expedition. When we related our tale of frustration, he bolstered our good judgment by telling us about two army officers who were blown off and killed the preceding August in a similar storm.

Our train's swaying motion soon had us in dreamland, secure in the belief that our adventures were behind us. Alas, our train was late arriving in Tokyo and we had to look for immediate accommodations to conform to the midnight curfew. With only ten minutes to the witching hour, an M.P. directed us to a small Japanese hotel, a ryokan. Here, we slept on bamboo rugs, our heads resting on pillows stuffed with sand pebbles. Our breakfast was rice balls and fish, instead of bacon and eggs. It turned out to be the perfect curtain closer to a memorable weekend.

Our mountain climbing days were over. True, the six of us hadn't reached the top like so many of our shipmates. The effort alone would have to be triumph enough. John Robben wrote a fine account for the *Champ*'s newspaper, and my short story made it into a local daily in the Bronx. It wasn't exactly the *New York Times* best-seller list, but at least it showed that our Fordham University English courses hadn't gone to waste.

Chapter 30

Hong Kong Holiday

Back on the *CHAMP*, we'd scarcely regained our sea legs when we received some glorious news. During our next liberty stop in Japan, we'd transfer our Corsair squadron back to the *Boxer*. More importantly, we'd pick up over a hundred army, navy, and Marine Corps veterans of Korea and transport them to Hong Kong for an eight-day R & R. No one had expected anything approaching this astounding change of itinerary, and it turned out to be the perfect tonic to jolt us out of our doldrums.

While we were in Sasebo, taking on some stores, there was a British carrier in the harbor. We never operated with them up north, as they worked another part of the coast. This was the first Royal Navy ship I'd seen since leaving Port Said.

I didn't have liberty, so I was sitting in the cool Ready Room, watching Rhonda Fleming give us butterflies in our groins. "Jungle Jim" Herman (our skipper) came in and tapped me on the shoulder. I knew it was trouble. "Jack, I hate to break up your dreams, but CAG just called and wants each team to delegate an aircrewman to show some of your limey counterparts around the ship. You're the only one on board from VC-12, and I know we won't be ashamed of you. So, quick like a rabbit, change into undress whites, and hop up to the quarterdeck." There went my afternoon with Rhonda and all those beautiful dreams. Two or three of the other guys heard Jungle Jim and gave me the razz. "Don't drink too much tea, Jack."

By the time I got up to the hangar deck, the three British airmen were waiting for me. There was supposed to be another AC from the *Champ*, but he never showed. The OOD said, "Don't wait, you show them around." I asked him if there was any kind of a program, but he said no, just use your head and answer their questions. It's a good will gesture to promote allied unity.

Trying to make the best of a lost afternoon, I engaged them in conversation and found they were a fascinating bunch. They were in their thirties, and none had served less than eight years. They'd all seen combat, and since I was a World War II buff, I was in my glory.

One of them had been on board the carrier *Ark Royal* when she caught the *Bismarck* in 1941, and he told me some exciting stories about flying as a radioman/gunner in the backseat of one of those fiber-covered biplanes. I showed them around the flight deck, the hangar deck, our electronics shop, and finally inside the backseat of an AD4W. They were interested in everything. After an hour, we repaired to the library and had a few Cokes before returning to the quarter deck.

I was kind of sorry to see them go. As we were saying our good-byes, their senior man asked our OOD if they could return the compliment and take me back to their carrier. Our officer of the deck said he saw no reason why not and told me to have a good time, being sure to return to the *Champ* by 1700. Their launch had us on board the HMS *Ocean* in no time, and they gave me their 25-cent tour. I was surprised at how small their carrier was, about two-thirds the length of *CVA-39*. What had taken me an hour, they did in twenty minutes, explaining that it was much too hot to crawl around aircraft. As it turned out, they'd also been conned into this excursion by some PR type and would much rather have spent the day relaxing. They led me to their "canteen," as they called it, and I expected a cool soda to quench my thirst. Instead, they had a regular bartender, who asked what I wanted. My look of surprise left them laughing, and then it dawned on them that American ships were dry, but the British Navy wasn't. I had a Scotch and water, and they drank some vile-looking dark beer. We exchanged sea stories for the rest of the afternoon, and I almost needed help getting down their accommodation ladder into the boat. Luckily, the same OOD was on our quarterdeck, and when he returned my salute and smelled my breath, he just winked and said, "Sailor, I'd watch that cough medicine if I were you. It can make you dizzy."

I returned to the Ready Room. There was another movie on, this time with Ava Gardner, but the best part of my day was "breathing" on my shipmates, who'd given me the bird. I told them, "That was the best 'tea' I ever had."

As we left Sasebo with our new guests on board, the ship took on the trappings of a pleasure cruise. Except for one day's flight operations in each direction (which incidentally was a great treat for the ground troops), it was holiday routine all the way. Our galley laid on plenty of steak and ice cream, and there were extra movies and bingo. After the harsh combat conditions of Korea, these guys must have thought they had died and gone to heaven.

Sailing south in the China Sea, I noticed what I thought was an officer wearing "suntans" staring at me among the sunbathers on the flight deck. He looked vaguely familiar. His opening line was, "Don't call me sir, I'm an enlisted man just like you. Don't let this uniform fool you." Comparing notes, we discovered we'd been in Great Lakes together in the late summer of 1950. It all seemed so long ago.

Jack Burgess was two years younger than me, but looked every bit of thirty-five. His hair had turned completely white. A premed student before the war, he'd become a hospital corpsman and had served with the marines in Korea. That explained the suntans, since navy personnel attached to the Corps wore the marines uniform. We remembered a lunch I'd had at his house at Oak Park, near Chicago, and tried to recall some of the other recruits at boot camp. "Popeye" and the "Armed Guard" came quickly to mind. Neither of us had ever run into any of the boys from Company 248. I showed him around the ship and took him into the backseat of a Skyraider. He couldn't begin to imagine flying off this deck.

Later, one of his buddies filled me in on some things that had puzzled me. Burgess had been wounded three times. He could have gone home after the first wound but insisted on returning to his unit. His combat experiences had netted him the Silver and Bronze Stars and three Purple Hearts, in addition to all that white hair. In all our talks, he'd never even hinted at any of this.

At eighteen knots, it took us two-and-a-half days to reach Hong Kong. Those lingering sunsets on the China Sea were breathtaking. In the early evenings, all hands on deck were struck silent by the unfolding panorama of clouds, sea, and sky. When the fiery red ball finally dropped below the horizon, night came swiftly, changing the ocean into the color of steel. Our guests were particularly fascinated by the flying fish. Some would sit the whole afternoon, watching them on our bow wave. A few needed to be convinced that they weren't, in fact, birds.

On the Sunday before we reached our destination, an interesting item appeared in *The Lectern*, Chaplain Kelly's weekly parish bulletin. It said, "Next Sunday, something Catholic. A collection! We're raising some money for a mission church in Kowloon, and I don't want to see any coins!"

I should note that Mass and Protestant services were held every Sunday on the hangar deck, except when preempted by flight operations. Attendance was voluntary, but a surprisingly large crowd turned out, week after week. Chaplain Budd, the Protestant padre, had the use of the band, but the Catholics sang just as lustily, if not more so. Prior to the start of services, Father Kelly would hold last-minute confessions for those who'd missed him earlier. There were no dark alcoves here. You just walked up in plain sight and related your sins. It was yet another barrier broken by the navy.

While I always attended Mass, I somehow felt my most sincere praying was done in the backseat of a Skyraider. In the air, I had this strong feeling of being closer to God, and it wasn't only the altitude. Considering all the rash promises made to the Almighty from that vantage point, I often thought it would be only appropriate to change the plexiglass bubble (in the backseat) to stained glass when these 4Ws finally made it to a museum.

Just after dawn on the last day of September, the humped shapes of a series of islands came out of the shimmering mist. A magnificent sunrise transformed this landscape into the soft, liquid tones of a living Monet. Hong Kong had been endowed with the most beautiful harbor in the Far East. Jaded as we were after nearly girdling the globe, we would have had to be blind not to glory in that sight.

Entering the anchorage, we had two panoramas to choose from. On our right lay the island of Victoria, also known as Hong Kong Island. Rising almost vertically from the waterfront, row upon row of banks, hotels, and apartments edged up the hillside, finally giving way to the natural greenery near the summit. Vying for our attention was Kowloon, the city directly across the harbor, which was attached to the Chinese mainland. Not as dramatic at first sight, it still held the promise of great shopping, exotic eating, and it was, according to the old-timers, the closest approximation to the real China around today.

Everyone on board had impossible expectations, but somehow they were all realized. Hong Kong was accustomed to delivering the impossible. It was a never-never land come true.

The travel booklets handed out by the *Champ*'s information office were more a hindrance than a help. With so many spectacular sights to see, there was really no logical place to begin. This was a port for plunging right in. One could close one's eyes and thrust a pin anywhere on the map. It was that good.

A ship's notice put Kowloon out of bounds to all officers and men in uniform, but fortunately, we'd had the foresight to pick up some slacks and sport shirts in Japan. We were among the very few whitehats roaming the streets of the mainland. This directive gave us the advantage of a lot less competition and doubled our bargaining chips.

The big attractions filled our card that first morning. From a ride to the summit on the Peak Tram, to the weird Tiger Balm Gardens,

we tried to absorb all the sights, sounds, and smells of this unbe-
lievable metropolis. The real sights, the ones that remained in our
memories forever, were those found on every street. Life here was
lived under the sky. With the city's normal population swelled to
nearly double, the less affluent merchants and hawkers took to the
teeming streets and alleys to set up shop.

Wood carvers, jade dealers, bird-sellers, and purveyors of everything edible overflowed the narrow sidewalks. We didn't walk, we
oozed our way along in this mass of humanity, trying to remain alert
enough not to miss anything. It was a losing battle. After five or six
blocks, we were drained physically and emotionally. The brain can
absorb just so many images before its circuits become overloaded. If
you have ever tried to "do" a major museum in one day, you know
what I mean.

We decided to pull over onto a "siding" for some badly needed refueling. Over an open brazier, lamb with curry was being roasted,
and we washed it down with some good English beer. In that blazing sun and humidity, it was just what the doctor ordered.

Back on board, John Williford found the name of a good tailor
recommended by an editor friend of his dad, and we planned to
order our "tailor-mades" the next day. Before we could make decisions on jackets, trousers, and sweaters, however, John Robben
strongly suggested that we buy some tickets which were being sold
through his office for a tour conducted by a smashing Eurasian
guide. When it came to girls, most sailors exaggerate, but here his
description was, if anything, understated. She was stunning. We
decided to combine the two outings, doing the tailoring in the morning and the tour in the afternoon. Lee, the guide, said she was not
due to work the next day, but if we could gather up a few more
sailors, she'd give us a privately escorted tour. Her girlfriend, who
was a mother's helper to a teenage British girl, would accompany us.
It was obvious after a few minutes what had changed her mind. She
was stuck on Williford. The rest of us were just window dressing.

Early the following morning, Murphy, Danny (of Coke fame),
Robben, Williford, and I took the liberty boat to Victoria. There we
quickly boarded the Star Ferry to Kowloon. On board, we changed
into our civilian garb. We felt like different people. No saluting for
openers.

Hong Kong harbor was alive with every imaginable kind of vessel, from tiny bumboats to massive gray warships. A great number
of smaller craft scurried in and around the anchored ships, barely
missing one another in the choppy waters. The ferry cost the equivalent of 2 cents (U.S.) and was, without a doubt, the best buy in the

Crown colony. Our only regret was that the ride lasted less than ten minutes.

Once ashore, Williford (our undisputed Hong Kong leader) hailed a taxi, and in no time at all we were at Harialea's, probably the finest clothier in the Far East. The Indian owners said they were familiar with John's referral and laid out the red carpet. Later, we figured they'd do the same thing for any group of Americans, the dollar being as strong as it was. Before they showed us their inventory of woolens and silks, they plied us with drinks and cigarettes. Pretty young Chinese girls appeared carrying gleaming trays of small sandwiches and a selection of hot delicacies called dim sum. This was our first taste of shopping Hong Kong style, and we were sold.

When it was time to get down to business, just about every one of us made a serious logistical error. For the last six months, we'd all been running up and down ladders in a heat and humidity that burned every ounce of fat from our bodies. We forgot we were ordering tailor-made clothes for what would shortly be a civilian way of life, with all the attendant bulges in our waist lines. Most of us had been away so long, it was hard to think in those terms. I weighed 153 pounds. Six months after my discharge I was nearly 200 pounds and couldn't close the gorgeous cashmere jacket I had purchased. Well, it was fun while it lasted.

After we had dropped a couple of paychecks, our hosts took us to a Russian restaurant for an enormous lunch. We reboarded the Star Ferry and in a short time found Lee, looking even more radiant in the sunlight. The three girls, with the five of us in tow, drew admiring glances from the hundreds of sailors cruising Kings Road. Victoria was awash in white uniforms.

Lee's tour took us past double-decker trams and encompassed the cathedral, the cenotaph, and finally the botanical gardens, where we all had a drink. The cenotaph was a particularly impressive war memorial commemorating the thousands of British Empire troops who had died defending this colony in the first few days after Pearl Harbor. Hong Kong had been the scene of some of the bitterest fighting, and although the outcome was never in doubt, the British fought well against overwhelming odds. The Japanese had expected a walk-through, but when the Allied troops fought them for every yard, they became enraged, committing some of the worst atrocities of the war. Scores of captured soldiers were thrown from the cliffs above Repulse Bay. Twelve years had erased all signs of battle, and the average officer or whitehat would never have imagined how much blood had flowed in these streets now thronged with sailors and tourists.

Later in the afternoon, we took a drive to Repulse Bay for a swim.

The white sandy beach ringed a protected lagoon, and with water temperatures in the 80s, none of us wanted to leave. Towards sunset, we decided to take the girls to dinner as a way of saying thanks. Williford had made a reservation in a top restaurant overlooking the harbor. When we arrived, the maitre d' welcomed us but then quickly drew John aside. He'd be happy to accommodate the five men in our party, he said, but were we aware our guide was perhaps the most notorious prostitute in all Hong Kong? We were speechless.

Lee may have guessed what had transpired, for she remarked that this was a lovely place, but much too expensive. She and her friends would be uncomfortable knowing we'd spent so much money. Besides, she knew a fabulous floating restaurant in Aberdeen that was unique to the colony and had some of its finest food. This quickly saved us from a potentially embarrassing situation, and we were all visibly relieved. After another elaborate dinner (this time Chinese) in spectacular surroundings, we took Lee back to the ferry terminal. She went home to Kowloon; we went home to the ship, ending a memorable day. The mystery of her double life was left unsolved.

The next day brought still another surprise in a place that was turning the eye-popping into routine. Since our anchor had splashed into the harbor three days before, we'd been surrounded by tiny boats of every description. Some of these bumboats would lay off our accommodation ladder, offering to take anyone ashore who didn't want to wait for the next liberty launch. Most of this floating market was manned by merchants who'd hold up everything from silk pajamas to teakwood chests. Once a price was agreed on, the merchandise would be hauled up by line. For security reasons, the boats were not permitted to tie up to the *Champ* but had to keep their distance. Later in our stay, a full-scale oriental bazaar was set up on the hangar deck, and hundreds of watches, silks, cameras, and chests changed hands amid much good-natured haggling. It was a case of "If Mohammed couldn't come to the mountain...."

What came alongside this morning was none of these, but was, in its own way, the most exotic craft in the harbor. Here was a sampan loaded to the gunnels with ship's painters who, without setting a foot on board, were going to paint the 880-foot hull of the *Lake Champlain*. What made it all the more fascinating was that the entire crew was composed of women. They were called, appropriately enough, "Mary Soo's Side Cleaners."

We supplied the paint, Navy Gray, and they supplied the skill and the sweat. Wide brushes extended from tapered bamboo poles, up to thirty feet long. The finished job couldn't have been neater had they been doing the Sistine Chapel. Our hull was given two coats.

The price? Our garbage. After all the leftovers from noon chow were delivered, three Chinese women would painstakingly separate the vegetable, the bone, the meat, and the starches into large metal cans. This was recycling at its best, and these people had been doing it for centuries.

Near the end of our stay, there was a big Communist holiday, celebrating the October revolution. To avoid any incidents during the parades, all liberty was canceled. Not even officers were permitted ashore. This was at the direct request of the British government, which had to maintain good relations with the mainland.

It became a day to complete all the chores we'd been postponing. In our eyes, seeing Hong Kong was a once-in-a-lifetime event, far more important than writing letters, sewing socks, or catching up with *War and Peace*. Now we were given that day. For most, it was a chance to catch up on sack time.

In my three years in the navy, I'd met almost all the old gang from New York City. Dick Landy at Great Lakes, Corky Kern at Memphis, Hal Atkins at Norfolk, and Don Roller (same squadron, same shop) at Quonset Point. The odds on this happening again were almost too great to calculate.

I was stretched out in my rack that October morning, trying to coax a slight breeze through the open port, when Ruprecht, a quartermaster 2d class, came into the compartment and stopped at my side. "You'll never believe this, Jack," he said. In my time in the navy, I'd heard every ploy for getting someone out of their rack, so I smiled and said, "What won't I believe?" I wondered what kind of wild story he'd dreamed up. Ruprecht said, "I know this sounds crazy, but a freighter just entered the harbor and someone on their bridge wanted to know if you were on board. I wrote down the exact message: 'Is Jack Sauter, VC-12 on board?' I replied, 'Affirmative,' and the sender said he'd come over later in the day." Ruprecht looked serious, but I'd been burned before. "Oh yeah, and what was his name?" Without a moment's hesitation, he replied, "I can't pronounce it, but it's spelled Czu...." I stopped him in midsentence and leaped out of my rack. Nobody could make up a name like that. I bounded up the ladder to the bridge, where through the telescope, I identified the freighter as the *Flying Eagle*, Harold Czubaruk's ship. Halfway around the world, another buddy had found me. Ripley would have smiled.

The *Lake Champlain* was restricted, but when Harold appeared on the quarterdeck, he convinced the OOD that we wouldn't go ashore, but only to his ship for a visit. Luckily, the officer was a pilot from VC-33 who knew me. He'd make an exception, if I'd give him my word I wouldn't go into Hong Kong. I agreed, and off we went in the bumboat. Over a bottle of Scotch in Harold's cabin (he was second mate), we celebrated the circumstances that had brought us together. Fortunately, he'd remembered the *Champ*'s number. Even more astonishing was the fact that out of 3,500 men his message was received by one of the few who knew me. When Ruprecht said I wouldn't believe this, he didn't know how true it was.

Hal filled me in on everyone at home and said he'd seen Marianne six weeks before. She looked terrific and missed me. Two out of two. It was a memorable reunion, as we discussed old times and old pals. We'd known each other since we were ten years old and, among other adventures, had spent V-J evening in Times Square together. One last note on the coincidence. It was fortunate that this was a Communist holiday. If I'd been on liberty, we'd never have met because the *Flying Eagle* was sailing the next day.

Back with the gang, I tried more shopping, but the heat and humidity finally drove us from downtown. We took a cab to the Repulse Bay Hotel and rented cabanas. Here, in between some delicious swims, we were served lunch and drinks on our private terrace. I have a photo from that afternoon, and none of us looked like an enlisted man. The Chinese staff treated us like kings, and I guess that's what we were, kings for a day.

Williford was, in many ways, more than a 24-hour king; he was our indisputable leader. Maybe not in any formal sense, but he had a lot more experience than the rest of us combined. John's family had traveled extensively, and he possessed a maturity far beyond his years. Like most of my shipmates, I'd taken our weekly paper *The Champ* for granted. It wasn't until I had an opportunity to view the efforts of other carriers and battleships that I realized what special talents our editor had.

John had a particular knack of encompassing every facet of our daily lives in a way that satisfied everyone, from messcook to Air Group commander. Whether it was Commander Hunley's "You and Your Health" or the "Chaplain's Corner," there was literally something for all hands. He compressed every imaginable interest into a four-page booklet and still found room for a crossword puzzle, baby pictures, and a couple of shapely pin-ups.

In the course of our eight-month deployment, every department was highlighted, including all the squadrons and teams of the air group. But in spite of this universal appeal, what I remember most was the way he highlighted those unique people in our midst, like Norm Bricker, the Olympic equestrian, and "Pop" Snow, our shoemaker, who at 56 was undoubtedly the oldest man on board.

Author at the Tiger Balm Gardens, Hong Kong, October 1953.

Although he could write up a storm, John displayed a real sense of humanity for those less gifted. He designed the paper so it could be easily folded and mailed home, thereby providing a regular conduit of news from the crew to their loved ones. For that part of the complement to whom letter writing was one step from the Chinese water torture, John was a Godsend.

Our final day in Hong Kong was spent collecting our "tailor-mades," revisiting the Tiger Balm Gardens, and taking a last lingering look from the peak above the harbor. Sipping some fantastic concoction, we toasted the best and most exotic port we'd ever seen. More than one guy would have welcomed another rendezvous with Lee, but that was wishful thinking.

As the liberty launch moved away from the pier, we gazed back, trying to burn this last image into our collective memories. In the late evening, the harbor seemed softer and less frenzied. On the roads circling the island, headlights flashed on and off, shining briefly like fireflies. Hong Kong, like most cities on the water, was best seen at night. Necklaces of sparkling lights draped the black hills, resembling some giant string of pearls. Bigger "diamonds" flashed along the waterfront: the hotel marquees and neon boulevards, all evolving into an Oriental "Great White Way." Closer in, the sampans and bumboats carefully picked their way through the crowded anchorage, their solitary beacons thrusting fingers of light on the rippling dark waters.

Chapter 31

A Last Look

OUR HIGH SPIRITS WERE DAMPENED on the return voyage when another sailor fell over the side during the night. Unfortunately, his disappearance wasn't noticed until morning muster at 0800. Any attempt at rescue seemed futile, but nonetheless we notified all ships and aircraft on our track to keep a sharp lookout. He was never found.

With hundreds of men sleeping on the flight deck on those hot, humid evenings, it was assumed that he'd lost his footing on one of the ladders leading from the catwalk and had fallen into the sea. The distance was about eighty feet, and the chance of surviving such a fall was pretty slim. Of course, there was a possibility, however remote. Many of us were haunted by thoughts of him floating in the China Sea, watching the carrier fade into the night. We could think of better ways to die.

Returning to Yokosuka, our visitors disembarked, and we regained our full complement of aircraft. Our stint as a "cruise liner" was over. During our three-day layover, the *Champ* was restored to her status as a fighting ship, and we sailed once more into the waters off Korea. Task Force 77 was down to two carriers and six destroyers and now spent only three weeks at sea before being rotated. Bill Munroe quipped that since we had only half our original ships, perhaps we should call ourselves Task Force 38 1/2.

Life once again fell into the old, well-worn pattern, with training missions and drills day in and day out. We had to be careful not to relax completely. Death could still claim you six different ways on the flight deck, even without the bombs and rockets. Also, our pilots had to gather up every ounce of skill to bring their planes back safely on board.

Our team worked with the ease of a well-oiled machine, and by now we knew even the smallest idiosyncrasy of each pilot. From a distance, it would appear that every carrier landing was the same, but from our vantage-point, there were major differences.

Some pilots took pride in catching the same wire almost every landing. Others had difficulty maintaining a steadily decreasing speed and altitude, and as a result the approach was a series of spurts and stops. Mr. Madison, if nothing else, was consistent. Worried about the possibility of being low and slow, the most fatal of all mistakes, he always came in high. Once over the deck, he'd nose it over and boom, we'd be down. To say it was a hard landing was the understatement of the cruise. Watching the faces of the metalsmiths (who were responsible for the landing gear) said it all. They were waiting for the day the landing struts would go right through the wings. Those of us who shared the flight learned to brace ourselves, lifting our hindquarters a few inches off the seat. This way, we weren't forced to eat noon chow standing up. Whatever each pilot's method, they all worked. During the entire cruise, none of our planes so much as caught a barrier.

One of our navigational flights carried me over some small island off the coast of South Korea. Those wooded green hills, ringed with the pounding surf, were a pleasant contrast to the endless ocean. We went round and round a few times, trying to pick out some individual buildings. When we finally leveled off and headed back on course, we flew very low over a small fleet of fishing smacks returning with their catch. On each and every deck, there was absolute panic, a multitude of praying, and white flag waving.

It took us a few moments to solve this mystery, but Mr. Quinn finally figured it was our radome that was bothering them. They probably thought it was an atomic bomb and that after a few dry runs, we would be ready to drop it ... on them!

When *CVA-39* eased into her berth under the massive cranes of Yokosuka, we noticed a new arrival. Across the pier sat USS *Oriskany* (CVA-34), our relief. She was more than a welcome sight, she was our ticket to home.

Personnel that had been detached to Korea returned to the *Champ*. Missing was one F3D Skynight, with the pilot, Lt. (j.g.) Robert Brick, and his aircrewman, Linton Smith, chief aviation electronics technician of VC-4. They had been flying night missions over North Korea and were shot down by heavy flak on 2 July 1953.

So the final tally was taken. Nine men would not return home. Of these, five were direct combat deaths. Four pilots and one aircrewmen paid the price of liberty. On the *Champ*, at least, the aircrewmen losses continued at the high rate set in World War II.

Those last few precious days were a time for tying up loose ends, for finally buying that Noritake china or one of those exquisite kimonos. Each of us tried to find room in an already-stuffed cruise box to fit some of those irresistible Japanese dolls or miniature sampans. The names on the bottom of our gift list had to settle for small. Among the more popular items were Zippo lighters (with the *Champ*'s logo), wristwatches, and elaborately carved penknives.

It was also a time to say good-bye to Tokyo, Yokohama, and, of course, Yokosuka. A time to bid a sad farewell to a favorite baby-san or bartender and a time to regret not having taken that last R & R or not having experienced the real Japan, away from the port cities. Would we ever get another chance for a bath at the Tokyo Osen or a trip to Nikko? Most of us couldn't wait for the lines to be singled up and to see the coastline disappear behind our fantail, but there were some who were leaving with real regret. For many on board, Yokosuka and her people had become a second home, a home not easily duplicated 20,000 sea miles from here. Mostly, there was a quiet gentleness in these people that would be sorely missed in the weeks and months ahead.

The men of the *Champ* had always felt welcome here, and sadly this could not always be said for American liberty ports. No matter how noisy or (at times) rough and ready we were, we found the Japanese ever kind and polite, waiting to minister to our individual needs and satisfy our whims. Feelings ran deep on that morning of 17 October 1953, as we watched the coastline fade into the misty horizon.

But there was another side of the coin. With each turn of the screws, Task Force 77 and all it had meant to us faded further from our memory: no more bomb runs, no more darken ship, no more Korea. As the ship turned her prow into the deeper blue waves of the Pacific, an almost audible sigh of relief could be heard from every compartment. We were really going home.

CAG, the Air Group Commander, notified us that in compliance with new economy regulations, air operations on the return trip would be held no more than once a week. This would be just about sufficient for all the flying personnel to earn their flight pay. At the same time, this directive effectively changed the aircrewmen into passengers for the long voyage home. With all this free time to fill, I volunteered my services to the newly formed cruise book staff.

Chapter 32

Retracing Our Steps

As FAR BACK AS ANYONE COULD REMEMBER, all large naval vessels (cruisers, battleships, and carriers) published cruise books to commemorate their voyages. These books became the premier souvenir, neatly packaging all one's memories into one convenient volume. With the exception of a handful of old-timers, everyone signed on to buy one. For a great number on board, this would naturally resemble their high school yearbook, only now it would relate their adventures as men, not boys.

Besides chronicling all our exotic ports of call, each shipboard division was featured at work and at play. Finally, everyone from the skipper on down sat for a formal portrait, much like those class pictures of grammar school days. This project touched the heart of every whitehat. The whole effort was accomplished by the officers and men, with no outside professional help.

I never discovered when this custom started, but we had some excellent examples going back to World War II. One, from the USS *Iowa* (BB61), was as professional a job as I'd ever seen. Weighing over a pound, with a bronze silhouette of the ship mounted into the front cover, it easily held its own with the best college yearbooks. From a naval historian's point of view, these were as prized as a latter-day Rosetta Stone. If the men of the *Enterprise* (CV-6) wrote one (and I certainly hope they did), one could record almost the entire Pacific War, from Pearl Harbor to Japan, just from that one ship.

The closest the navy came to a "universal cruise book" was one produced by Edward Steichen at the end of the war. Steichen, one of the world's great cameramen, headed up the navy's photographic division. From a fantastic collection of prints (most of which he took himself), he fashioned a unique pictorial record of the U.S. Navy and Marines, in every theatre of operations. Near the end of the war, he offered it to a publisher, with the proviso that a soft-cover copy be furnished to every sailor and marine, free of charge.

The *Lake Champlain* couldn't brag of having a Steichen, but we did have access to hundreds of professional prints amassed by our photographic department. These were heavily leavened with the snapshots of the crew. The photos we used were half official and half crew donations, and all were enlarged by the photo department to eight by ten.

Working on the cruise book, was, next to flying, my most rewarding experience on the *Champ*. Our nine-man staff included three officers. Lt. Cmdr. Wicker and Lt. (j.g.) Elliott ran the photo lab, and Ensign Bill Ward had a real flair for good short prose. After our initial meeting, everything was on a first name basis. Since we were all volunteers, there was no need for musters and other time-wasters. If you didn't feel the urge to show up, no one put you on report. It was strictly a labor of love, and when we got hold of a good idea, we often worked into the night.

To give the staff ample room to work without interruption, we were allotted the use of the Flag Plot and the admiral's quarters, both of which were now vacant. More than twice the area of our berthing compartment (which, incidentally, housed twenty-five men), the admiral's plot was more than adequate for our task. The old lesson that rank hath its privileges wasn't lost on us. When we weren't actively laboring on the book, it was a convenient hideaway to write letters or drink coffee after lights out. The adjoining quarters even boasted a real full-size bath tub.

Dave Crosby, a navy journalist, was the driving force behind the project. A whiz at magazine layout, he produced drawings that were striking and humorous. If there was one indispensable man, it was Dave. Bill Ward and John Williford followed closely on Dave's heels and were aided by John Robben, George Walls, Don Caulfield, and myself. We all gilded the book with some prose and layout ideas, but since the aim was essentially visual, our writing efforts were in the end simply window dressing. Still, it was a new experience, and it gave us a tremendous sense of pride and accomplishment to see it take shape.

As we sailed south again into the China Sea, the oppressive humidity returned. For a short while in Japan, we'd felt the first stirrings of autumn, and it was pure heaven. A glance at the map showed us that before we could turn west, we still had hundreds of miles to travel south, and south meant hot and hotter. We moved so far down the charts, we nearly recrossed the equator. Gratifying as it might have been to be on the opposite side of a Shellback ceremony, it wasn't in the cards. The few uninitiated souls on board just weren't worth the trouble.

For six days and nights, *CVA-39* cut a solitary wake on this flat tropic sea. For the first time since leaving Norfolk, we were without an escort. With no plane guard destroyer to rescue a downed airman, flight ops were put on hold. While no one in the air group complained, I'm sure the ship's company considered us about as useful as a space heater.

This enforced idleness soon took its toll. We began to measure the interminable length of this long voyage home. The number of days and hours was painfully large. Some masochists even figured out the minutes. They were lucky not to have been heaved over the side.

A week to the day after leaving Yokosuka, we entered the Singapore Straits. Right on schedule, our escort appeared—four sleek destroyers boiling up on our port quarter, Gattling, Dortch, Dashiell, and Caperton. They made up Destroyer Squadron 30, and they would shepherd us to within a few miles of Mayport.

Our task unit was again sailing in historic waters. Twelve years before, in December 1941, the British battleships *Prince of Wales* and *Repulse* had been sunk by Japanese torpedo planes in little more than an hour. Three days earlier, similar aircraft had wiped out our battleline at Hawaii. At the time, many "battleship admirals" said Pearl Harbor didn't prove anything about the vulnerability of capital ships to air power. These vessels had, after all, been sitting at anchor.

Now, on the open seas, two combat-hardened BBs were dispatched with scarcely a loss, leaving nothing larger than a cruiser to face the Imperial Fleet (carriers had yet to prove themselves). Battleships would still serve, and serve well, in the war ahead, but they would no longer venture forth alone without air cover.

Singapore, our next stop, was Britain's largest Far Eastern base and still a Crown colony. Although not as exotic as Hong Kong, it remained a fabulous sight to see, and there were still enough attractions to wear out a dozen tour groups. Besides its own Tiger Balm Gardens and Chinese quarter, it boasted an array of immaculately preserved Victorian buildings. Along the main road, a variety of shops offered high-quality British and Oriental goods. It was open house at every club, and the British navy followed suit with their usual hospitality, not to mention their fine beer.

My second afternoon was spent in the hills outside town. At a monkey forest, we were overwhelmed by these friendly but persistent creatures. At first we didn't see any animals, but after our guide produced some bananas, all hell broke loose. Families of monkeys were instantly on us, and after the initial panic wore off, we reveled in their antics. They had absolutely no fear of man. A couple of sailors lost sunglasses and white hats, but all were eventually recovered.

That evening, at the famous Raffles Hotel, we all met for a huge dinner, well-irrigated by the namesake drink of the city: Singapore Sling. At our table were Rich Murphy, Danny Klein, John Williford, Al Pengelley, and Lt. (j.g.) Cummings, the latter a naval officer returning with the *Champ* to the States. Back on board, we caught the tail end of a show by a contingent of Highlanders, complete with kilts and bagpipes.

Leaving Malaysian waters, we steamed due west for the first time on our long odyssey. In the late afternoon, we stared for minutes on end as the flying fish put on their usual show. Across this flat glassy sea, they seemed to glide forever. If the sun was right, rainbows danced in the bow wave, launching these winged fish through a halo of brilliant color. Those of us in the air group had a special affinity for these unusual creatures. If one looked at the basics, we shared some extraordinary similarities. We both flew over water, and each of us skillfully employed our folding wings. The *Lake Champlain* was solidly back in the Indian Ocean, and each dusk would find us heading directly into the setting sun.

Ceylon had been our first Far Eastern port, and as it turned out, it would be our last. By now, all hands were experts at bargaining. Some of the more affluent sailors bought star sapphires and ivory, and even those who were nearly broke returned with miniature wooden elephants. This animal proved to be the national symbol, and when a count was taken in a ship's lottery, it was revealed we'd purchased over 4,000.

A few hardy souls returned to Kandy, the ancient capital, but I stayed close to Colombo. I spent the whole day out at the Mount Lavinia Hotel, a cool oasis in the blazing sun. The dark sands were covered with very white British women. Although they wore extremely modest one-piece bathing suits, it was the largest concentration of Caucasian women I'd seen since leaving the States. Their sight was a sharp reminder of what I'd been missing all these months, and I too started calculating the time remaining. The souplike water of the Indian Ocean wasn't my idea of refreshment, so I stayed on the terrace. Sipping Scotch and soda, I spent my lazy afternoon watching the colonialists enjoy the last days of their fading empire. It was glorious just being away from the ship, even for a few hours.

Under lowering clouds, we eased out of Colombo harbor on the morning of 3 November. It would be two weeks before we set foot on land—another continent, a world away.

One welcome dividend of this course was the regaining of all the time we'd lost on the outward journey. We'd steamed through so many time zones, it scarcely mattered which one we were in. It was too bad we hadn't crossed the International Date Line. We'd done just about everything else, including the equator and the Suez Canal. Sailing across the Pacific would have also meant a stop in Hawaii, and a transit of the Panama Canal. Those were the only major spots we'd missed. Last year at this time, I was steaming high above the Arctic Circle.

As the *Champ* moved away from the subcontinent and into the vast reaches of the ocean, all the clocks seemed to slow down at once. Did these new hours have 100 minutes? A large map was displayed on the hangar deck, illustrating the homeward course of the ship. Every day after the noon sighting, someone from navigation would move the little model ship ever so slightly on the red track. Moans would rise from the chow line, which snaked passed this spot. "Are we going backward or what?" "Did you guys forget to raise the anchor?"

Our one day's flight operations before reaching the Suez Canal did little to break the monotony. Even from 5,000 feet, this tropical ocean seemed endless. Above the clouds, the radar revealed nothing but our five tiny blips, seemingly stuck to the screen. Bill and I thought the flight would cool us down, but the brutal humidity stayed with our Skyraider all the way.

The crew read, played cards, stood in line for everything from chow to Cokes, and listened to music piped over the ship's radio. In the Flag Plot, our cruise book retreat, we had a RCA 45-RPM record player that we'd removed from the old compartment.

Each team that had left Quonset had been issued a cruise kit, sort of a Care package for swabbies. In it were a couple of sets of Monopoly, Acey-Deucy, playing cards, the RCA player, and about a dozen records. I often wondered how that officer chose these records. Did he really give any thought to the kind of music that would come close to satisfying the taste of twenty-five young men from all parts of the country? With the exception of one disk of Montavani (a big favorite), the remainder couldn't have been further from their liking. Every last record was an original cast Broadway show, including *Oklahoma, South Pacific, Gentlemen Prefer Blondes,* and *Annie Get Your Gun.* Except for one or two songs, the team loathed them. Bill Munroe rescued the disks before they were thrown over the side, as had been suggested more than once. A week out of Norfolk, Radio Central started playing Patti Page, Tony Bennett, Eddie Fisher, and Vaughn Monroe, and the RCA was abandoned.

In the early months, we listened to our phonograph in a winch room that adjoined our first compartment. Later it graced the admiral's quarters. We wrote letters after lights out to the music of Broadway, over and over and over. Bill and I got so we could sing every lyric and learned to appreciate the creative skills of a Hammerstein, Porter, or Berlin. Munroe insisted that with a name like Hammerstein, he had to be the composer of the "Anvil Chorus."

Working on the cruise book helped pass the time, but there just wasn't that much prose to be written, and my talents didn't extend to layout and art work. In either case, the project was well served by the indispensable Dave Crosby. On that interminable stretch of sea, the *Champ* did a pretty good imitation of the Ancient Mariner's "painted ship upon a painted ocean." Little incidents stood out like oases in the desert.

One day on a chow line that snaked around and down two decks, a scene unfolded right out of Mack Sennett. As usual, to ease the tedium, our band played marches, songs, and sometimes even drifted into a jam session. Nevertheless, I'd seen lines in doctor's offices move faster. Unknown to us, about three hundred kapok life jackets had been stored under a tarpaulin on a sloping bulkhead above the hangar deck. No doubt someone believed they'd come in handy in a major disaster, or, more likely, the deck force couldn't find anywhere else to store them. A quick release line designed to act as a lanyard hung down toward the deck. Someone had untied this release from the upper stanchion, and now it dangled about six feet above us.

A couple of energetic types decided to liven things up. They grabbed a sailor's white hat and tossed it back and forth just above his outstretched hands. In a leap to snare it, the hapless swabbie grabbed the quick release by mistake and buried us in kapok, band and all. As if by magic, two Masters at Arms (our police) appeared and immediately set half the chow line to work restoring the jackets to their original perch. Ordinarily, there would have been a lot of "pissin and moanin," but all hands pitched in with a gusto that took everyone by surprise—anything to break up the monotony. Back on line, many of us were astounded that, even after 180 days, no one had noticed those life jackets. The *Lake Champlain*, it seemed, still held some surprises.

On a more personal level, John Robben was down in the dumps. At first, I thought it was just the humidity, but it went deeper than that. He finally admitted that he hadn't received a letter from Margie in nearly a month. When the word got around, sailors started to tease John that the next word he'd receive would be a "Dear John" letter. (In reality, every letter he got was a "Dear John.") Locked in the clutches of misery, he was the target of every innocent remark. Eventually, he discovered that his girl had forgotten to change the fleet post office from San Francisco to New York when we left Japan, and in due time he was buried with mail.

In this oppressive humidity, our only relief was the open air. If the hangar deck was our meeting hall and theatre, the flight deck was our front and backyard. It was a place to get away from it all. More so, it was a place to be alone with your thoughts or to just stare at the sea. It was also the only spot on CVA-39 that boasted clean, pure air, except during flight operations, when the pungent smell of burnt kerosene from the jets hung over everything. Below decks, there was always the smell of a thousand bodies: some freshly showered, some sweat-soaked or coated with grease. The hangar deck, in spite of being open on the sides, still reeked of oil and hydraulic fluid.

Over everything else, at almost any hour of the day, wafted the odor of whatever was on the menu. Frying bacon or hamburgers relayed their mouth-watering smells of hot, burning grease. It always gave me an appetite. Other times, it was fried onions, lamb chops, or pea soup.

In the narrow passageways where the air hung heavy, the sickeningly sweet smell of soybeans was inescapable. It took me a while to trace this unusual scent, but I finally discovered it came from scores of foam canisters stored every twenty or thirty feet. In the event of a gasoline fire, the contents of this mixture would be fed into a nearby hopper, producing the element necessary to control these blazes. This foam, as it happened, had a soybean base. There appeared to be no end to these cans, stacked like jars of preserves, waiting to be opened.

To escape these hundred and one "perfumes," we fled to the flight deck. Walking through that last hatch was like stepping out of a tunnel. After the dark passageway, the sight of that unlimited expanse of sea and sky always raised the lowest spirit.

When the carrier was underway, a strong breeze blew, generated by the ship's speed. If one stood poised at the forward edge of the deck, the air was best—clean and pure, untainted by man. It carried only the pristine smell of the sea. Sometimes, late in the day, as the clouds gathered on the horizon, the ocean turned to the color of burnished metal. Standing there with the wind in your face, watching the deep swells marching toward the bow, you wouldn't change places with anyone in the world. After evening chow, those who weren't keen on the movies would gather on the flight deck or in gun tubs for long bull sessions. Our conversations often lasted well into the night. In these latitudes, the punishing heat and humidity drove everyone except watchstanders out of their steaming compartments. With only the sound of the rushing sea, the talk flowed under a night sky pale with starlight. The mood we shared was one of time out of time.

Men formerly tight-lipped opened up and revealed sides of themselves we scarcely imagined. The intimacy of some of the remarks startled us at first, but that comforting blackness had a way of softening the shock and releasing any inhibitions. Perhaps the priests and psychiatrists had known this all along.

One night, "Preacher" Williams, my favorite pilot, sat with us and set the tone for the evening. Was this recent conflict a just war? All thought it was, but many were bitter about the unfairness of the selection system. Everyone knew a friend who'd avoided the service through various ploys ranging from joining an exempted union to doing graduate work. It might have been legal, but was it moral?

Williams made an interesting point. Liberally quoting from the Bible (and shaming all the Catholics in the process), he asked us if we were truly our brother's keeper? If we were, was it morally defensible to wiggle out of military duty, when someone else had to take your place and maybe lose his life? How different was this than eating another man's rations on a life raft?

Williams was an oddity, even for a mustang (an officer who comes up through the ranks). Short and slight, his sandy hair made him look even younger. He could get away with this in a flight suit, but in dress blues he resembled a teenager trying to pass as a naval officer. But behind that look was a sharp incisive mind. Deeply religious and well read, he hardly fit his chosen role. "Preacher" Williams was one for the books.

When the lieutenant went below, his remarks fueled the discussion well past midnight. The "Preacher's" stock rose in my book. Aside from being a terrific pilot, he was one of the finest individuals I've ever known, in or out of uniform.

Chapter 33

Europe Again

ONE DAY AFTER WE'D ALMOST GIVEN UP HOPE, the endless horizon was broken by a ridge of faraway mountains. In a few hours, we left the Indian Ocean behind and entered the Red Sea. For the first time in many days, we had company as tankers and cargo ships appeared, all heading in our direction. Binoculars were uncased, and it became an interesting pastime to identify their nationality. It was apparent that most of the world's merchant vessels were registered in only a few countries. Aside from Great Britain, most of the ships flew a flag unknown to most of us. My aircrewman's course came in handy, as flag identification was part of the curriculum. I readily recognized the red and white stripes with a single star as the Liberian ensign. One of our navigation friends explained "flags of convenience" and why shipping companies sometimes registered ships in other countries to avoid taxes and costly safety requirements.

During the night, we approached the Suez Canal at reduced speed so we could traverse it during daylight hours. For the umpteenth time, all hands bedded down in their fetid berthing spaces, most wearing little or nothing.

At about 0200, lights were turned on all over the ship, as hundreds of sailors rummaged through their lockers for shirts and blankets. Since sunset, the temperature had dropped forty degrees. In late November the mercury dipped well into the 50s at night, and in the desert the humidity was nearly zero. The tropics were behind us.

Our second Suez Canal transit couldn't have been more different from the first. The cool breeze wafting across the flight deck was a sharp and delightful contrast to the blazing heat and scorching sun of the previous May. As we were more relaxed (and now veterans of the exotic), we enjoyed the desert cruise simply for what it was, a leisurely passage from one world to another. A few dhows and a handful of Arabs leading camels broke the endless plain, and the 103 miles were covered without a break. Ninety-nine years before,

Ferdinand De Lesseps had obtained the rights to build the waterway from the viceroy of Egypt. Entering Port Said, we passed his monument. I remembered the movie *Suez*, with Tyrone Power. It was too bad we didn't have a print on board. It would have given us a sense of living history.

Dropping our pilot, we increased revolutions and set a course due west across the Mediterranean. This deep blue sea was far different from the tropical waters we'd just left. The air was sharp and crisp, and foul weather jackets appeared for the first time since the Atlantic crossing seven months before. Everyone's spirits rose visibly in direct proportion to the falling mercury and humidity.

Villefranche in the south of France was Sixth Fleet headquarters and our next liberty stop. Located in the crook of a spectacular promontory, it lay almost perfectly centered between Nice and Monaco. What names! Here was the heart of the fabled Riviera we'd all heard and read so much about. Fitzgerald, Hemingway, and Maugham had each left their mark cataloguing this dream oasis of the very rich. As we steamed within sight of land, it didn't take any great stretch of the imagination to see why this was the most famous playground in Europe, if not the world.

A rocky range of cliffs marched right up to the sea, where they suddenly halted, as if by command. Whitewashed villages crowned each hilltop, with their ancient stones springing straight out of the mountainside. Terraced ramparts once used to repel Saracens now stood peacefully, silhouetted against a cloudless sky. There were none of the sandy beaches we were accustomed to, but sumptuous villas dotted a magnificent shoreline that had never felt a flake of snow. Nice and Monte Carlo easily satisfied that most secret yearning of all those poor souls raised in frigid climates: a warm city.

There are some who fantasize about life on a desert island, but come seven o'clock, they're hunting for a good restaurant. I could guarantee that no one in our task group was looking for a desert anything.

For the first time since leaving the States, we wore dress blues emblazoned with rows of service ribbons and set off on a short taxi ride to Nice. The temperature was in the low sixties, but a warm sun gave us a splendid day to sightsee. Our first order of business was a place for an outdoor drink, and our driver took us directly to the Negresco Hotel.

Four of us (Murphy, Danny, Hal, and I) drank a bottle of champagne on the terrace. It was almost December, but with that warm sun and the effects of all that marvelous bubbly, I could have dozed right off. True as this was, it was hard to think of napping with the view we had. Across the boulevard was the Mediterranean, and closer in was the promenade, sporting scores of smartly dressed French-women, every last one (it seemed) being led by a poodle.

We shopped for perfume, gloves, and other small gifts. Beyond these items, there wasn't much to buy in a France still struggling to regain its place as the arbiter of style and grace in the world. There was little doubt the country was suffering the effects of a long war and occupation, but behind these poorly stocked counters were some startlingly beautiful girls. In one parfumerie, the proprietor and his attractive daughter spoke excellent English, and they plied us with information on good restaurants and shopping. John Robben was so impressed with this girl that he, Williford, and Murphy took her to dinner. Later, he passed her name on to a close friend who was about to embark on his first visit to France. The friend ended up marrying her.

After lunch, we took the train to Monaco. We couldn't enter the casino in uniform, but we found the steep, narrow streets held far more charm. Pint-size outdoor cafés sat on every corner, their tables filled with locals scanning the morning papers and smoking Gualoises. We watched the changing of the guard at the Royal Palace and drank espresso out of toy cups. Old men in black berets played boules in the open spaces, and the smell of roasted chestnuts filled the air. There was no disagreement; we all wanted to return.

At the suggestion of Father Kelly (a gourmet if I ever saw one), we dined that evening at La Reynaud, in the outskirts of Nice. I'm sure we would have ordered steak and eggs, the sailor's response to waiters the world over, were it not for his recommendations. I had a fish soup for a starter, followed by roast lamb (gourmet that I was, I thought it was veal), a salad, and dessert. All this was washed down by a local white wine and a digestif forced on us by the proprietor. There may have been some officers in civies, but we were the only American sailors in attendance. Our ribbons drew questions about where we'd been, and since the French were heavily involved in Indo-china, our response drew applause from the patrons, and after-dinner drinks from the owner. The Korean War had ended four months before, but these people hadn't forgotten. From past experience, we knew the French weren't famous for either embracing strangers or buying drinks, so this warm reception was exceptional.

The next day, while most of the liberty party took a bus tour to Grasse, Murph and I (at Kelly's urging) headed for the hilltop towns of Vallauries, Vence, and St. Paul. The journey up into the hills above Nice was an adventure in itself. Our road, an old national route, was probably built in Roman times. It rose sharply through olive groves and vineyards. There was little traffic. The tourists had all gone north in early October.

Murphy commented on the almost complete lack of new construction. All the buildings, it seemed, had the patina of age, a phenomena shared the country over. One imagined that the French had a special spray that made everything look centuries old.

Anyone who liked pottery would love Vallauries. After an hour, I didn't care if I ever saw another pot, but I came away with a ceramic bee for Marianne. Vence and St. Paul were something else. We could have spent a year instead of an afternoon. Rich and I drank some wine at an outdoor café above the ramparts. Later, we became more intoxicated with the view. Spread out in the afternoon sun, a long green valley stretched into the distance, dotted with massive stone farmhouses whose red tile roofs shimmered in the late autumn sun. Inside St. Paul, there appeared to be a church on every corner, and we wondered who supported them all. There was hardly a soul in sight. Later, in Vence, in yet another chapel, we watched a wizened artist paint panels on the pillars. Murph and I weren't particularly impressed with his work. To our eyes, it resembled a geometric design more than a creative piece of art, and after a few minutes we went on our way. Back on board, comparing notes with Father Kelly, we discovered that we wouldn't have made very good art critics. The old man in Vence had been Henri Matisse.

CVA-39 pulled up her anchor and sailed out of Villefranche on the morning of 18 November, starting the last lap of our long deployment. There wasn't a man on board who wouldn't have gladly passed up our next port, Lisbon, to get to Mayport four days earlier. Home was just over the horizon.

I thought it especially apt that our last stop should be the birthplace of Vasco de Gama and Prince Henry the Navigator. The *Lake Champlain* was steaming further than any other carrier in the Korean War, Norfolk to Yokosuka and back.

CVA-39 sailed through the straits of Gibraltar, and Africa faded from view. The *Champ*'s prow cut into huge rollers which announced, in no uncertain terms, that we'd put "Mare Nostrum" behind us. We returned to the Atlantic as a ship of peace. How different it seemed from the ocean we crossed seven months before.

Into the mouth of the Tagus sailed our travel-weary crew, eyes straining to see ahead for the first glimpse of Lisbon. Here was an almost unknown country. Portugal had yet to be invaded by hordes of tourists, or in fact by anyone. Being neutral in World War II had shielded it from the limelight. The small country was the best-kept secret in Europe.

An agricultural country of scarcely three million, known primarily for wine and cork, Portugal was far overshadowed by Spain, its huge neighbor to the east. Having little of Spain's bloody past, all of Portugal's history, it seemed, was made far across the sea. Its people were great sailors and explorers who left their mark and language on three continents. Portugal's former colonies included Timor and Macao in the Pacific, Angola in Africa, and, of course, Brazil in South America. Even in India, Goa flew the flag of Portugal.

With mild sunny days and cool nights, Lisbon offered dozens of diversions, all new to our eyes. The city had everything: palm-tree shaded boulevards, vast plazas flanked by huge outdoor cafés, and rows of quality stores. Even a quick glance revealed the fine craftsmanship of this small but proud nation. Unusual touches set it apart. The Eiffel-built elevator in the heart of downtown carried shoppers from one level of the city to another. In a capital built on seven hills, this was no frill. Miniature trams ran alongside mosaic sidewalks. On these, pedestrians strolled, scarcely ten feet from gliding swans on a brook in the marginal. The people were friendly, the food was enjoyed, and the price was right.

One of the sailors from the Gatling tipped us off about a place that had to be seen to be believed. Located in the Alfama (the old quarter) was a big sprawling café. It was filled with swabbies, tough-looking locals, and buxom women, any one of whom looked able to take on the whole task group. Halfway down the back wall, a full-size lifeboat hung from real davits. Inside the boat, a five-piece jazz band blasted lustily away, limiting all conversation to lip reading. No one was here to do much talking anyway, and the harried bartenders were kept running. We tried something highly recommended by the destroyer sailors that we couldn't pronounce. It was sort of a Portuguese ouzo that you didn't want to get too close to an open flame. One sip cleared your sinuses and anything else that might have been clogged.

Later in the day we stumbled onto a much quieter place, an underground restaurant with food to match its atmosphere. Our lack of the language posed a problem until the owner took us into his larder and motioned for us to pick out what we wanted. Using this crude pantomime, we dined so well that we vowed to return. For the next three nights, with our party growing larger with each meal, we ate in this cavelike bistro near the fleet landing.

One evening, in the midst of gorging ourselves on roast pork, John Robben nudged me and said, "My God Jack, look at the girl who just walked down the stairs." I turned and almost went into shock. There was Marianne, or at least a facsimile so close she could have convinced me. Of course, she was a local, but it left me shaken for the rest of the night. The odd part was that John had never met my girl, but had only seen photographs. The resemblance was uncanny.

On the third day of our stay, five hundred men from the ship went to Fatima with Father Kelly to visit the shrine. I joined Rich Murphy and a much smaller group for a tour of the countryside surrounding Lisbon. It turned out to be a memorable excursion. I never dreamed there were so many sights within an hour's drive of the capital.

Our tour bus stopped first at a bizarre rock formation near Cascais that is called the Boca de Inferno, or "Mouth of Hell." Massive waves smashed into the cliffs, carving out caves and niches and sending sheets of spray far above our observation terrace. The impact sounded like thunder. Next we all had lunch at the Palacio Hotel in Estoril and toured its Casino. Sintra, in the hills, boasted a fairy-tale castle and handsome buildings painted in gaily-colored pastels. On the return trip, the driver stopped the bus to show us how cork was grown. Harvested only once every few years, it was the country's largest cash crop. If nothing else, this told us something about the Portuguese economy.

On our final evening, in our favorite restaurant, a small band of singers sang fado songs, a kind of Portuguese lament. It was a deeply moving performance, even though the sole recognizable melody was "April in Portugal." Better still, the group had a large stock of recorded fados at giveaway prices. Most were sung by Amalia Rodriguez, and we bought his entire stock.

These fados perfectly suited our mood. If there was ever a time to be melancholy, it was now. The cruise was nearly over. Home was ten days away, and our thoughts were way out across the ocean. It was so close, but we were emotionally beyond getting excited. We'd thought about it, planned for it, and dreamed of it a thousand times over in these past seven months. There was nothing left. We were dry.

To liven our mood, the owner and his family joined us at the end of the meal, drinking toasts of port which he had graciously supplied. We responded by leaving all our cigarettes and the remnants of our escudas on the table. As we slowly walked toward the stairs, there wasn't one of us who wasn't deeply moved. In spite of the language barrier, we'd learned to love these people. Four days earlier, no one could have imagined a scene like this.

As our liberty boat left the commercial pier, the *Champ*, ablaze with floodlights against the black river, stood out like a welcoming beacon. Her anchor chain straining against the current, it looked as if she too couldn't wait to begin this last leg of our long journey. No matter how good the liberty port, it was always good to go home.

Quarters for leaving port was dismissed, just as the river met the sea. Lisbon was almost out of sight, but many of us waited for the view of the lighthouse at the mouth of the Tagus. Silently, we all stood there, watching the last vestige of continental Europe disappear into the distance. Each man was alone with his thoughts. It was a time to remember and a time to look ahead. There wasn't a man whose life hadn't changed one way or another since we left Norfolk, and it was difficult to put this in context. It would take much longer than an hour on the flight deck. For some, it would take a lifetime.

Chapter 34

Homeward Bound

A NEW FEELING ENCOMPASSED THE *CHAMP*. In nine days, we'd be home, or at least in Mayport, Florida. The day before, our air group would fly away to Jacksonville, Oceana, Atlantic City, and Quonset Point. I guess this first feeling was one of relief, as if some giant weight had been lifted from our shoulders.

One sailor said it was as if he'd been holding his breath all this time and now he could finally let it all out. Some pessimist quipped, "There's still a chance our orders could be changed, like replacing some CV that broke down in the Med." No one even wanted to think about that possibility. But whatever the individual feelings, and there was probably a different one for each of the 3,500 men on this ship, the U.S.A. was getting closer with every turn of the screws. The skies were never bluer, the stars never brighter, as the distance narrowed, hour by hour, day by day. Even the sound of the engines seemed to be saying, "going home, going home."

The mild microclimate of Portugal behind us, the Atlantic winds of near winter closed off the flight deck for late night meetings. Our little band found a protected area in Hangar Bay II, not far from the Coke machine, and the discussions continued. It was a time to draw the threads together. Before Lisbon, in addition to the moral questions we occasionally pondered, the talk was mostly of the last port, the next port, our girls, and home. Now, we spoke only of the last two. Within our group, there'd be no next ports. The airdales would say good-bye to the *Champ* at Mayport and probably never set foot on her again. Those who did remain were essentially short-timers and wouldn't make another cruise. Only Lt. Williams would stay in the navy. This was his chosen career, his life. For the rest of us, the road ahead was not that certain.

As the western sky darkened, the air turned noticeably colder. We'd gone almost full circle, returning to the Atlantic on a reciprocal course. One night on the hangar deck, we tried in a bull session to put the past eight months into some sort of perspective. It wasn't easy.

While there were a few diehards who thought the whole effort had been a colossal waste of time, most of us took the opposite tack. In fact, it was soon apparent that the doubters were dissenting purely for the sake of being different.

The gray winter ocean made it hard to remember what it had been like in the heat and humidity of the summer, a summer that never seemed to end. But remember we did, and other things as well. For instance, those chow lines that snaked endlessly and moved with the speed of an hour hand. To some, it seemed as if they lined up for breakfast and found dinner waiting in the galley. One friend said he'd read a complete set of pocket classics during the eight months of shuffling across the deck. Others had made instant friendships born of conversations sparked by the sheer boredom of it all.

For many, the worst memory was the sweltering heat and the nonstop sweating. Always the sweating. Climbing into your damp rack after a lukewarm shower and finding your pillow saturated a few minutes later. You flipped it once or twice and finally gave up. It seemed as if there was no place on board you could be dry and cool. For the aircrewmen, briefings in the air-conditioned Ready Room were treasured beyond belief. All the while, the *Lake Champlain* seemed to be locked in a Turkish bath, a bath that enveloped the ship from the Red Sea to Japan and back.

Still others recalled the lack of sleep, the stumbling around in a daze. The worst period had been those last days on the line, when it seemed we rearmed and replenished every night. The crew busted their chops on the hangar deck, working like zombies well into the morning.

But now it was all behind us, and feelings of satisfaction started to emerge, first from one and then from another. In spite of our reticence and fear of being laughed at, a consensus was formed. We'd been part of a great undertaking.

Danny Klein said he first felt that way when he served in the "Big One" eight years earlier. He had thought that nothing else in the rest of his life would come close to that experience. Now he shared that same emotion.

John Robben and I believed that we'd been given a rare opportunity to see a world and live a life neither of us had ever dreamed of. More important, we'd been able to get off the treadmill of our former lives and in some sense stand frozen in time. This cruise would remain the benchmark of all memories.

"Preacher" Williams put it most eloquently. He said we probably didn't appreciate the rare chance we'd been given to taste combat, even if it was vicarious for most of us. We'd served faithfully and unselfishly in a great moral struggle, and we'd always be able to look people in the eye and say we were proud to have played an active role (only the "Preacher" could get away with lines like that).

Sure we suffered hardships, he said: empty loneliness, cramped quarters, dull food, and the terrible heat. But we shouldn't think of these things as wasted time. In the years to come, we'd look back on this period as one of the most treasured chapters in our lives. We were fortunate to have been in Korea because we could directly relate our work, no matter how tedious or routine, to helping put those planes in the air. It would be more difficult to understand what we had contributed if we had been stuck on some supply ship that never saw Task Force 77 or in some state-side training base. We'd been given an opportunity offered to but a few in every war.

Lt. Williams went into second gear. "I've been reading some articles in *Time* magazine, and some other so-called 'respected' newspapers. They make me sick. They're questioning the very worth of our effort. What did it get us, they ask? Was it worth losing all those young men?"

His face took on an expression I'd only seen on Bishop Sheehann's face during one of his television sermons. Williams said our cause was to resist aggression and help a small nation maintain its integrity. It was only exceeded by our brilliant stroke to make this a United Nations effort, not just an American one. Skeptics had warned that the UN would collapse the first time it was tested, just like its predecessor, the League of Nations.

Instead, we had British carriers alongside the *Valley Forge* in the early days of the war. As the conflict progressed, we were joined by French, Turkish, Canadian, and other forces.

The "Preacher" had given us much to chew on, and no one looked ready to expand on his critique. Finally, Rich Murphy summed it up for all of us with one final remark. It couldn't be improved on.

Just barely suppressing that ever-present Irish grin, he said, "I've had to put up with a ton of chickenshit since I came on board, but do you know something? I wouldn't have missed this for all the world."

As the last few days peeled off, we started to sense these great friendships would soon be only a memory. Some of us remembered the pain of high school graduation, when the close ties of four years were suddenly cut, and we had to start the whole process all over again. This was very different. These last seven months were no high school trip. We had worked and played and drank together, and we had shared life and death experiences. For someone who hadn't been in the service, it would be nearly impossible to understand how we felt about each other. We had revealed more of our inner selves than we'd ever do again to any other human being, and that's what made the parting so tough.

Radio Central put us in a homecoming mood by playing the latest hits of the day. Every passageway resounded to our own versions of "How Much Is That Doggie in the Window?" "Unchained Melody," "Wanted," "My Truly Fair," and "You Belong to Me." Perhaps we weren't as mellow as, say, Vaughn Monroe, but our efforts were certainly as enthusiastic. That last song was a favorite. Marianne had often quoted it in her letters: "Fly the ocean in a silver plane.... But remember darling all the while, you belong to me." In the midst of all these melodies from the Hit Parade, a bit of nostalgia was introduced. In the last seven months, we'd heard one song more than any other. Some of us reflected that for all its popularity on the *Champ*, we'd never hear it at home. It was "China Night." Sung in Japanese, its haunting melody made it the "Lilli Marlene" of the Korean War. I doubt if one man in 10,000 knew the words, but we fashioned our own lyrics to that sweet, high-pitched Oriental warbling. Every time the record was played on Radio Central, a dozen voices would chime in with, "I ain't got no yo yo."

All of us on the cruise book staff went into high gear. For those who were departing the ship at Mayport (and that was the lion's share), it was a last sprint. We didn't want to leave Dave Crosby in the lurch. On the whole, we'd done a job we could be proud of. The main outline was finished, the illustrations were chosen, and the writing was completed. We didn't have a product ready for the presses, but the staff members had carried the book about as far as they could.

Now a professional editor would scan it and turn it over to a publisher. These people who specialized in yearbooks and cruise books knew enough not to overrefine the manuscript. The flavor of the original had to be pretty much left alone, or it could be easily improved to death. In the end, the publishers did a beautiful job. They printed 99 percent of the original. Looking back after forty years, I think it has held up exceptionally well, uniquely capturing the spirit and flavor of those seven months between the covers of one slim volume. Months later, in recognition of my efforts, a complimentary copy arrived at my home, in addition to the one I'd ordered. My name was embossed in gold.

By the third day out from Lisbon, some of the squadrons started to assemble their gear for transport. The moving process had begun.

As the chow line wound its way past the huge map on the hangar deck, the band kept us jumping with appropriate melodies like "Carry Me Back to Old Virginia," "Sidewalks of New York," and "California Here I Come." Each one was met with cheers and jeers. They never seemed to come up with one that satisfied all of us. I suggested "Going Home," but the chief musician just ignored me. Actually, all the cheering and jeering added immensely to the holiday spirit that was now running unchecked throughout the ship.

On the 29th, we refueled our destroyers for the last time, and our decks were crowded with sightseers snapping away with all those expensive German and Japanese cameras. There was hardly a man who didn't sport a Canon or a Leica. As a farewell gift, each destroyer was sent 10 gallons of ice cream, and this gesture was met with a thunderous roar. Looking down on those small ships rising and falling with every swell, while we remained steady as a rock, we generated a lot of respect for these "real" sailors who earned every cent of their sea pay. On these rare occasions, we all felt like brothers under the blue.

The next day, flight operations were held. It'd been a long time, and a few of the landings were a little rough. All came back to roost safely, however. There's always that unspoken fear at the end of a combat deployment that after surviving the tough part of the war, fate would step in and claim an airman in some simple training exercise. George, Bill, and I all flew because we were not involved in the "fly away" December 3. It was just a routine flight, with nothing to see but the gray Atlantic. We'd forgotten how uncomfortable the "poopy suits" could be, and there was much moaning and groaning. Mr. Quinn reminded us that pretty soon we'd be struggling in and out of them a few times a week at Quonset. This information was met with more groans that were even louder.

At the time, George and I didn't think about it, but this was to be our last carrier takeoff and landing. Had we remembered, I'm sure we would have had a little party or ceremony, even if it meant only drinking a few Cokes. One thing could always be said of carrier operations: they never, but never, got dull.

More than anything else, this act of flying from the ship's deck set us apart from the other 99 1/2 percent of the crew. For us "sailors in the sky," it made all the difference. It turned a routine four-year enlistment into a memorable adventure. In spite of the "poopy suits," night cat shots, the "heart-in-the-mouth" approaches, and the 0400 flight quarters, we wouldn't have traded one minute of it. Nothing would ever replace the generous fellowship in naval aviation, nor that special feeling when the wheels left the deck and you were airborne.

Even in the midst of our packing, there was one surprise left up the *Champ*'s sleeve that would rivet the attention of the entire crew. The last bingo game.

During the cruise, Father Kelly had allotted most of the take to the nightly winners, with some of the money going to the ship's benevolent fund. Crafty Irishman that he was, he held back $1,500 for a last grand jackpot to generate interest. Fill the card—winner take all. Did I say generate interest? The turnout so far exceeded the expectations that two hundred would-be players had to be turned away. If Hollywood had written the script, it couldn't have had a happier ending. A married seaman apprentice (the poorest guy in the navy) won the whole wad. For him, it was about 18 months pay. Kelly had a money order sent to his wife to make sure the lucky whitehat would enjoy his winnings. While most of the crew thought this was prudent, some of the old married hands said that this was the trouble with having an unmarried Catholic priest run things. A married chaplain would have known better than to send all that money to a sailor's wife.

Father Kelly, in his more conventional role at Sunday Mass, re-minded us not to forget the nine men who would not be returning home with the ship to Mayport. Some were still in North Korea, and some were at the bottom of the sea. Anyone of us could be in their place.

The familiar sound of the bugle call announced flight quarters. It would be the last time for this air group on the *Champ*. All our pilots, two chiefs, and two first class ATs would fly out. They'd be home three days before the rest of us. While the attack and fighter squadrons would return to Jacksonville, a short drive from Mayport, the VCs had a longer road to cover and had to wait for air transport. Our team had the farthest distance to travel, to Rhode Island. After all this time at sea, it would have been great to land in New York City, doing an imitation of the returning troops from World War II, but it was not to be.

At last, all the planes that could fly were ready for the ultimate launch. Everyone who could cajole a spot on the island was up there to have one last look. Most of the planes were emblazoned with mes-sages and graffiti. Some were carrying so much contraband that we wondered how they got airborne. This final operation came off with-out a hitch, and after one farewell flyover, the air group headed west and out of sight.

A strange calm descended on the *Lake Champlain*. Our flight and hangar decks were empty, and our footsteps echoed on the steel plates. No more tie-downs to trip over. No more pools of oil to step around. The ship felt like an empty house on moving day. It was eerie.

I started to sort through all the odds and ends I'd collected over these last eight months. After each liberty, I'd toss the contents of my pockets into my cruise box. Now, it was time to catalog and pack all this flotsam and jetsam of the seven seas: photos, liberty cards, postcards, foreign money, M.P.C.s, and hand bills from places like "No Squeak Fong" (a Hong Kong store). Among the more unusual were cards written in Chinese and English, stating on one side, "Give this to your rickshaw driver," and on the other, in both languages, "Take this man to the fleet landing." There were labels from wine and beer bottles, copies of *The Champ* newspaper, memorial sheets for men killed in action or lost at sea, about sixty 8 × 10 official navy photographs that had not been needed for the cruise book, and lastly, the nearly 300 letters I'd received from friends and family, but mostly from Marianne.

I reread all the letters, kept all of Marianne's, and the most interesting of the remainder. All my color slides had been sent home directly from Kodak in Rochester, so I'd never laid eyes on them. Marianne and Margie, John Robben's girlfriend, had viewed them at his home in New Rochelle with our parents. After spending about an hour sifting through all these odd pieces, I decided to throw them all in the bottom of my box and sort them out when I got home. I eventually did. They now comprise three huge albums with over two hundred leaves and nearly a thousand pictures.

Farewell geedunk parties were held, and we toasted ourselves with Coke, vowing lifelong friendship. After I left the *Champ*, I figured I'd never see anyone in the ship's company again, except possibly a few New Yorkers.

In the early afternoon of the air group's departure, our escorts blew their sirens and swung smartly away, heading north to Philadelphia. I stood there for a long time watching them disappear. The *Lake Champlain* was going to be alone for the last four hundred miles.

My reverie was shattered by a screaming voice from a speaker right next to my head. "Relieve the watch, second section." How many times had I heard these calls and seemingly hundreds of others? "Clean sweep-down, fore and aft. Empty all G.I. cans and butt-kits." "The smoking lamp is out (or lighted) in all authorized spaces." "Movies will commence at 1900. The movie for tonight is...." (Once, the announcement should have been, "The movie for tonight is *She Wore a Yellow Ribbon*," but it came out, "*She Lost Her Yellow Panties*." No one ever discovered who the prankster was.) "Rosary will be held on the fantail in five minutes." "Mail call, Mail call. All divisional mail personnel to the mail room." And, last but not least, the favorite call of all hands, "Liberty will commence for the first and third sections immediately."

At dusk on this final day at sea, I headed up to the flight deck. So many times I had walked this space, listening to the wind whistle through the tie-downs. How many days had I picked my way around the parked planes, watching the endless sea and the sky? Tonight the deck was clean, the only sound coming from the wind in the rigging high above. Our radar antenna rotated silently in the near darkness. Even the sea was calm.

I wasn't the only one walking the deck. At a time like this, it seemed half the ship had the same idea. There wasn't a better place on board to sort out old memories and think about tomorrow. It was still hard to accept that, for all practical purposes, this great voyage was over. I should have felt elated, but I didn't. There were too many different emotions pulling on me at the same time. A major part of my life was ending, and the future was filled with uncertainty.

For the last three-and-a-half years, my every move had been planned. There were few decisions, and they affected only me. Soon I'd be married and taking on a whole new set of challenges. Nothing I'd learned in AT school would be of much help there. My only consolation was that Marianne was meeting me on exactly the same terms. She had no more experience at this sort of thing than I did. I guess nobody does until they jump in. Regardless of all these nagging doubts, there was no hesitation on my part. I really wanted to get married.

Chapter 35

Home Again

THE *LAKE CHAMPLAIN* WOULD BE MY LAST SHIP. I'd spent 218 days on her in the great adventure of my life. I didn't want to spend any extra time, but I didn't regret one minute of the voyage. The statistics of the trip were mind-boggling.

From the moment we left Norfolk until our landfall at Mayport, the *Champ* had logged 71,780 nautical miles, a distance three times around the earth at the equator. We'd spent 161 days at sea, twenty-eight of them in the combat zone. Our air group flew 2,244 combat sorties, dropping 1,350 tons of bombs and firing 1,106 rockets in close support of our ground forces. Although we were in combat the shortest time of all the carriers, we held the record for the most sorties flown in one day. During our tour on the line, Task Force 77 also flew the most flights of the entire conflict.

The air group distinguished itself with 5,559 landings and only five barrier crashes. The crew topped that in their own fashion, consuming 134,880 hot dogs and 256,000 cups of ice cream and washing it down with 1,002,100 Cokes. Sadly, there are no figures for Tums or Pepto-Bismol!

Unfortunately, there are no figures comparing mail in against mail out. From my end, I sent 124 letters to Marianne and received 82 in reply. I guess that on my end there was more going on, or I was just hornier.

Sheer numbers alone can't tell the whole story, however. No mere collection of facts could do more than jog the memory, for each man had his own story to tell. All of us changed in the end, and most, I'm sure, came home with a fuller appreciation of the world and its peoples. Closer to the mark, and far more important, we returned with a better understanding of ourselves. And now it was all coming to an end.

The atmosphere on a ship the night before landfall is one of quiet expectation. For those in the air group, it was doubly so. We all hoped to be gone tomorrow. Cruise boxes packed and flight bags bulging, we wandered the *Champ* for the last time, exchanging addresses and drinking in memories that would have to last a lifetime. Even our mess deck looked good, as the smell of frying pork chops and baked beans greeted us. A multitude of transfers would lift these poor messcooks out of their miserable jobs and replace them with some of the scores of new recruits waiting to report aboard.

I returned the last of my library books and had a cup of coffee with Danny and John Robben. The library had been a Godsend, keeping me well supplied with good reading. Leaving those shelves was like saying good-bye to an old friend.

Nobody felt much like sleeping, and the talk went on well into the morning. I can't recall any conversation that didn't start with, "You know the first thing I'm going to do when I get home?" Finally, even the diehards gave up, and the only sounds on the *Champ* were the ship's ventilators humming in the night.

Without realizing it, we were also saying good-bye to the *Champ*, and it wasn't an easy parting. For those who've never been to sea, it's nearly impossible to appreciate the emotional attachment a sailor has for his ship. After a few months, those steel plates, boilers, and ventilators become imbued with a nobility, strength, and grace that defies description. The ship takes on human qualities, just like a favorite car. It was easy to imagine the pounding of the engine was the beat of a heart, and in a way, I guess it was.

We'd come a long way together and shared many dawns. How tiny the ship used to look from 5,000 feet, but how welcome too. Now, after eight months, the *Champ* had become home.

To most people, it would seem odd to describe all these steel plates and narrow passageways with a word as tender as "home," but home she was, every bit as much as my apartment in New York. The flight and hangar decks held the special nooks and hidden corners we came to call our own. And just as in my own room, I could navigate these spaces in total darkness. It was a radar of familiarity.

Sure, we used to gripe about her, as I'm certain all sailors have done since the days of sail. But nevertheless she was ours, and we were going to miss her. She'd been good to us. She'd taken us clear across the world and into combat. And now she'd safely carried us almost back to our doorstep.

Just outside Mayport, we slowed to pick up our pilot and U.S. Customs personnel. About half an hour later, two tugs appeared off the breakwater, ready to ease us past those last few hundred yards of open water. Without our usual flock of planes, we couldn't execute Operation Pinwheel, even if we wanted to.

Just before breakfast, I went up on deck and couldn't see anything in the morning mist. From the sounds of the engines, I knew we were close. After a few minutes, I could just make out a long, low shoreline behind scores of screeching gulls. The guy behind me said disgustedly, "I know it's home and all that, but what a dump! The mud flats outside my town in Texas are better looking than this."

I wasn't searching for postcards. We'd had more than enough of those, including Hong Kong, Gibraltar, and Athens, some of the most beautiful ports in the world.

Our bow swung at the tug's urging, and a long pier loomed into sight. The sound of band music came across the narrowing strip of water, and all at once we knew we were really back. Hundreds of cheering people stood behind a long row of pretty baton twirlers from the local high school. Banners were held high that proclaimed "Welcome Home" and "Well Done." The band struck up "Anchors Aweigh" and suddenly we all had trouble focusing on the wild crowd below.

Emotional reunions were the order of the day, but no one in VC-12 was part of them. In fact, watching all those sweet embraces made it all the more painful to be so near and yet so far. Over a thousand miles lay between this dock and Quonset Point, and we had to wait for air transport to take us home. In the late afternoon, we got the news: all bad. Our aircraft had some problems, and we wouldn't be departing until the next day. More groans. Liberty was granted to all hands, but I elected to stay on board.

I'd visualized my homecoming a thousand times, but Mayport was not part of it. I didn't want to spend my first night in some small town. I stayed on board (the only one from the air group who did, it turned out) and kept an eye on our mound of cruise boxes and parachute bags piled high on the hangar deck. One of the boxes held the three .38 cal. pistols we had to carry in the war zone. When the squadron was still here, they were safely stored in the Ready Room. Now, with all our "birds" gone, they again became our responsibility. The last thing we needed was to lose those weapons so close to home.

The next morning at muster, Chief Rogers told us we could load our gear on waiting trucks after breakfast. We all made a beeline for the trucks before someone else grabbed them. Breakfast could wait until we got to the airfield. As it developed, there were ample vehicles to go around, and we were soon on our way to N.A.S. Jacksonville. Our detachment was airborne at 3 P.M. We made one stop at N.A.S. Anacostia (Washington, D.C.) and finally landed at Quonset Point about six hours later.

After the transport fiasco, good news greeted the team when we arrived on this Saturday night, December 5, 1953. Cmdr. Herman had arranged basket leave for all hands, commencing immediately. Handing over our pistols to the OOD, George and I dropped our gear in lockers and hurriedly changed into dress blues. A taxi took us to Providence, where we caught the train to New York. While waiting for the train, I called Marianne and told her I'd be home sometime that night and that I'd go straight to her house.

After waiting all that time, the train seemed to take forever. I thought about other train rides: the Pullman to boot camp, the rides to Glasgow and Paris, the trips in Japan, and finally, the runs along the Riviera and Portugal. But none were more emotionally draining than those five hours on the longest Saturday night of my life.

When we reached Grand Central, George wanted to share a cab to save money. Normally a great idea, but not tonight. I had a dull ache in my gut from anxiety, and every minute counted.

As my taxi wound itself through the nearly deserted streets of Throggs Neck, it suddenly dawned on me that Marianne and I were practically strangers, that letters, no matter how passionate, were a poor substitute for the real thing. I needed a strong opening line to prove to her in no uncertain terms that her man was back. My mind raced through a hundred movies, and everything from "Dr. Livingston, I presume" to "Why ask for the stars, when we already have the moon?" flashed by. All were discarded. It would have to be original and dramatic.

Finally the taxi arrived at that familiar house and after a few words with the cabbie, I bounded up the stairs. The house was dark, and it took a couple of sharp knocks on the door to get any action. At last, a sleepy Marianne stood before me. My first words were, "Honey, do you have five bucks. The driver doesn't have change for a twenty."

Opening lines forgotten, I had Marianne in my arms, crushing the breath out of her. The poor girl had fallen asleep (it was 4 A.M.), but she was soon fully awake. Suddenly, feeling the touch of her hair on my face, the warm lips, the familiar scent, and her wet cheeks on mine, brought everything flooding back. This time, it was no illusion. I was really home. We kissed and talked, and kissed and talked, waiting for dawn. My ache gradually disappeared with the morning light, and I felt as though all my dreams had come true on the same day.

Marianne and I were engaged for Christmas. One day while walking near Rockefeller Center, we met Hal Holman, up from Norfolk on leave. Marianne took him aside and invited him to my surprise bachelor party that evening. Hal had lost some of his shyness after eight months at sea, but apparently not all of it. He never showed up.

After my leave, I returned to VC-12 and resumed working nights. I picked up exactly where I'd left off the previous March. The few of us that hadn't been sucked up in the accelerated separation were looked on a little differently. Of all the swabbies who'd come in during the Korean War, we were among the very few in the Atlantic Fleet who sported combat ribbons. While it didn't make us heroes, we were held in some awe by those who'd never seen the Pacific. After a few drinks, we told appropriate "sea stories" (over and over).

Two of the ribbons, the United Nations and the Korean Service medals, were oddly the same color code, blue and white. The latter held a solitary battle star. Our most exotic decoration turned out to be a parting gift from Syngman Rhee: the Korean Presidential Unit Citation. Its vivid colors stood in stark contrast to the other war "fruit salad," and it even boasted a miniature South Korean flag in its center. Later, we discovered we were entitled to the China Service Medal. We'd earned this during one boring stretch on the way to Hong Kong, when we alerted the Formosan defense force with some planes from our air group. It gave us a strange feeling, knowing we could win a medal just for sailing a few miles off course. Later, many years later, we would learn that some of us earned other medals for having flown "x" number of missions in the war zone and having received a letter of commendation. It never brought us any more money or veteran's benefits, but I don't think we were looking for anything extra. We'd acquired a lot more important things than ribbons and medals: self-confidence, discipline, and a maturity lacking in those who stayed behind. I think we all chalked up those four years as simply doing our duty. There were no big parades, but neither did anyone berate us for serving. Our war wasn't as long or as popular as World War II, but I guess most people looked on it as sort of a continuation.

The last sixteen weeks were routine—flying training missions and maintaining the equipment. Some of the sailors about to enter separation started gathering souvenirs. Volt-ohm meters and soldering irons would mysteriously disappear, "blown over the sea-wall by a turning up AD4W." I felt funny about taking government issue. Perhaps I had too ingrained a sense of affection for Uncle Sam, I don't know. But I still wanted something to take home that would always remind me of the Skyraider, which, like nothing else, had shaped my enlistment. In the end, I picked up an aircraft clock. Had it been for sale, I'd gladly have paid the few bucks it was worth, but the bureaucracy wasn't set up that way. I just dropped it in my flight jacket pocket.

My old friends disappeared one by one, like some endless game of musical chairs. When George was separated before Christmas, I lost my best friend in the squadron. Everyone was given an accelerated discharge as an economy move. My enlistment would be shortened by two months, and my target date was 15 June. In January, John Robben married Margie, the girl of his dreams. Williford and I served as ushers, and now I regretted having to wait those extra months.

Those final weeks dragged. I did my job, but for all practical purposes, my navy career was over. Marianne tried to involve me in all the sensitive diplomacy that goes into making up a wedding reception list, but fortunately the navy kept me occupied right up to the last few days, when it was too late to change anything. The women in the family were all excited about the wedding, which was set for May 1. I was too, but for different reasons.

In March, suddenly, and for no logical reason, I developed a dread of flying. I convinced myself that having survived all the crazy experiences over the last three years, I was destined to die on some routine training mission. I kept this to myself of course, but quietly arranged to be occupied when I was scheduled for a flight. On night check, they expected you to arrange your own flight time, anyway. I gave up two months flight skins.

As it turned out, I wouldn't fly again for thirteen years. During that time, our trips to Europe were made by ship, and we traveled to Florida by car or train. I finally broke the ice in 1967, when, having been separated from Marianne for the first time since we were married, I flew to Miami. This proved, that for me at least, the sex drive was stronger than the drive for self-preservation.

At last the big day arrived, bright and sunny. Don Roller, my old buddy who'd been discharged two years earlier said, "What more appropriate date could an airedale get married on than Mayday?"

Standing there at the front of the church, waiting for my bride, I suddenly felt real fear. Typhoons and night catapult shots paled in comparison to what I was about to embark on. But as I looked at Marianne walking towards me, radiant in that long white gown and beautiful beyond description, all my fears vanished. I took my second oath in four years. This one would have far more reaching consequences and last a lifetime.

After a month's honeymoon in Florida (I had a lot of accumulated leave), we stopped by Norfolk to visit John Robben and Margie and show Marianne the *Champ*. The ship was in drydock, covered with scaffolding, and like a woman in the middle of fixing her hair, she was in no shape to be seen. But see her we did, crawling over cables and around air-compressors. The flight deck was filled with construction huts and the sound of hammering. In desperation, we went below to the library, where I introduced my bride to Dave Crosby, one of the few men on board whom I still knew. Dave wondered aloud how I'd snared Marianne. He said her pictures didn't do her justice. She was a knockout.

Looking around after we'd made our good-byes, I found it hard to believe that this was the same ship I'd called home for over 200 days. I was to walk the decks one more time before she went to the breakers, but that was down the road.

The *Champ* was a ship of records. From her (almost) Blue Ribband crossing in 1945 to being the carrier with the most Korean combat sorties on one day (during our deployment), she made a name for herself. She also set records for making the longest cruise in distance from home port to Korea of all the CVs participating in the war, for being the largest ship to transit the Suez Canal, and for being the only large carrier never to have her flight deck canted. She remained the last true Essex class CV right to the end in 1966.

In addition to being part of our naval quarantine during the Cuban Missile Crisis, the *Champ* was the carrier used to retrieve our first astronaut, Alan Shepard. Later she served the same purpose for Gemini 5.

On 4 June 1954, I left Quonset Point for the last time. I was in dress blues, but I was a civilian. In September of the following year, the *Champ* was in New York for a visit and we went on board, this time with my daughter Karen, who was six months old. While walking down the flight deck, Marianne tripped on one of the arresting wires and fell, sending Karen tumbling ahead of her. Solicitous officers quickly took them below to the dispensary where everyone checked out OK. When one of the pilots discovered I'd flown from this ship, he winked and said, "You're certainly breaking her in right. Imagine catching the second wire on your first approach."

The day I was discharged, I packed away my blues with the two red chevrons of an AT2. I'd made 1st class the end of May, but didn't have enough time left to make it permanent. I had to settle for the satisfaction of knowing I made it. I removed the three rows of ribbons and aircrew wings and placed them in a jewelry case. Today, more than forty years have passed since I stood in that recruiting station on lower Broadway. Time has tarnished the silver wings and faded the color from the ribbons. But the memory remains, bright as ever, of the pride I felt in being one of the chosen few, one of the "sailors in the sky."

Epilogue

OVER THE PAST FORTY YEARS, I have regrettably fallen completely out of touch with most of the people in this story. There are others whom I know about only secondhand (alive and dead), and finally, there are those precious few who are as close to me today as if they were standing on the fantail of the *Champ* in the China Sea.

To begin with, I'm sorry to report that Captain Schaeffer was killed in Okinawa in a helicopter crash in 1958. I'll always remember him as the best C.O. I ever had, and a man who never forgot the people under him. He combined efficiency with compassion and endeared himself to every man on board.

Don Roller is the only navy friend with whom I have maintained a continuing relationship. He went to work for General Electric (who made our radar) after leaving VC-12 in 1952, and he settled in Syracuse, where he and his wife Dot raised four children. Don retired a few years ago, and we still get together on occasion.

I lost all touch with most of my shipmates within a few years of my discharge. George Walls went into separation before I returned from Christmas leave in December 1953 and disappeared into the wilds of New Jersey. I tried to trace him a few times, but my attempts were frustrated by the fact that I didn't know in what county he resided. In 1992, my old high school, Cardinal Hayes, published a 50th anniversary directory. I'd forgotten that George had also gone there (I was two years his senior), but glancing at the book one day, I found his name. I wasn't sure it was the same person, so I wrote him a letter. A few days later, George called me at the office, and we spoke for nearly two hours. We met at last at the *Lake Champlain* Association reunion in Burlington, Vermont, in September 1991. He'd followed along Don Roller's path, choosing an engineering career, although with Bell Labs.

I thought this meeting was a stroke of fate, but it was only a foretaste of a fantastic series of reappearances of long-lost whitehats.

As I was recovering from my heart surgery, I was astonished to hear from John Robben, whom I'd last seen in 1960. He wrote to me after my operation, and our correspondence has continued unbroken all this time. John was perhaps the most successful of all of us in fulfilling his dream of becoming a writer. He'd published a book in 1972, another piece in the *Reader's Digest*, and numerous articles in such prestigious publications as the *New York Times*. Although he manages his own business, John still finds time to write a lively column for his Connecticut newspaper. He's been married to Margie (the recipient of all his letters) for 40 years. They have five fine children and a flotilla of grandchildren.

Through John, I've made contact with Rich Murphy, Chaplain Kelly, and John Williford. Unfortunately, John Williford died before he had a chance to answer my first letter. I also learned that Danny Klein had passed away sometime earlier.

When the *Lake Champlain* Association was formed a few years ago, I became the historian, no doubt because I'd saved more stuff than anyone else. It's been a labor of love, and I've learned a great deal about the history of the *Champ*, particularly in the early days of her career. My heaviest contributors are those who served aboard her in World War II.

Marianne and I have also been happily married for forty years, and we have three marvelous children. I've made a career of insurance, just completing thirty-nine years as an agent with State Farm Mutual. We've been fortunate enough to have been able to travel extensively, and I've revisited many of the places I once thought I'd only see as a whitehat on liberty.

Hong Kong had probably changed the most, but in 1982 it was every bit as spectacular as it was in 1953. I even took Marianne for a swim at Repulse Bay, but the water wasn't as clean as I'd remembered it. The Peak Tram was still a thrill, and we managed to dine in some of the same spots I'd remembered so well. We spent a week in Tokyo, but I couldn't locate any of my old haunts. Maybe it was just as well. I'd always thought I'd like to give Fujiyama another try, but we never had the time. One night in Osaka, I discovered the Japanese hadn't lost their obsession for pachinko, and it seemed half the city was perched in front of those machines.

We had better luck in Europe, where we got to know Paris and places like Nice, Monaco, and Lisbon intimately. We once even dined at Le Reynaud near Villefranche where 35 years before, on the advice of Father Kelly, I'd experienced my first good French meal. I never did get back to Ceylon (now Sri Lanka) or Singapore, but I guess one can't be greedy.

Although I've had luck in renewing old friendships, I never thought I'd set foot on any of the ships I served in after my last visit to the *Champ* in 1956. But chance or fate deemed otherwise.

In December 1991, Marianne and I joined a group of historians and World War II buffs in Hawaii for the fiftieth anniversary of the Japanese attack on Pearl Harbor. We spent a nonstop week attending all the ceremonies and touring the battle sites. Mostly, it was a once-in-a-lifetime opportunity to meet the surviving participants, including those from the other side. John Finn, Medal of Honor December 7, 1941, personally described how he felt standing on that exposed runway dueling with the Japanese fighters strafing his PBYs. When I asked what motivated him to put his life on the line, he replied, "I guess I was just damn angry." Another thrill was seeing the great battleship *Missouri* underway, leaving Pearl Harbor for Bremerton and deactivation.

On the return flight home, we decided to stop over one day in San Diego to help break up the jet-lag. Flying into the airport, we approached low over North Island, where two carriers were berthed. Marianne had the better view and recognized the number "41" illuminated on the superstructure. It was the *Midway*.

When I called the next morning about going on board, I was told the ship was closed to visitors because it was being prepared to go into mothballs. I used every bit of salesmanship I'd acquired over the years and persuaded the OOD that since it was my only chance to see the first carrier I'd flown from, he should make an exception. He eventually found some transport and with a 2d class yeoman as a guide, we boarded a carrier I'd last set foot on in October 1952.

We had an extended tour and visited every area that wasn't taken up by yard workers, including the flight and hangar decks. Better still, the yeoman told us we could take all the photos and video we wanted because all the sensitive equipment had already been removed. The *Midway* had had some major changes since I'd last walked its decks, but then I guess the same thing could be said about me. Seeing her again was an unexpected delight, and I'm grateful to all on board who went the extra mile for an old shipmate.

I've crossed the Atlantic a few times by ocean liner, a much more luxurious mode of travel than a CVA or CVB, but not nearly as exciting. There are still times when I wish I could crawl back into that rear compartment, strap myself in, and look forward to that indescribable feeling of flying off a carrier. When I look back on my years in naval aviation, I have only a sense of deep pride and fulfillment: I never had any regrets. As another whitehat in this story said so well, "I wouldn't have missed it for the world."

Bibliography

Books

Blair, Clay. *The Forgotten War.* New York: Doubleday, 1987.

Bryant, J. *Aircraft Carrier.* New York: Random House, 1954.

The Champ, Cruise Book of the USS *Lake Champlain*, 1954.

Cressman and Wenger. *Steady Hands and Stout Hearts.* Missoula: Pictorial Histories Publishing Co., 1989.

Dept. of the Army. *Korea 1950.* Washington, D.C., U.S. Government Printing Office, 1982.

Field, J. A., Jr. *U.S. Naval Operations in Korea.* Washington, D.C., U.S. Government Printing Office, 1962.

Hallion, R. P. *U.S. Naval Air War in Korea.* Baltimore: Nautical Aviation Publishing Co. of America, 1986.

Jackson, B. R. *Douglas Skyraider.* Fallbrook: Aero, 1969.

Messimer, Dwight. *In the Hands of Fate.* Annapolis: Naval Institute Press, 1985.

Morrison, S. E. *U.S. Naval Operations in World War II.* Boston: Little, Brown, 1962.

Phillips, Christopher. *Steichen at War.* New York: Harry Abrams, 1982.

Polmar, Norman. *Aircraft Carriers.* Garden City: Doubleday, 1969.

Reese, Lee F. *Men of the Blue Ghost.* San Diego: Lexington, 1982.

Stafford, Edward. *The Big "E."* New York: Ballantine, 1962.

Y'Blood, W. T. *Hunter-Killer.* Annapolis: Naval Institute Press, 1983.

Magazines and Periodicals

Esders, Wilhelm G. "Torpedo Three and the Devastator." *The Hook* (August 1990).

Military History
of the Author

Jack Sauter enlisted in the 107th Infantry, New York National Guard (Old Seventh Regiment), in October 1947. He served as a rifleman and later as part of an 81mm mortar platoon.

At the outbreak of the Korean War, he was released from his regiment and enlisted in the U.S. Navy at New York on 6 August 1950. After completing his recruit training on 27 October 1950, he was sent to the Naval Air Technical Training Command at Millington, Tennessee. After graduating from Airman Primary School in January 1951, he was selected for Aviation Electronics Technician School (A) at the same facility. This course was 28 weeks and upon graduation Sauter, now rated ATAN (aviation electronics technician airman), was sent to Norfolk for more advanced radio and radar training at Fleet Airborne Electronics Training Unit, Atlantic (FAETULANT). This school provided intensive instruction on carrier-based radio and radar.

At the end of this course Sauter was assigned to regular naval aviation duty with Composite Squadron 12 (VC-12) at N.A.S. Quonset Point, R.I. In addition to maintaining radio and radar, his duties included flying training missions in airborne early warning and anti-submarine warfare from Douglas Skyraider aircraft (AD4-W). In December 1951 Sauter was returned to N.A.S. Norfolk for eight weeks of early warning radar school. Early in 1952 he was rated aviation electronics technician 3rd class (AT3) and started a program that led to his designation as aircrewman.

On 25 August 1952 he was assigned to the USS *Midway* (CVB-41), as part of a special team from VC-12. For seven weeks *Midway* took part in Operation Mainbrace, fleet exercises that involved other heavy units of the U.S. and British navies and ranged from the British Isles to the Arctic Circle.

Returning to Quonset Point he was later detached for a brief assignment in the Caribbean on USS *F.D. Roosevelt* (CVA-42) in January 1953. The following month Sauter became part of a new team being formed for duty aboard USS *Lake Champlain* (CVA-39) that would take him to Korea and Task Force 77. Departing Norfolk on 26 April, the *Lake Champlain* sailed over 20,000 miles with stops at Gibraltar, Athens, Port Said, Colombo, Ceylon and Manila, before reaching Yokosuka on 9 June 1953. The *Lake Champlain* completed two combat tours with Task Force 77 as flagship before the war ended on 27 July. Sauter flew 21 ASW and AEW missions as part of his team. In June he was rated AT2, and in August he was designated Combat Aircrewman.

He returned to N.O.B. Mayport, Florida, on 5 December 1953 and resumed his duties at N.A.S. Quonset Point, R.I. He was honorably discharged on 4 June 1954.

Index